BAKE

BAKE

Beautiful baking recipes
from around the world

This edition published by Parragon Books Ltd in 2013 and distributed by

Parragon Inc.
440 Park Avenue South, 13th Floor
New York, NY 10016
www.parragon.com/lovefood

LOVE FOOD is an imprint of Parragon Books Ltd

ISBN: 978-1-4723-1971-5

Printed in China

New recipes written by Edward Gee

Edited by Fiona Biggs

Created by 99 PAGES

Notes for the Reader

This book uses standard kitchen measuring spoons and cups. All spoon and cup measurements are level unless otherwise indicated. Unless otherwise stated, milk is assumed to be whole, eggs are large, individual vegetables are medium, and pepper is freshly ground black pepper. Unless otherwise stated, all root vegetables should be washed in plain water and peeled prior to using.

For best results, use a food thermometer when cooking meat and poultry. Check the latest USDA government guidelines for current advice.

Garnishes, decorations, and serving suggestions are all optional and not necessarily included in the recipe ingredients or method.

The times given are only an approximate guide. Preparation times differ according to the techniques used by different people and the cooking times may also vary from those given. Optional ingredients, variations, or serving suggestions have not been included in the time calculations.

Recipes using raw or very lightly cooked eggs should be avoided by infants, the elderly, pregnant women, convalescents, and anyone with a weakened immune system. Pregnant and breast-feeding women are advised to avoid eating peanuts and peanut products. People with nut allergies should be aware that some of the prepared ingredients used in the recipes in this book may contain nuts. Always check the packaging before use.

Contents

Contents

Baking

BAKING — THE HISTORY OF HUMANITY

Bread, cakes, and biscuits are a central feature of almost every food culture, whether in the Americas, Europe, Africa, Asia, or Australasia. In fact, baking is one of the principal achievements in the history of humankind.

Historians speculate that Egyptians found the existence of natural yeast by chance. On a warm day, the yeasts that occur naturally in flour caused it to ferment before baking. In the Middle Ages, bread baking with yeast was already highly developed. Thousands of recipes from this era still exist in some part of Europe.

Many customs and traditions have been and still are associated with baking. Baked goods have traditionally been viewed as a symbol of the gods, because ancient cultures believed that the gods invented the art of baking and then taught it to the people. The Greeks worshipped Demeter, the goddess of grain and fertility. The Roman goddess of agriculture was called Ceres. The word "cereal" derives from her name.

Over the centuries, thousands of recipes for bread have evolved all over the world. Although the origins of baking are unclear, there are few civilizations where baked goods are not a staple food. Ever since we ceased to be nomadic, we have been cultivating cereal grains. The grain obtained was usually eaten raw and whole and was not very easy to digest. At some point people had the idea of grinding the grain between two stones and then mixing it with water. Between BC 6000 and 3000, this method spread throughout the East to Egypt, China and India. By adding water, milk, and fat to the ground grain, a dough mixture was made that is still a basic component of the daily diet of 60 per cent of the world's population today.

However, at that time, bread and cakes in the modern sense were unknown. The mixture was baked into small, round cakes on heated stones or placed in hot ashes. Archaeological findings in Bulgaria show that a type of basic ceramic oven was already in use around BC 300. Another early type of oven was known as a tube oven—these were heated from within and flat bread was placed on the outside. In India, a similar process is still used, with flat bread being cooked on the walls of mud huts that are heated by the sun.

Early flat bread was an ideal food for taking on long distance journeys as its low water content meant that it kept fresh for a long time. This made it a practical food for Bronze Age hunters in around BC 2000 and it was also later used by the Vikings. In Finland and some Alpine countries, there was also a hole in the center of the bread that was used for stringing it up to protect the bread from mice. The holes that are still to be found in bagels are a relic of this practical, everyday solution.

Archaeological artefacts from different parts of the eastern Mediterranean suggest that dough mixture was fermented to leaven for the first time in around BC 1800. This discovery is attributed to the Egyptians who noticed that dough that was left standing for longer periods was looser. Their logical conclusion was that a looser dough would produce a softer bake, rather than hard flat breads—this observation led to the development of early leavened breads and, eventually, cake!

In Egypt in BC 1500, clay ovens were developed and they began to be used in people's homes. In BC 1000, portable ovens, which were 3-foot tall pots made of stone or metal, were also created. This ground-breaking invention was followed in rapid succession by improvements in milling and baking technology. The Greeks took their lead from the Egyptians and started leavening the flour to produce sourdough. The Germans also got in on the act and introduced leavened bread in BC 800. In around 50 AD, the Romans began to sift the crushed, wholemeal grains. By 400 AD, there were already more than 250 bakeries in Rome, some of them large factories, grinding and processing up to 30 tons of grain daily.

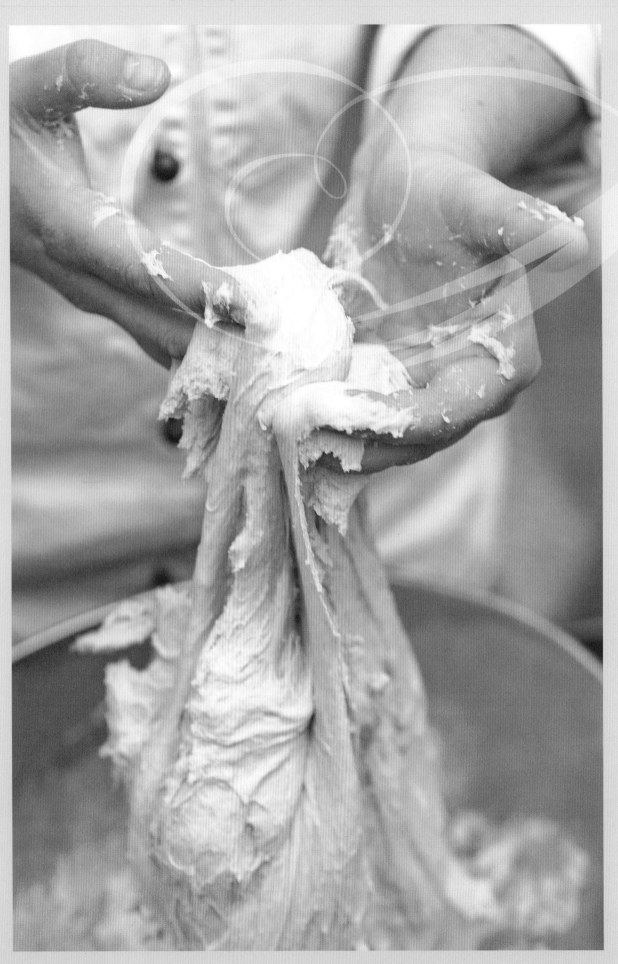

One of the most recognized and outstanding accomplishments by the German chemist Justus Liebig (1803–1873) was the invention of a nitrogen-based fertilizer. This developed into a product that started to be used in baking instead of yeast, for people who found yeast's strong fermentation flavor undesirable. This product was baking powder, which was revolutionary in home baking.

However, for the majority of the population, good quality leavened bread still remained out of reach for many hundreds of years. It wasn't until the sixteenth century that flat breads were gradually replaced by leavened breads in Northern and Central Europe, and fine bread was still only eaten at court. This meant that social class could be assessed by the type of bread people ate: the harder and rougher the bread, the lower a person's status.

Documents on brewing beer from the beginning of the sixteenth century provide accurate information about the development of the systematic cultivation of yeast, which meant that leavened bread soon became more widely available. Rapid increases in population brought about the transition from baking at home to baking in commercial bakeries, so as to guarantee a daily supply of bread. Improved sifting devices, mechanized roller mills for grinding the grain, and harvest machines all contributed to making the flour finer still.

In the early nineteenth century, German chemist Justus Liebig made the groundbreaking discovery that potassium salt added to soda loosened the batter in a similar way to yeast. This discovery led to the use of baking powder in baking, still an essential ingredient today. It ensures that a mixture rises well, giving a light and fluffy result. This advance led, inevitably, to the baking of cakes on an industrial scale, adding sweetness and luxury to the lives of generations.

The road from the first dough mixture to the bread and elaborate cakes of today was a long and tortuous one. It is no wonder that a food whose production was associated with so much effort has always been held sacred. Grain and bread are often mentioned in the Bible; it shows how people's concern for their "daily bread" dominated their thoughts. Each crop failure was a threat to their very existence. This explains the line in the "The Lord's Prayer": "Give us this day our daily bread". Bread was, quite simply, a necessity of life. Marriages were often concluded with a symbolic handing over of bread, with the groom giving some bread to the bride at the altar to show his willingness to feed the family in the future. In some cultures a wheat sheaf replaces the bridal bouquet, symbolizing the desire for close ties—an entire life as close and united as the grains in the ear and in the bread. Even today, the beautiful Russian blessing for newlyweds or new homeowners: "May bread and salt never be missing from your home", is still alive. "Good luck" bread has a coin baked into it and is given at a christening or to those moving into a new home. Plaited bread is still used to decorate wedding tables, and dough is plaited into wreaths for the harvest festival.

THE NORTH AMERICAN
Way
of
Baking

It is impossible to pinpoint the one and only symbol of American and Canadian baking traditions, due to the fact that different parts of these two vast countries bear the influences of diverse immigrant cultures over the centuries and are also subject to widely varying geographic and climatic conditions. With about 50 million Americans of German origin and another 30 million being of English or Irish descent, it is self-explanatory that the North American baking culture has a predominantly European background, with the exception of the southern states, which have a strong Latin American influence. With delicate cupcakes and vibrant red velvet chocolate cakes, Americans hold true to their famous love of detail and live up to their reputation as baking artists ... Whether a piece of banana bread for breakfast, a slice of traditional New York cheesecake after lunch, a cupcake on the fly while doing the afternoon shopping, or a hearty pie for dinner—Americans love to bake, and the possibilities are endless.

The United States has developed its own baking style, which is much more than just fast food. Bagels and donuts are world famous for their special flavor. They are just two of many real American baked goods.

1.

4.

4.

Black Bottom
PECAN PIE

SERVES 6–8

PREP TIME: 40 minutes,
plus 1 hour to chill

COOKING TIME: 30 minutes

Pecans are a favorite because of their subtle, nutty-sweet taste and their similarity to the European walnut. Pecan trees grow mainly in the southern United States and are even the official state tree of Texas. The nuts are extremely nutritious and are an excellent source of Vitamin E. In this recipe, pecans and chocolate are brought together to make a delicious sweet pie.

1. To make the dough, put the flour, salt, and sugar into a bowl and mix to combine. Add the butter and mix in with your fingertips or an electric mixer until the mixture resembles coarse bread crumbs. Carefully add the water, 1 teaspoon at a time, until the mixture just begins to crumble. Add more water, if necessary, to achieve the right consistency.

2. Turn out the dough onto a lightly floured work surface and knead until pliable. Shape it into a ball, sprinkle with a little flour, wrap in plastic wrap, and chill in the refrigerator for at least 1 hour.

3. Preheat the oven to 350 °F. Grease a 9-inch round fluted tart pan. Remove the dough from the refrigerator and let warm up to room temperature. Roll out the dough on a lightly floured work surface and ease it into the prepared pan.

4. To make the filling, put the chocolate chips and cocoa powder into a bowl set over a saucepan of barely simmering water and stir until melted. Spread the mixture over the bottom of the unbaked pastry shell.

5. Put the eggs, brown sugar, and granulated sugar into a medium bowl and beat to combine. Add the corn syrup and melted butter and mix until incorporated. Stir in the nuts, then pour the filling into the pastry shell.

6. Bake in the preheated oven for 30 minutes, or until the filling is just set. Remove from the oven and place on a wire rack to cool in the pan. Serve cold.

INGREDIENTS

pastry dough
*2⅓ cups all-purpose flour,
plus extra for dusting*

1 teaspoon salt

1 teaspoon sugar

*2 sticks chilled butter, diced,
plus extra for greasing*

*⅓–½ cup iced water,
plus extra if needed*

filling
½ cup milk chocolate chips

2 tablespoons unsweetened cocoa powder

4 eggs

¼ cup firmly packed light brown sugar

⅓ cup granulated sugar

½ cup light corn syrup

4 tablespoons butter, melted

1½ cups pecan halves

New York

CHEESECAKE

SERVES 10

PREP TIME: 40 minutes, plus 2 hours to cool and overnight to chill

COOKING TIME: 55 minutes

INGREDIENTS

*1 stick butter,
plus extra for greasing*
1¼ cups finely crushed graham crackers
1 tablespoon granulated sugar
4 cups cream cheese
1¼ cups granulated sugar
2 tablespoons all-purpose flour
1 teaspoon vanilla extract
finely grated zest of 1 orange
finely grated zest of 1 lemon
3 eggs
2 egg yolks
1¼ cups heavy cream

The typical New York-style cheesecake is rich, with a dense and particularly creamy consistency. This is because cream or sour cream is added to the batter instead of cottage cheese or cream cheese alone. The brave also add a good pinch of salt to the crust to balance out the tender, creamy sweetness of the cake.

1. Preheat the oven to 350 °F. Melt the butter in a small saucepan. Remove from the heat and stir in the crushed cookies and sugar. Press the cookie mixture tightly into the bottom of a 9-inch round springform cake pan. Place in the preheated oven and bake for 10 minutes. Remove from the oven and let cool on a wire rack.

2. Increase the oven temperature to 400 °F. Use an electric mixer to beat the cheese until creamy, then gradually add the granulated sugar and flour and beat until smooth. Increase the speed and beat in the vanilla extract, orange zest, and lemon zest, then beat in the eggs and egg yolks, one at a time. Finally, beat in the cream. Scrape any excess from the beaters of the electric mixer into the mixture. It should be light and fluffy—beat on a faster setting if you need to.

3. Grease the sides of the cake pan and pour in the filling. Smooth the top, transfer to the oven, and bake for 15 minutes, then reduce the temperature to 225 °F and bake for an additional 30 minutes. Turn off the oven and let the cheesecake stand in the oven for 2 hours to cool and set. Chill in the refrigerator overnight before serving.

4. Slide a knife around the edge of the cake, then unclip and release the springform and transfer the cake to a plate to serve.

1.

1.

3.

2.

2.

4.

Chocolate *Cupcakes*

At first glance, cupcakes look a lot like muffins. But these little cakes are sweeter and have a softer batter. They are in fact a completely different experience from a muffin. Covered with a cloud of frosting, in this case a chocolate buttercream, they provide a taste experience that is hard to beat.

1. Preheat the oven to 350°F. Place 14 paper liners in a muffin pan.

2. Sift together the flour, baking powder, and cocoa powder into a large bowl. Add the butter, granulated sugar, and eggs and beat until smooth. Fold in the melted chocolate.

3. Divide the mixture evenly among the paper liners. Bake in the preheated oven for 15–20 minutes, or until risen and firm to the touch. Transfer to a wire rack and let cool.

4. To make the frosting, put the chocolate into a heatproof bowl. Heat the cream in a saucepan until boiling, then pour it over the chocolate and stir until smooth. Let cool for 20 minutes, stirring occasionally, until thickened. Put the butter in a bowl, stir in the confectioners' sugar, and beat until smooth. Beat in the chocolate mixture. Chill for 15–20 minutes.

5. Spoon the frosting into a pastry bag fitted with a large star tip. Pipe swirls of frosting on top of each cupcake. Decorate with chocolate shapes and gold candied balls, if using.

MAKES 14

PREP TIME: 25 minutes, plus time to chill

COOKING TIME: 15–20 minutes

INGREDIENTS

1 cup all-purpose flour

1½ teaspoons baking powder

1½ tablespoons unsweetened cocoa powder

1 stick butter, softened, or ½ cup soft margarine

½ cup granulated sugar

2 extra-large eggs, beaten

2 ounces semisweet chocolate, melted

frosting

6 ounces semisweet chocolate, finely chopped

1 cup heavy cream

1¼ sticks unsalted butter, softened

2¼ cups confectioners' sugar, sifted

chocolate shapes and gold candied balls, to decorate (optional)

Apple Pie

SERVES 6

PREP TIME: 40 minutes,
plus 30 minutes to chill

COOKING TIME: 50 minutes

INGREDIENTS

pastry dough

2¾ cups all-purpose flour,
plus extra for dusting

pinch of salt

6 tablespoons butter or
margarine, diced

⅓ cup lard or white
vegetable shortening, diced

⅓ cup cold water

beaten egg or milk,
for glazing

filling

5–6 Granny Smith or other cooking apples
(about 1¾–2½ pounds), peeled, cored,
and sliced

⅔ cup granulated sugar,
plus extra for sprinkling

½–1 teaspoon ground cinnamon,
apple pie spice, or ground ginger

"As American as apple pie" is a phrase common among all Americans. Apple pie symbolizes the warmth of the hearth as the center of family life. Old-fashioned family values, with the mother baking delicious comfort food homemade from simple and affordable ingredients, often during difficult economic times, are still relevant in today's busy times.

1. To make the dough, sift together the flour and salt into a bowl. Add the butter and lard and rub in with your fingertips until the mixture resembles fine bread crumbs. Add the water and gather the mixture together into a dough. Wrap in plastic wrap and chill in the refrigerator for 30 minutes.

2. Preheat the oven to 425°F. Thinly roll out two-thirds of the dough on a lightly floured surface and use to line a deep 9-inch pie plate or pan.

3. To make the filling, place the apple slices, sugar, and spice in a bowl and mix together thoroughly. Pack into the pastry shell to come up above the rim. Add 1–2 tablespoons of water if the apples are not juicy.

4. Roll out the remaining dough on a lightly floured surface to form a lid. Dampen the edges of the pie rim with water and position the lid, pressing the edges firmly together. Trim and crimp the edges. Use the trimmings to cut out leaves or other shapes to decorate the top of the pie. Dampen and attach. Glaze the top of the pie with beaten egg, make one or two slits in the pastry, and place the pie plate on a baking sheet.

5. Bake in the preheated oven for 20 minutes, then reduce the oven temperature to 350°F and bake for an additional 30 minutes, or until light golden brown. Serve hot or cold, sprinkled with sugar.

1.

3.

4.

Chocolate Chip

COOKIES

The chocolate chip cookie is still a newcomer to the baking world. It was only in 1930 that Ruth Graves Wakefield first concocted these little delights in her Toll House Inn in the village of Whitman, Massachusetts. Apparently, some small pieces of chocolate accidentally fell into the dough, but she baked the cookies anyway, not wanting to waste the dough. It has been the official cookie of the state of Massachusetts since 1997.

1. Preheat the oven to 375 °F. Lightly grease two baking sheets.

2. Place all of the ingredients in a large mixing bowl and beat them until well combined.

3. Place tablespoons of the mixture on the prepared baking sheets, spaced well apart to allow for spreading.

4. Bake in the preheated oven for 10–12 minutes, or until golden brown. Transfer to a wire rack and let cool.

MAKES 8

PREP TIME: 10 minutes

COOKING TIME: 10–12 minutes

INGREDIENTS

unsalted butter, melted,
for greasing
1⅓ cups all-purpose flour, sifted
1 teaspoon baking powder
½ cup (1 stick) margarine, melted
⅓ cup firmly packed light brown sugar
¼ cup granulated sugar
½ teaspoon vanilla extract
1 egg, beaten
¾ cup semisweet chocolate chips

1.

3.

Donuts

WITH CINNAMON SUGAR

Donuts are omnipresent in the United States and Canada. These donuts, with the characteristic hole in the middle, are a tasty and easy variation of fritters. It's possible that American-style donuts date back to Polish *pączki*, which have been around in Eastern Europe since the Middle Ages.

1. Sift together the flour, sugar, and salt into a mixing bowl and stir in the yeast. Stir in the milk, butter, eggs, and lemon rind, mixing to a soft, sticky dough.

2. Turn out the dough onto a lightly floured work surface and knead until smooth. Return to the bowl, cover, and let stand in a warm place for about 1 hour, or until doubled in size.

3. Turn out the dough onto a lightly floured work surface and knead again for 5 minutes, until smooth and elastic. Roll out to a thickness of ½ inch. Stamp out 3-inch circles with a cutter, then cut a 1-inch circle from the center of each.

4. Place the rings on a baking sheet lined with wax paper, cover, and let rise in a warm place for about 1 hour, until doubled in size.

5. Heat the oil for deep-frying in a deep fryer or deep saucepan to 350–375 °F, or until a cube of bread browns in 30 seconds. Add the donuts, in small batches, and fry, turning once, for 3–4 minutes, until golden brown.

6. Remove the donuts with a slotted spoon and drain on paper towels. Toss the donuts in the sugar-and-cinnamon mixture until lightly coated. Serve warm.

MAKES 12–14

PREP TIME: 25 minutes, plus 2 hours to rise

COOKING TIME: 15–20 minutes

INGREDIENTS

4 cups all-purpose flour, plus extra for dusting
⅓ cup granulated sugar
½ teaspoon salt
2¼ teaspoons active dry yeast
¾ cup lukewarm milk
5 tablespoons unsalted butter, melted
2 eggs, beaten
finely grated rind of 1 lemon
sunflower oil, for deep-frying

cinnamon coating
¼ cup granulated sugar
1 teaspoon ground cinnamon

BLUEBERRY & CRANBERRY
Squares

MAKES 12

PREP TIME: 20 minutes

COOKING TIME: 25–30 minutes

INGREDIENTS

*1½ sticks unsalted butter, softened,
plus extra for greasing*
¾ cup granulated sugar
1 teaspoon vanilla extract
3 eggs, beaten
1⅓ cup all-pupose flour
1¼ teaspoons baking powder
⅓ cup dried cranberries
1¼ cups fresh blueberries

frosting

*1 cup mascarpone cheese,
or cream cheese*
¾ cup confectioners' sugar

Blueberries are native to the eastern half of North America. They were once cultivated from low-lying plants in the coastal forests of the new continent. The little berries are rich in nutrients and add a powerful, unique aroma to many baked goods, especially when mixed with cranberries, a related fruit.

1. Preheat the oven to 350°F. Grease a shallow 7 x 11-inch rectangular cake pan and line with wax paper.

2. Put the butter, sugar, and vanilla extract into a large mixing bowl and cream together until pale and fluffy. Gradually add the eggs, beating well after each addition.

3. Fold in the flour and baking powder with a metal spoon, then stir in the cranberries and ⅔ cup of the blueberries.

4. Spoon the batter into the prepared pan and spread evenly over the bottom. Bake in the preheated oven for 25–30 minutes, or until risen, firm, and golden brown. Let cool in the pan for 15 minutes, then turn out and transfer to a wire rack to cool completely.

5. To make the frosting, beat together the mascarpone cheese and sugar until smooth, then spread it over the cake with a spatula.

6. Sprinkle the remaining blueberries over the cake and cut into 12 squares to serve.

Fudge Blondies

4.

MAKES 9

PREP TIME: 30 minutes

COOKING TIME: 40–45 minutes

INGREDIENTS

*1 stick butter, softened,
plus extra for greasing*
1 cup firmly packed light brown sugar
2 extra-large eggs, beaten
1 teaspoon vanilla extract
2 cups all-purpose flour
1 teaspoon baking powder
*4 ounces soft butter fudge,
chopped into small pieces*
*½ cup coarsely chopped
macadamia nuts*
confectioners' sugar, for dusting

Similar to brownies in shape and texture but made with chunks of fudge and macadamia nuts instead of chocolate.

1. Preheat the oven to 350 °F. Grease a shallow 8-inch square cake pan and line with parchment paper.

2. Put the butter and brown sugar into a large bowl and beat with an electric mixer until pale and creamy. Add the eggs, one at a time, beating after each addition until combined, then add the vanilla extract and stir to mix. Sift together the flour and baking powder into the mixture and beat until combined.

3. Add the fudge and chopped nuts and stir together until combined. Spoon the batter into the prepared pan and smooth the surface.

4. Bake in the preheated oven for 40–45 minutes, or until risen and golden brown. Let cool in the pan, then dust with sifted confectioners' sugar to decorate and cut into squares.

Pumpkin Pie

SERVES 8

PREP TIME: 25 minutes

COOKING TIME: 1 hour

INGREDIENTS

all-purpose flour, for dusting
1 store-bought rolled dough pie crust
*1 (15-ounce) can pumpkin
(not pumpkin pie filling)*
2 eggs, lightly beaten
¾ cup granulated sugar
1 teaspoon ground cinnamon
½ teaspoon ground ginger
¼ teaspoon ground cloves
½ teaspoon salt
1½ cup canned evaporated milk

eggnog whipped cream
1½ cups heavy cream
⅔ cup confectioners' sugar
1 tablespoon brandy, or to taste
*1 tablespoon light or dark rum,
or to taste*
*freshly grated nutmeg,
to decorate*

Pumpkin pie is a popular dessert, especially during Halloween, Thanksgiving, and Christmas. After all, late fall is the time of the year when pumpkins, which have been grown in North America for thousands of years, are ready for harvest. The recipe, however, probably traveled to the Americas from Britain in around 1800, where this pie has been baked since the sixteenth century.

1. Preheat the oven to 400 °F. Lightly dust a rolling pin with flour and use to roll out the dough on a lightly floured work surface into a 12-inch circle. Line a 9-inch deep pie plate or pan with the dough, trimming the excess. Line the pastry shell with parchment paper and fill with pie weights or dried beans.

2. Bake in the preheated oven for 10 minutes. Remove from the oven and take out the paper and weights. Reduce the oven temperature to 350 °F.

3. Meanwhile, put the pumpkin, eggs, sugar, cinnamon, ginger, cloves, and salt into a bowl and beat together, then beat in the evaporated milk. Pour the filling into the pastry shell, return to the oven, and bake for 40–50 minutes, until the filling is set and the tip of a knife inserted in the center comes out clean. Transfer to a wire rack and set aside to cool completely.

4. While the pie is baking, make the eggnog whipped cream. Put the cream into a bowl and beat until it has thickened and increased in volume. Just as it starts to stiffen, sift over the confectioners' sugar and continue beating until it holds stiff peaks. Add the brandy and rum and beat, being careful not to overbeat or the mixture will separate. Cover and chill until required. When ready to serve, grate some nutmeg over the whipped cream. Serve the pie with the cream.

Devil's Food

CAKE

SERVES 10

PREP TIME: 40 minutes,
plus time to cool

COOKING TIME: 35–40 minutes

INGREDIENTS

*5 ounces semisweet chocolate,
broken into pieces*
½ cup milk
2 tablespoons unsweetened cocoa powder
*1¼ sticks unsalted butter, softened,
plus extra for greasing*
⅔ cup firmly packed light brown sugar
3 eggs, separated
¼ cup sour cream or crème fraîche
1⅔ cups all-purpose flour
1 teaspoon baking soda

icing

5 ounces semisweet chocolate
½ cup unsweetened cocoa powder
¼ cup sour cream or crème fraîche
1 tablespoon light corn syrup
3 tablespoons unsalted butter
¼ cup water
1⅔ cups confectioners' sugar

This classic American cake has a moist and dark chocolate sponge smothered in a rich and creamy chocolate frosting. It is a great cake to serve for a birthday celebration because it can be made in advance and is easy to slice!

1. Preheat the oven to 325 °F. Grease two 8-inch cake pans and line with parchment paper.

2. Put the chocolate, milk, and cocoa powder into a heatproof bowl set over a saucepan of barely simmering water and heat, stirring, until melted and smooth. Remove from the heat.

3. In a large bowl, beat together the butter and brown sugar until pale and creamy. Beat in the egg yolks, then the sour cream and melted chocolate mixture. Sift in the flour and baking soda, then fold in evenly. In a separate clean bowl, beat the egg whites until they hold stiff peaks. Lightly fold into the mixture.

4. Divide the batter between the prepared cake pans, smooth the surfaces, and bake in the preheated oven for 35–40 minutes, or until risen and firm to the touch. Let cool in the pans for 10 minutes, then turn out onto a wire rack to cool completely.

5. To make the frosting, place the chocolate, cocoa powder, sour cream, light corn syrup, butter, and water in a saucepan and heat gently until melted. Remove from the heat and sift in the confectioners' sugar, stirring until smooth. Cool, stirring occasionally, until the mixture begins to thicken and hold its shape.

6. Split the cakes in half horizontally with a sharp knife to make four layers. Sandwich the cakes together with about one-third of the frosting. Spread the remainder over the top and sides of the cakes, swirling with a spatula.

2.

3.

5.

Snickerdoodles

MAKES 40

PREP TIME: 15 minutes,
plus 1 hour to chill

COOKING TIME: 12 minutes

INGREDIENTS

2 sticks butter, softened
¾ cup granulated sugar
2 extra-large eggs, lightly beaten
1 teaspoon vanilla extract
3¼ cups all-purpose flour
1 teaspoon baking soda
½ teaspoon freshly grated nutmeg
pinch of salt
½ cup finely chopped pecans

cinnamon coating
1 tablespoon granulated sugar
2 tablespoons ground cinnamon

A snickerdoodle is a cookie with a cracked surface flavored with cinnamon. It probably originated with the European immigrants to New England, who loved giving fanciful names to their recipes. It might also be a corruption of the German schneckennudeln, a larger cinnamon-flavored baked item, usually made with a yeast dough.

1. Put the butter and sugar into a bowl and mix well with a wooden spoon, then beat in the eggs and vanilla extract. Sift together the flour, baking soda, nutmeg, and a pinch of salt into the mixture, add the pecans and stir until thoroughly combined. Shape the dough into a ball, wrap in plastic wrap, and chill in the refrigerator for 30–60 minutes.

2. Preheat the oven to 375 °F. Line two to three baking sheets with wax paper.

3. For the cinnamon coating, mix together the sugar and cinnamon in a shallow dish. Scoop up tablespoons of the cookie dough and roll into balls. Roll each ball in the cinnamon mixture to coat and place on the prepared baking sheets, spaced well apart to allow for spreading.

4. Bake in the preheated oven for 10–12 minutes, until golden brown. Let cool on the baking sheets for 5–10 minutes, then use a spatula to carefully transfer the cookies to wire racks and let cool completely.

1.

3.

Pumpkin

WHOOPIE PIES

2.

3.

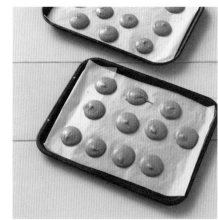

Whoopie pies were born in New England or Pennsylvania and have a sweet creamy filling between two cake halves. Farmers would be given these by their wives as part of their packed lunch—apparently their response was to shout out "Whoopee!" with joy.

1. Preheat the oven to 350°F. Line two to three large baking sheets with wax paper. Sift together the flour, baking powder, baking soda, cinnamon, and salt.

2. Put the sugar and oil into a large bowl and beat with an electric mixer for 1 minute. Add the egg and vanilla extract and beat until incorporated, then beat in the pumpkin. Stir in the sifted flour mixture and beat until thoroughly incorporated.

3. Pipe or spoon 24 mounds of the batter onto the prepared baking sheets, spaced well apart to allow for spreading. Bake, one sheet at a time, in the preheated oven for 8–10 minutes, until risen and just firm to the touch. Let cool on the sheets for 5 minutes, then use a spatula to transfer the cakes to a wire rack and let cool completely.

4. To make the cinnamon-and-maple filling, put the cream cheese and butter into a bowl and beat together until well blended. Beat in the maple syrup, cinnamon, and confectioners' sugar until smooth.

5. To assemble, spread or pipe the filling over the flat side of half the cakes. Top with the remaining cakes.

MAKES 12

PREP TIME: 30 minutes

COOKING TIME: 10 minutes

INGREDIENTS

2¼ cups all-purpose flour
½ teaspoon baking powder
½ teaspoon baking soda
1½ teaspoons ground cinnamon
¼ teaspoon salt
1 cup firmly packed light brown sugar
½ cup sunflower oil
1 extra-large egg, beaten
1 teaspoon vanilla extract
½ cup canned pumpkin
(not pumpkin pie filling)

cinnamon & maple filling

1 cup cream cheese
6 tablespoons unsalted butter, softened
2 tablespoons maple syrup
1 teaspoon ground cinnamon
⅔ cup confectioners' sugar, sifted

1.

2.

3.

Key Lime *Pie*

This pie, going back more than a century, is named after the limes that grow on the Florida Keys. The plant is thornier and its fruit doesn't last as long as the standard lime, but it is a popular ingredient because of its pronounced sour-bitter taste. The Key Lime Pie has been the official pie of the State of Florida since 2006.

1. Preheat the oven to 325 °F. Lightly grease a 9-inch tart pan, about 1½ inches deep. To make the crust, put the cookies, sugar, and cinnamon into a food processor and pulse until reduced to fine crumbs—do not overprocess to a powder. Add the melted butter and process until combined.

2. Transfer the crumb mixture into the prepared tart pan and press over the bottom and up the sides. Put the pan on a baking sheet and bake in the preheated oven for 5 minutes. Meanwhile, to make the filling, beat together the condensed milk, lime juice, lime rind, and egg yolks in a bowl until well blended.

3. Remove the tart pan from the oven, pour the filling into the crust, and spread out to the edges. Return to the oven for an additional 15 minutes, or until the filling is set around the edges but still wobbly in the center. Let cool completely on a wire rack, then cover and chill for at least 2 hours. Spread with whipped cream and serve.

SERVES 8

PREP TIME: 30 minutes,
plus 2 hours to chill

COOKING TIME: 20 minutes

INGREDIENTS

crumb base

25 (about 6 ounces) graham crackers or gingersnaps

2 tablespoons granulated sugar

½ teaspoon ground cinnamon

5 tablespoons butter, melted, plus extra for greasing

filling

1¾ cups canned condensed milk

½ cup freshly squeezed lime juice

finely grated rind of 3 limes

4 egg yolks

whipped cream, to serve

Red Velvet

CAKE

SERVES 12

PREP TIME: 20 minutes

COOKING TIME: 25–30 minutes

INGREDIENTS

2 sticks unsalted butter,
plus extra for greasing
¼ cup water
⅔ cup cocoa powder
3 eggs, beaten
1 cup buttermilk
2 teaspoons vanilla extract
2 tablespoons red food coloring
2¼ cups all-purpose flour
⅓ cup cornstarch
1½ teaspoons baking powder
1⅓ cups granulated sugar

frosting
1 cup cream cheese
3 tablespoons unsalted butter
3 tablespoons confectioners' sugar
1 teaspoon vanilla extract

The classic reddish-brown color of this cake comes from the chemical re-
action of the anthocyanins found in the cocoa with an acid (for example,
buttermilk). To add to the effect, red food coloring is often added to the
recipe in North America.

1. Preheat the oven to 375 °F. Grease two 9-inch cake pans and line with
    parchment paper.

2. Place the butter, water, and cocoa powder in a small saucepan and heat
    gently, without boiling, stirring until melted and smooth. Remove from
    the heat and let cool slightly.

3. Beat together the eggs, buttermilk, vanilla extract, and food coloring in a
    bowl until frothy. Beat in the butter mixture. Sift together the flour, corn-
    starch, and baking powder, then stir quickly and evenly into the mixture
    with the granulated sugar.

4. Divide the batter between the prepared pans and bake in the preheated
    oven for 25–30 minutes, or until risen and firm to the touch. Let cool
    in the cake pans for 3–4 minutes, then turn out onto a wire rack to
    cool completely.

5. To make the frosting, beat together all the ingredients until smooth. Use
    about half of the frosting to sandwich together the cakes, then spread the
    remainder over the top, swirling with a spatula.

2.

3.

4.

Banana

BREAD

SERVES 6

PREP TIME: 20 minutes

COOKING TIME: 45 minutes

INGREDIENTS

1 cup vegetable shortening,
plus extra for greasing
½ cup granulated sugar
1¼ cups all-purpose flour
1 tablespoon baking powder
1 teaspoon baking soda
1 teaspoon salt
2 tablespoons water
2 eggs
3 ripe bananas, mashed

Banana bread has been a classic in North American cookbooks since the 1930s, when baking powder and baking soda became popular leavening agents. This quick-to-prepare bread uses completely ripe bananas—the riper the better. The result is moist, sweet, banana deliciousness!

1. Preheat the oven to 325 °F. Grease an 8½-inch loaf pan. Put the vegetable shortening and sugar into a large bowl and beat together well, then add the flour, baking powder, baking soda, and salt and mix to combine. Add the water and eggs and beat until light and fluffy.

2. Add the bananas and mix to combine. Spread the batter in the prepared pan. Use a spatula dipped in a little oil to score an impression along the center of the loaf.

3. Bake in the preheated oven for 45 minutes, until a toothpick inserted into the center comes out clean. Remove from the oven and let cool in the pan for 10 minutes, then turn out onto a wire rack and let cool completely. Cut into slices and serve.

1.

2.

2.

Cup

OF HOPE AND

Joy

The cupcake is a traditional American baked good that has recently become a phenomenon all over the world. From cupcake cafés to cupcake decorating parties, cupcakes are now everywhere; however, their spiritual home is the United States.

Cupcakes makes the world go round! This idea was supported by TV series like 'Sex and the City' and, ever since, the whole world has been talking about cupcakes.

The well-known theory that chocolate contains substances that make you happy can serve as an excuse to indulge now and again. Probably the same can be said about a treat that has come much into vogue during the last few years: the cupcake. A small, sweet snack for premeditated bursts of happiness. Cupcakes are colorful, pretty little cakes with sweet decorations and an almost irresistible creamy frosting. However, contrary to what you would think, they are not a new invention. The first formal reference to them can be found as early as 1928 in Eliza Leslie's American cookbook Receipts, although with a somewhat puritanical formulation: "The cupcake, as the name already reveals, is fabricated in a cuplike baking pan." If we left it at that, they would admittedly be just too similar to muffins. However, to begin with, their taste is different. Their dough is softer, and, they are crowned with an opulent and sweet, buttercream topping decorated with fruit, sugar pearls, or sugar flowers. Cupcakes were popular in England and were first known as "fairy cakes." The cupcake euphoria that swept over Europe from the United States at the beginning of the new century has since made cupcakes a popular anytime treat across the capitals of Europe.

The fact is, that these little cakes have by now even found their way into the general vocabulary and that the term "cupcakes" has become one of the most popular terms of endearment in the United States. Surely the enthusiasm for the television series "Sex and the City," the first season of which was broadcast in the United States, Great Britain, and Australia in 1997, is partly responsible for this. In the series, the single Carrie Bradshaw and her friends bought cupcakes from the Magnolia Bakery. Ever since, the whole world has been talking about cupcakes, because they—like any other fashionable accessory—symbolize a little piece of everyday luxury. And the best part is everyone can afford this luxury, because one can reward oneself without a bad conscience. In other words, personal happiness is within everyone's reach—but especially if it is edible. Cupcakes make the world a happier place.

Peanut Butter
S'MORES

SERVES 4

PREP TIME: 5 minutes

COOKING TIME: 1 minute

INGREDIENTS

½ cup smooth peanut butter
8 graham crackers
*4 ounces semisweet chocolate,
broken into squares*

Peanut butter, that all-time American favorite, is also an important part of many baked goods. In 1884, Canadian Marcellus G. Edson filed a patent for the nutritious, tasty food product, but the recipe for peanut butter is mostly attributed to cereal magnate John Harvey Kellogg (1895).

1. Preheat the broiler to medium. Spread the peanut butter on one side of each cracker. Place the chocolate pieces on four of the crackers and invert the remaining crackers on top.

2. Toast the s'mores under the preheated broiler for about 1 minute, until the filling starts to melt. Turn carefully. Serve.

Classic

VANILLA CUPCAKES

This recipe was once a must-have for American children's parties. Vanilla is the traditional flavor used for these little cakes, which are lighter and sweeter in taste than the muffins they resemble. Plus, they're always topped with frosting. Cupcakes were named after the cups in which they were originally baked, although today standard muffin pans can be used.

1. Preheat the oven to 350 °F. Place 12 paper liners in a muffin pan.

2. Put the butter and granulated sugar into a bowl and beat together until pale and creamy. Gradually beat in the eggs and vanilla extract. Sift in the flour and baking powder, then fold in gently.

3. Divide the batter evenly among the paper liners and bake in the preheated oven for 15–20 minutes, or until risen and firm to the touch. Transfer to a wire rack and let cool.

4. To make the frosting, put the butter into a bowl and beat with an electric mixer for 2–3 minutes, or until pale and creamy. Beat in the cream and vanilla extract. Gradually beat in the confectioners' sugar and continue beating until the buttercream is light and fluffy.

5. Use a spatula to swirl the frosting over the tops of the cupcakes. Decorate with the sprinkles.

MAKES 12

PREP TIME: 25 minutes

COOKING TIME: 15–20 minutes

INGREDIENTS

1½ sticks unsalted butter, softened
¾ cup granulated sugar
3 extra-large eggs, beaten
1 teaspoon vanilla extract
1⅓ cups all-purpose flour
1¼ teaspoons baking powder

frosting

1¼ sticks unsalted butter, softened
3 tablespoons heavy cream or milk
1 teaspoon vanilla extract
2⅓ cups confectioners' sugar, sifted
sprinkles, to decorate

2.

5.

3.

4.

5.

Boston CREAM PIE

SERVES 10

PREP TIME: 40 minutes,
plus time to cool

COOKING TIME: 20–25 minutes

This has been the official cake of the State of Massachusetts since 1996. It was supposedly invented by the French chef at the Parker House Hotel in Boston when it opened in 1856. He replaced the heavy filling between two layers of cake with a light vanilla pastry cream and topped it all with a rich chocolate glaze.

1. Preheat the oven to 350°F. Grease two 9-inch cake pans and line with parchment paper.

2. Place the eggs and sugar in a heatproof bowl set over a saucepan of simmering water. Beat with a wire whisk until the mixture is thick and pale and leaves a trail when the whisk is lifted.

3. Sift in the flour and fold in gently. Pour the butter over the mixture in a thin stream and fold in until just incorporated. Divide the batter between the prepared pans and bake in the preheated oven for 20–25 minutes, or until light golden and springy to the touch. Let cool in the pans for 5 minutes, then turn out onto a wire rack to cool completely.

4. To make the pastry cream, beat together the eggs, sugar, and vanilla extract. Blend the flour and cornstarch to a paste with ¼ cup of the milk, then beat into the egg mixture. Heat the remaining milk until almost boiling and pour onto the egg mixture, stirring continuously. Return to the saucepan and cook over low heat, beating continuously, until smooth and thickened. Pour into a bowl and cover with damp wax paper. Let stand until cold, then fold in the whipped cream.

5. To make the glaze, put the chocolate, corn syrup, and butter into a heatproof bowl. Heat the cream until almost boiling, then pour it over the chocolate. Let stand for 1 minute, then stir until smooth.

6. To assemble, sandwich the sponges together with the pastry cream. Spread the chocolate glaze over the top of the cake.

INGREDIENTS

4 extra-large eggs, beaten
⅔ cup superfine sugar
1 cup all-purpose flour
3 tablespoons butter, melted and cooled, plus extra for greasing

pastry cream
2 eggs
¼ cup superfine sugar
1 teaspoon vanilla extract
2 tablespoons all-purpose flour
2 tablespoons cornstarch
1¼ cups milk
⅔ cup heavy cream, softly whipped

chocolate glaze
4 ounces semisweet chocolate, grated
1 tablespoon light corn syrup
2 tablespoons unsalted butter
⅔ cup heavy cream

Berry *Muffins*

MAKES 12

PREP TIME: 20 minutes

COOKING TIME: 20–25 minutes

INGREDIENTS

1¾ cups all-purpose flour

2 teaspoons baking powder

½ cup ground almonds (almond meal)

⅔ cup granulated sugar, plus extra for sprinkling

1¼ sticks butter, melted

½ cup milk

2 eggs, beaten

2 cups mixed berries, such as blueberries, raspberries, blackberries, and cranberries

The American muffin is the result of the invention of baking powder in 1856 by Harvard professor Eben Norton Horsford, one of the founders of modern nutritional science. With berries added to the batter, this muffin bursts with the warmth and freshness of summer.

1. Preheat the oven to 375 °F. Place 12 paper liners in a muffin pan.

2. Sift together the flour and baking powder into a large bowl and stir in the ground almonds and sugar. Make a well in the center of the dry ingredients.

3. Beat together the butter, milk, and eggs and pour into the well. Stir gently until just combined; do not overmix. Gently fold in the berries.

4. Divide the batter evenly among the paper liners. Bake in the preheated oven for 20–25 minutes, or until light golden and just firm to the touch. Serve warm or cold, sprinkled with sugar.

2.

3.

4.

Black & White

COOKIES

MAKES 20

PREP TIME: 20 minutes

COOKING TIME: 15 minutes

INGREDIENTS

*1 stick unsalted butter,
softened, plus extra for greasing*
1 teaspoon vanilla extract
¾ cup granulated sugar
2 eggs, beaten
2⅓ cups all-purpose flour
½ teaspoon baking powder
1 cup milk

icing

1¾ cups confectioners' sugar
½ cup heavy cream
⅛ teaspoon vanilla extract
*3 ounces semisweet chocolate,
broken into pieces*

These cookies originated in New York State, where they are also known as half moons. They come in different taste variations, but what sets them apart is their black-and-white icing. Only one question remains: Which side do I bite first? Or should I just bite them both at the same time?

1. Preheat the oven to 375°F. Grease three baking sheets. Put the butter, vanilla extract, and granulated sugar into a large bowl. Beat with an electric mixer until light and fluffy, then add the eggs, one at a time, beating after each addition until combined.

2. Sift together the flour and baking powder and fold into the creamed mixture, loosening with milk as you work until both are used and the batter is of dropping consistency. Drop heaping tablespoons of the batter on the prepared baking sheets, spaced well apart to allow for spreading. Bake in the preheated oven for 15 minutes, or until turning golden at the edges and light to the touch. Transfer to wire racks to cool completely.

3. To make the icing, put the confectioners' sugar into a bowl and mix in half the cream and the vanilla extract. The consistency should be thick but spreadable. Using a spatula, spread half of each cookie with white icing. Put the chocolate into a heatproof bowl set over a saucepan of barely simmering water and heat until melted. Remove from the heat and stir in the remaining cream. Spread the dark icing over the uncoated cookie halves.

1.

2.

3.

MISSISSIPPI
Mud Pie

This dish was created by home bakers in Mississippi and was only published for the first time in 1970s. The pie is made using ingredients that are close at hand, and leftover cookies are often used in the recipe for the crust. This sticky chocolate pie is good with vanilla ice cream.

1. Preheat the oven to 400°F. To make the dough, sift the flour and cocoa powder into a bowl and stir in the sugar. Rub in the butter with your fingertips until the mixture resembles fine bread crumbs. Add just enough water to bind to a dough.

2. Roll out the dough on a lightly floured work surface to a circle large enough to line a 1¼-inch deep, 8-inch round tart pan. Use the pastry to line the pan. Prick the bottom with a fork, cover with a piece of wax paper, and fill with pie weights or dried beans, then bake in the preheated oven for 10 minutes. Remove from the oven and remove the paper and weights. Reduce the oven temperature to 350°F.

3. Put the chocolate and butter into a saucepan and heat over low heat, stirring, until melted. Put the sugar and eggs into a bowl and beat together until smooth, then stir in the chocolate mixture, cream, and vanilla extract.

4. Pour the chocolate mixture into the pastry shell and bake in the oven for 20–25 minutes, or until just set. Let cool.

5. To make the topping, whip the cream until it just holds its shape, then spread over the pie. Put the chocolate into a bowl set over a saucepan of barely simmering water and heat until melted, then spoon into a pastry bag and pipe decorations over the cream. Serve cold.

SERVES 6–8

PREP TIME: 30 minutes, plus time to cool

COOKING TIME: 35–40 minutes

INGREDIENTS

3 ounces semisweet chocolate
6 tablespoons unsalted butter
⅓ cup firmly light brown sugar
2 eggs, beaten
½ cup light cream
1 teaspoon vanilla extract

pastry dough
*1⅓ cups all-purpose flour,
plus extra for dusting*
¼ cup unsweetened cocoa powder
3 tablespoons packed light brown sugar
6 tablespoons unsalted butter
2–3 tablespoons cold water

topping
1 cup heavy cream
3 ounces semisweet chocolate

Chocolate Chip
MUFFINS

MAKES 12

PREP TIME: 20 minutes

COOKING TIME: 20–25 minutes

INGREDIENTS

2⅓ cups all-purpose flour
5 teaspoons baking powder
4 tablespoons chilled butter, diced
½ cup granulated sugar
*6 ounces milk chocolate,
chopped into chunks*
2 extra-large eggs, beaten
1 cup buttermilk
1 teaspoon vanilla extract

American muffins have a standard shape and batter, and they have to be made following a special "muffin method." The dry and wet ingredients are mixed separately and then stirred together briefly. If mixed for too long, too much gluten will be activated and the batter will become heavy. Muffins with chocolate chips are a classic.

1. Preheat the oven to 400 °F. Put 12 muffin cups into a 12-cup muffin pan.

2. Sift together the flour and baking powder into a large bowl. Add the butter and rub in to make bread crumbs. Stir in the sugar and chocolate chunks.

3. Beat together the eggs, buttermilk, and vanilla extract in a separate bowl. Make a well in the center of the dry ingredients and pour in the beaten liquid ingredients. Gently stir until just combined. Do not overmix.

4. Divide the batter evenly among the muffin cups. Bake in the preheated oven for 20–25 minutes, or until risen, golden, and just firm to the touch. Let cool in the pan for 5 minutes, then transfer to a wire rack to cool completely.

2.

2.

4.

2.

3.

3.

Maple & Pecan

BUNDT CAKE

The Bundt cake pan is a ribbed cake pan with a hole in the middle. It became popular in 1950s North America after kitchen appliance manufacturers Dalquist used it as part of their logo. This recipe with maple syrup and pecans gives this all-American cake shape an all-American taste. And, of course, it simply must have icing on top.

1. Preheat the oven to 325 °F. Grease a 2-quart Bundt pan and lightly dust with flour.

2. Put the butter and brown sugar into a bowl and beat together until pale and fluffy. Gradually beat in the eggs, then stir in the nuts, maple syrup, and sour cream. Sift in the flour and baking powder, and then fold in thoroughly.

3. Spoon the batter into the prepared pan and gently smooth the surface. Bake in the preheated oven for 45–50 minutes, or until the cake is firm and golden and a toothpick inserted into the center comes out clean. Let cool in the pan for 10 minutes, then turn out onto a wire rack to cool completely.

4. To make the icing, mix together the confectioners' sugar, maple syrup, and enough water to make a smooth icing. Spoon it over the top of the cake, letting it run down the sides. Decorate with chopped nuts and let set.

SERVES 10

PREP TIME: 30 minutes,
plus time to cool

COOKING TIME: 45–50 minutes

INGREDIENTS

1¾ sticks butter, softened,
plus extra for greasing

1 cup firmly packed light brown sugar

3 extra-large eggs, beaten

½ cup finely chopped pecans,
plus extra, coarsely chopped, to decorate

¼ cup maple syrup

⅔ cup sour cream

1¾ cups all-purpose flour,
plus extra for dusting

1¾ teaspoons baking powder

icing
⅔ cup confectioners' sugar, sifted

1 tablespoon maple syrup

1–2 tablespoons lukewarm water

CHOCOLATE & CHERRY

Brownies

MAKES 12

PREP TIME: 30 minutes

COOKING TIME: 45–50 minutes

INGREDIENTS

6 ounces semisweet chocolate, broken into pieces

1½ sticks butter, plus extra for greasing

1 cup granulated sugar

3 extra-large eggs, beaten

1 teaspoon vanilla extract

1 cup all-pupose flour

1 teaspoon baking powder

1 cup pitted fresh cherries

3 ounces white chocolate, coarsely chopped

Do you like your cake on the sticky side? Then the brownie will be just your thing. This brownie is rich and sweet with a moist, dense center. The cherries add a sweet freshness and heighten the typical brownie experience.

1. Preheat the oven to 350 °F. Grease a shallow 9½ x 8-inch cake pan and line with parchment paper.

2. Put the semisweet chocolate and butter into a large, heatproof bowl set over a saucepan of barely simmering water and heat until melted. Remove from the heat and let cool for 5 minutes.

3. Beat the sugar, eggs, and vanilla extract into the chocolate mixture. Sift in the flour and baking powder, and then fold in gently. Pour the batter into the prepared pan. Sprinkle the cherries and white chocolate over the top.

4. Bake in the preheated oven for 30 minutes. Loosely cover the tops of the brownies with aluminum foil and bake for an additional 15–20 minutes, or until just firm to the touch. Let cool in the pan, then cut into pieces.

2.

3.

3.

Canadian

BUTTER TARTS

MAKES 16

PREP TIME: 30 minutes,
plus 30 minutes to chill

COOKING TIME: 15 minutes

INGREDIENTS

1 egg

½ cup firmly packed light brown sugar

2 teaspoons light corn syrup

1 tablespoon butter

1 teaspoon vanilla extract or 1 vanilla bean, scraped

1 cup golden raisins

pastry dough

2⅓ cups all-purpose flour, plus extra for dusting

1 teaspoon salt

1 cup vegetable shortening

1 egg

3 tablespoons cold water

These little tarts are among the few recipes that are uniquely Canadian in origin and are a highlight of the early cuisine of this North American country. In this version, the inside is filled with a rich mixture of light corn syrup, brown sugar, and golden raisins—a true Canadian original.

1. To make the dough, sift together the flour and salt into a large bowl, then add the vegetable shortening and mix until the mixture resembles bread crumbs. Mix together the egg and water in a separate bowl and add to the flour mixture, working it in until smooth. Wrap the dough in plastic wrap and chill in the refrigerator for 30 minutes.

2. Preheat the oven to 400 °F. Turn out the dough onto a lightly floured work surface, roll out and use a 3-inch cutter to cut out 16 circles, rerolling the trimmings, if necessary. Press the circles into 16 individual tart pans and trim the edges.

3. Put the egg, sugar, corn syrup, butter, and vanilla extract into a saucepan and heat over medium heat, stirring continuously, until the butter has melted. Divide the golden raisins among the tart shells. Pour in the filling so that the pastry shells are almost filled. Bake in the preheated oven for 10 minutes, until light golden brown. Remove from the oven and serve hot or cold.

2.

2.

3.

2.

4.

5.

MINI
Cherry Pies

The annual cherry harvest coincides with Independence Day (July 4) and Canada Day (July 1). These patriotic celebrations at the height of summer are great occasions for these wonderful fruity pies, especially when served with vanilla ice cream or whipped cream. Thanks to the freezer, these dark cherry pies can now be enjoyed year-round.

1. Preheat the oven to 350°F. Grease two 12-cup muffin pans.

2. Put the cherries into a mixing bowl. Stir in the cornstarch, preserves, and lime rind.

3. Thinly roll out half the dough on a lightly floured work surface. Use a 2½-inch fluted cookie cutter to stamp out 24 circles. Press the circles gently into the prepared pans, rerolling the trimmings, if necessary.

4. Brush the top edges of the pastry shells with a little of the egg yolk and water mixture, then spoon in the filling.

5. Thinly roll out the remaining dough on a lightly floured work surface. Use a 2-inch round cutter to cut out 24 circles, rerolling the trimmings, if necessary. Attach the circles as lids to the rim of the pies, wet the edges with a little water, then press together to seal. Use a heart-shape cutter to cut out mini hearts from the pastry and attach them to the lids with a little water. Brush the egg glaze over the pastry and sprinkle with granulated sugar.

6. Bake in the preheated oven for 15 minutes, or until golden. Let cool in the pans for 10 minutes, then loosen with a blunt knife and transfer to a wire rack to cool. Whip the cream until it holds soft peaks, then fold in half the lime rind and the confectioners' sugar. Sprinkle with the remaining lime rind. Serve spoonfuls of the cream with the pies.

MAKES 24

PREP TIME: 25 minutes

COOKING TIME: 15 minutes

INGREDIENTS

butter, for greasing
2 cups coarsely chopped, pitted cherries
2 teaspoons cornstarch
2 tablespoons cherry preserves
grated rind of 2 limes
1 sheet rolled dough pie crust, chilled
all-purpose flour, for dusting
1 egg yolk mixed with 1 tablespoon water, for glazing
granulated sugar, for sprinkling

to serve
1 cup heavy cream
grated rind of 2 limes
2 tablespoons confectioners' sugar

BREAKING
bagels

A bagel is only a good bagel when the hole in the middle is the right size. It has to be round, 2 inches high, and approximately two-and-a-half fingers across.

The ingredients? simple: Flour, salt, water, yeast, and malt. That's it. The whole thing is first boiled and then baked, so that at the end a golden ring comes out, weighing pretty much 4½ ounces. Not more, but not much less. And when you bite into it, there should be a slightly crunchy sound. If not, then the bagel is not really a good bagel. As is always the case with legendary recipes, the strangest stories are woven around its origins. In the case of the bagel, scientists and researchers have been trying for years to reconstruct its origins as accurately as possible. Yale University in New Haven, Connecticut, even went as far as to sponsor a Polish author named Maria Balinska in her research. The result was an entire book telling the "surprising history of a modest bread." Of course, Jewish bakers had something to do with it and

The bagel's history is long and has plenty of surprising facts. Some of them seem to be an invention, some of them are proven. It is very much influenced by Jewish heritage.

claim to have invented the bagel to celebrate the end of the Turkish siege of Vienna. This is doubtless part of the many legends and anecdotes surrounding the history of the bagel. It's now certainly beyond dispute that the bagel has a Jewish background. Linguists have finally concluded that the term comes from the Yiddish word *beigen* (bay-gen), meaning "to bend." According to another legend, the Polish baking family Beigel invented the bread for purely practical reasons. This version is based on the Jewish commandment to wash one's hands before eating bread. Since so many Jews were often on the road and the bagel dough was boiled before being baked, the bagel could no longer be considered bread per se, but rather a kind of pasta. This meant that it could be eaten while traveling when clean water was often not available to wash one's hands.

The first time the ring-shape bread was officially mentioned was in a 1610 regulation from the Jewish community of Krakow, Poland, which prescribed exactly what could and could not be eaten at the celebration of a boy's circumcision ceremony.

With the European emigration wave to the United States, the bagel not only traveled to the new world, but it also took on a life of its own. In the early 1900s, a bakery in Manhattan's Lower East Side with a staff of 300 and a baker's union determined the ingredients to be used for the bagel and how it was supposed to taste. The influence of the bagel bakers of Local 338 can also be measured by the fact that all of the bakeries in New York and the surrounding area in the 1920s meticulously adhered to the specifications for making the "original New York bagels." Although the Bagel Bakers Union has since disappeared with the appearance of bagel-baking machines in the 1950s, the making of a real bagel was, and still remains, an unwritten law. The New Yorkers themselves make sure that nothing changes in the good old bagel tradition.

On one occasion, when an attempt was made—for production reasons—to do away with the typical hole in the bread, a great outcry ensued in the press. Such aberrations were not real bagels and not worthy of New Yorkers, the writers declared. In fact, for a long time, the distribution of the bagels was limited to New York with its strong Jewish community. It was only with the emergence of fast-food chains that bagel sandwiches began to spread all over the country.

It should be noted that the bagel has nothing to do with its competitor, the donut. Although it has a similar shape, donuts are made of a completely different type of dough and are deep-fried in fat.

Little remains to remind us of the bagel's humble origins in Europe. In Austria, a croissant filled with nuts is still called a beugel. And in Hungary one can find the beigli, a poppy seed stollen, on supermarket shelves for Christmas.

Sourdough *Bread*

MAKES 2 LOAVES

PREP TIME: 30 minutes,
plus 4–5 days for starter and
2 hours 30 minutes to rise

COOKING TIME: 30 minutes

INGREDIENTS

3¾ cups whole-wheat flour
4 teaspoons salt
1½ cups lukewarm water
2 tablespoons molasses
1 tablespoon vegetable oil,
plus extra for brushing
all-purpose flour, for dusting

starter
¾ cup whole-wheat flour
⅔ cup white bread flour
¼ cup granulated sugar
1 cup milk

This was the most important bread for the gold prospectors in California and Canada because the sourdough, which relies on natural yeasts in the air to rise, was easy to make even out in the wilderness. In comparison to standard yeast breads, it has a distinctive, slightly sour taste.

1. For the starter, put the whole-wheat flour, white bread flour, sugar, and milk into a nonmetallic bowl and beat well with a fork. Cover with a damp dish towel and let stand at room temperature for 4–5 days, until the mixture is frothy and smells sour.

2. Sift together the flour and half the salt into a bowl and add the water, molasses, oil, and starter. Mix well with a wooden spoon until a dough begins to form, then knead with your hands until it leaves the side of the bowl. Turn out onto a lightly floured work surface and knead for 10 minutes, or until smooth and elastic.

3. Brush a bowl with oil. Form the dough into a ball, put it into the bowl, and put the bowl into a plastic food bag or cover with a damp dish towel. Let rise in a warm place for 2 hours, or until the dough has doubled in size.

4. Dust two baking sheets with flour. Mix the remaining salt with ¼ cup of water in a bowl. Turn out the dough onto a lightly floured work surface and punch down to back out the air, then knead for an additional 10 minutes. Halve the dough, shape each piece into an oval, and place the loaves on the prepared baking sheets. Brush with the saltwater glaze and let stand in a warm place, brushing frequently with the glaze, for 30 minutes.

5. Meanwhile, preheat the oven to 425°F. Brush the loaves with the remaining glaze and bake in the preheated oven for 30 minutes, or until the crust is golden brown and the loaves sound hollow when tapped on the bottom. If they need longer cooking, reduce the oven temperature to 375°F. Transfer to wire racks to cool.

1.

3.

4.

1.

2.

4.

5.

7.

Stromboli

WITH SALAMI, ROASTED PEPPERS & CHEESE

MAKES 1 LOAF

PREP TIME: 20–25 minutes,
plus 1 hour 10 minutes to rise

COOKING TIME: 30–35 minutes

This bread, which resembles a rolled-up pizza, is named after the volcano in Sicily. The dough and the ingredients are typically Italian, which makes sense, given that Italian immigrants to the United States invented the recipe in the 1950s.

1. Mix together the flour, yeast, and 1½ teaspoons of the salt, then stir in the oil with enough water to make a soft dough.

2. Knead the dough on a lightly floured work surface for about 10 minutes. Cover and let stand in a warm place for 1 hour, or until doubled in volume.

3. Lightly knead for 2–3 minutes, until smooth. Cover and let stand for an additional 10 minutes.

4. Roll out the dough to a 15 x 10-inch rectangle with a thickness of ½ inch.

5. Preheat the oven to 400°F. Spread the salami over the dough and top with the mozzarella cheese, basil, and roasted peppers. Season with pepper.

6. Grease a baking sheet. Firmly roll up the dough from the long side, pinch the ends, and place on the baking sheet, with the seam underneath. Cover and let stand for 10 minutes.

7. Pierce the roll deeply with the tip of a sharp knife several times.

8. Brush with oil and sprinkle with the remaining salt. Bake in the preheated oven for 30–35 minutes, or until firm and golden. Transfer to a wire rack and let cool. Serve the bread fresh and warm, cut into thick slices.

INGREDIENTS

3¾ cups white bread flour, sifted,
plus extra for dusting

2¼ teaspoons active dry yeast

2 teaspoons sea salt flakes

3 tablespoons olive oil,
plus extra for brushing

1½ cups lukewarm water

filling

3 ounces thinly sliced Italian salami

6 ounces mozzarella cheese, chopped

1 cup basil leaves

2 red bell peppers, roasted, peeled,
seeded, and sliced (or roasted red
peppers from a jar)

pepper, to taste

2.

3.

4.

5.

5.

Bagels

A bagel is the only bread in the world that combines fire and water as it is cooked in boiling water before being baked. Bagels were supposedly invented during the Turkish siege of Vienna in 1683. A Jewish baker wanted to please the horse-mad king and made a bread that looked like a bügel, the original German word for "stirrup."

1. Dust a baking sheet with flour. Put the flour, salt, sugar, and yeast into a large bowl. Mix together with your hands and make a well in the center.

2. Put the water into a bowl with 2 teaspoons of the malt extract, the egg, and butter, and stir to combine. Pour into the well and mix into the flour with your hands. The dough should be soft but sticky. If it is too dry, add a little more water. If it is too wet, work in a little more flour. Cover the bowl with a damp dish towel and let rise for about 10 minutes.

3. Turn out the dough onto a lightly floured work surface and knead for 10 minutes, until smooth. Return to the bowl and let stand at room temperature for 1–2 hours, until doubled in size. Turn out the dough onto a floured work surface, divide it into 12 pieces, and roll each piece into a ball. Cover with a dry dish towel and let stand for 10 minutes.

4. Lightly press the balls to flatten them, then use a floured finger to make a hole through the center of each ball. Gently rotate the bagel on your finger until the hole is 1 inch in diameter.

5. Preheat the oven to 400°F. Bring a large saucepan of water to a boil and stir in the remaining malt extract. Carefully drop the bagels into the boiling water and poach for 30 seconds on each side. Use a slotted spoon to lift them out of the water, shaking off any excess, then arrange them on the prepared sheet. Lightly brush them with egg white, sprinkle with the seeds, and bake in the preheated oven for 20–25 minutes, until golden brown. Remove from the oven and transfer to a wire rack to cool. Serve with butter and jelly, or cream cheese.

MAKES 12

PREP TIME: 60 minutes, plus 2 hours 20 minutes to rise

COOKING TIME: 21–26 minutes

INGREDIENTS

3¾ cups white bread flour, plus extra if needed and for dusting

1½ teaspoons salt

3 tablespoons sugar

2¼ teaspoons active dry yeast

1 cup lukewarm water, plus extra if needed

3 tablespoons malt extract

1 egg, beaten

2 tablespoons butter, melted

1 egg white, beaten

poppy seeds, sesame seeds, and sunflower seeds, for sprinkling

butter and jelly, or cream cheese, to serve

Zucchini Bread

SERVES 6

PREP TIME: 20 minutes

COOKING TIME: 40–50 minutes

INGREDIENTS

butter, for greasing

2 cups all-purpose flour

⅔ cup granulated sugar

1¼ teaspoons baking soda

1 teaspoon salt

½ teaspoon ground cinnamon

1 egg

⅓ cup vegetable oil,
plus extra for greasing

1 teaspoon vanilla extract or 1 vanilla
bean, scraped

½ teaspoon ground nutmeg

½ cup buttermilk

1 cup shredded zucchini

½ cup finely chopped walnuts

This bread is a cake in disguise: Like carrots, zucchini can be used to make not overly sweet baked goods, especially in the summer when the vegetable grows in abundance. The bread is extremely soft and moist, and it freezes well.

1. Preheat the oven to 325 °F. Grease a 9-inch loaf pan. Sift together the flour, sugar, baking soda, salt, and cinnamon into a large bowl. Put the egg, oil, vanilla extract, and nutmeg into a separate large bowl and mix to combine. Add the sifted ingredients and the buttermilk and mix well.

2. Gently stir in the zucchini and walnuts. Do not overmix.

3. Pour the batter into the prepared pan and bake in the preheated oven for 40–50 minutes, or until a toothpick inserted into the center of the bread comes out clean.

4. Let cool in the pan for 20 minutes, then turn out onto a wire rack and let cool completely.

1.

2.

3.

1.

2.

4.

5.

5.

Scallion & Parmesan
CORN BREAD

Corn bread dates back to Native American recipes and is a traditional basic foodstuff in the rural United States, especially in the South, because corn is cheaper than wheat. Formerly baked in a cast-iron skillet set over an open fire, the bread is now typically baked in a pan in the oven. This recipe is made with scallions and Parmesan cheese and is a hearty accompaniment to other dishes.

1. Preheat the oven to 375 °F. Grease a 9-inch square cake pan.

2. Sift together the cornmeal, flour, baking powder, celery salt, and pepper into a bowl and stir in ½ cup of the cheese.

3. Beat together the eggs, milk, and butter.

4. Add the egg mixture to the dry ingredients and stir well to mix evenly.

5. Stir in the scallions, then spread the batter evenly in the prepared pan.

6. Sprinkle the remaining cheese over the batter. Bake in the preheated oven for 30–35 minutes, or until firm and golden.

7. Cut the corn bread into 16 squares and serve warm.

SERVES 16

PREP TIME: 15 minutes

COOKING TIME: 30–35 minutes

INGREDIENTS

oil, for greasing
1 cup fine cornmeal
1¼ cups all-purpose flour
4 teaspoons baking powder
2 teaspoons celery salt
⅔ cup freshly grated Parmesan cheese
2 eggs, beaten
1¾ cups milk
4 tablespoons butter, melted
1 bunch scallions, chopped
pepper, to taster

THE LATIN FLAVOR

From the historic sights of Machu Picchu to the Carnival in Rio, South America offers a wide range of attractions as diverse as its food culture. The culinary selection ranges from filled burritos, Argentine steaks, and beans to sweet cookies and fruity cakes. The influence of European colonial rulers can often be detected in the way these baked goods are made, but they are still characterized by different eating habits and a huge variety of exotic ingredients. Corn is one of the staple foods of South America, and cornmeal is often used for pastries and cakes. So, in Colombia, the traditional stone-baked arepas are served for breakfast, and in the afternoons people have coffee with the traditional mantecada pound cake made from cornmeal. A speciality is dulce de leche, a confection that was said to have healing properties by ancient ayurvedic medicine. Dulce de leche is prepared by cooking milk, sugar, and vanilla for hours and is a component of many sweet foods. The traditional alfajores cookies and the many layers of the torta de hojas are coated with this sweet flavor.

Bright colors and full of life: Latin America's baking culture is greatly influenced by its colonial history. However, its own style has developed over the last few decades and the area now has many of its own baking traditions.

Tres Leches

CREAM CAKE

SERVES 12

PREP TIME: 30 minutes,
plus 30 minutes to stand

COOKING TIME: 30 minutes

INGREDIENTS

butter, for greasing
4 eggs
¾ cup granulated sugar
1 cup all-purpose flour
1 teaspoon baking powder
¼ teaspoon salt
⅓ cup milk
1 teaspoon vanilla extract
or 1 vanilla bean, scraped
2 egg whites
1½ cups evaporated milk
1½ cups sweetened condensed milk
¼ cup heavy cream
chopped candied cherries,
to decorate

topping
2½ cups heavy cream
3 tablespoons sugar

Different versions of this cake are found throughout the countries of Latin America. The Spanish name refers to the three types of milk used to soak the typical spongy dough. The method probably originates in Europe, where, for example, tiramisu is made in the same way.

1. Preheat the oven to 350 °F. Grease a 9-inch round cake pan. Put the eggs and sugar into a large bowl and beat together until doubled in volume. Slowly add the flour, baking powder, and salt, mixing well with a wooden spoon. Stir in the milk and the vanilla extract. Beat the egg whites until they hold stiff peaks, then gently fold into the mixture.

2. Pour the batter into the prepared pan, smoothing the surface. Bake in the preheated oven for 30 minutes. Remove the cake from the oven, prick all over with a fork, then transfer to a wire rack to cool.

3. Meanwhile, thoroughly mix together the evaporated milk, condensed milk, and cream.

4. Gradually pour the mixture over the top of the cooled cake, pausing after each addition to let it be absorbed, until the cake is completely saturated. Let stand for 30 minutes.

5. Meanwhile, to make the topping, whip the cream with the sugar until it holds stiff peaks. Just before serving, spread the cream over the cake, cut into 12 pieces, and decorate each piece with chopped candied cherries.

1.

2.

4.

1.

3.

7.

Oaxacan
COCONUT & CARAMEL CAKE

This dessert from the Mexican state of Oaxaca is a kind of crème caramel. When removed from the pan, the liquid caramel attractively decorates this dessert.

1. Preheat the oven to 325 °F. Put an 8-inch square cake pan into the oven. Put the sugar and water into a cast-iron nonstick saucepan and heat over medium heat, swirling the pan gently (do not stir) until all the sugar has dissolved. Turn up the heat and continue to swirl the pan gently while the syrup darkens to a deep amber.

2. Remove the hot pan from the oven (do not turn off the oven) and pour in the hot caramel, turning the pan around so that the caramel coats the bottom and sides as much as possible. Reserve any remaining caramel. Any parts of the pan that remain uncovered will need to be greased when the pan has cooled down.

3. Increase the oven temperature to 350 °F. Put the eggs and egg yolks into a medium bowl and beat to combine, then add the rum and allspice.

4. Put the cream, milk, and coconut milk into a small saucepan over medium heat, and bring to a boil, stirring continuously. Slowly pour the liquid into the egg mixture, stirring continuously.

5. Pour the batter into the cake pan together with the reserved caramel. Place the pan in a deep roasting pan, fill halfway with hot (not boiling) water, then carefully put it in the preheated oven.

6. Bake for 35 minutes, until a toothpick inserted into the center comes out clean. Remove from the oven and let cool in the pan, then transfer to the refrigerator to chill overnight.

7. Just before serving, use a knife to gently separate the custard from the sides of the pan and turn it out onto a plate. The liquid caramel will cover the custard. Sprinkle with the coconut, decorate with a Cape gooseberry, if using, and serve.

SERVES 6–8

PREP TIME: 30 minutes, plus 8 hours to chill

COOKING TIME: 45 minutes

INGREDIENTS

butter, for greasing, if needed
⅓ cup granulated sugar
⅓ cup water
6 eggs
3 egg yolks
¼ cup dark rum
½ teaspoon ground allspice
1½ cups heavy cream
1½ cups milk
1½ cups coconut milk, well stirred
2 cups toasted dry unsweetened coconut, for sprinkling
1 Cape gooseberry, to decorate (optional)

Mexican
WEDDING COOKIES

These delicate cookies are part of the Mexican wedding tradition, and they can be baked in different shapes. For special occasions, the cookies are made with high-quality butter, fine sugar, and choice nuts. Pecans are the key ingredient of these cookies from Mexico. When made with walnuts, they are called Russian tea cakes; with almonds and vanilla, they are the German Vanillekipferl (vanilla crescent cookies).

MAKES 30

PREP TIME: 20 minutes

COOKING TIME: 20 minutes

1. Preheat the oven to 300°F. Line two baking sheets with parchment paper. Put the nuts into a dry skillet over medium heat and cook, tossing occasionally, until toasted. Be careful that they do not burn. Let cool, then put them into a food processor with 2 teaspoons of the confectioners' sugar and pulse until finely chopped.

2. Put the butter, the remaining sugar, and the vanilla extract into a large bowl and beat with an electric mixer until creamy. Stir in the flour and the nuts.

3. With floured hands, form the dough into 30 finger-size rolls, then shape into crescents and place on the prepared sheets. Bake in the preheated oven for about 20 minutes, until lightly browned. Let cool slightly, then roll in confectioners' sugar to coat. Sprinkle again with confectioners' sugar just before serving.

3.

INGREDIENTS

1 cup pecans

⅓ cup confectioners' sugar, plus extra for coating and sprinkling

2 sticks butter, softened

1 teaspoon vanilla extract or 1 vanilla bean, scraped

2 cups all-purpose flour, plus extra for dusting

Torta de Hojas
LAYER CAKE

4.

SERVES 4

PREP TIME: 35–45 minutes

COOKING TIME: 3 hours 15 minutes

This "thousand leaves cake" is a popular dessert in Chile. It is a true labor of love, because each layer has to be baked individually and then they all have to be put together. Make the cake the day before you eat it. It will have set and will be easier to cut.

1. Heat the unopened can of condensed milk in a saucepan of boiling water for 3 hours, being careful that the water covers the can and topping up the water during the cooking, if needed. Carefully remove the can from the heat and let cool for 10–15 minutes.

2. Preheat the oven to 350°F. Line several baking sheets with parchment paper. Mix together the flour and baking powder and set aside. Put the butter into a large bowl and beat until creamy, then add the egg yolks, one at a time, beating after each addition until combined. Add the flour mixture and the milk and mix until a firm dough forms.

3. Divide the dough into 10 pieces and shape each piece into a ball. Flatten each ball into a 9-inch circle. Place on the prepared baking sheets and prick all over with a fork. Bake in the preheated oven for 5 minutes, then turn over and bake for an additional 5 minutes, until golden brown. You may have to do this in batches. Remove from the oven and transfer to a wire rack to cool.

4. Mix together the brandy and water in a small bowl. Place a pastry layer on a serving plate. Sprinkle with 1 tablespoon of the brandy mixture, then spread with 1½ tablespoons of the cooled condensed milk. Sprinkle with 1 tablespoon of the nuts. Repeat until all the layers have been used.

INGREDIENTS

1 (14-ounce) can sweetened condensed milk
4 cups all-purpose flour
2 teaspoons baking powder
1¾ sticks butter, softened
3 egg yolks
1 cup milk
5 tablespoons brandy
5 tablespoons water
⅔ cup coarsely chopped walnuts

SWEET CARAMEL
Pasteles

4.

MAKES 14

PREP TIME: 25 minutes, plus 30 minutes to chill

COOKING TIME: 15–20 minutes

INGREDIENTS

*3 cups all-purpose flour,
plus extra for dusting*
⅓ cup confectioners' sugar
1 teaspoon baking powder
¼ teaspoon salt
*2 sticks chilled butter, diced,
plus extra for greasing*
6–7 tablespoons iced water
1 pound soft caramel candies
2 tablespoons milk
½ cup dry unsweetened coconut
1 egg, beaten

Caramel means "burned sugar" in Spanish. The dry sugar, when heated, remains sweet but it also acquires its typical roasted aroma. In Argentina, pasteles are usually filled with soft and sweet caramel. This is a treat that's worth a little effort!

1. Put the flour, sugar, baking powder, and salt into a large bowl and mix together thoroughly. Add the butter and rub it in with your fingertips until the mixture resembles bread crumbs. Add the iced water, a teaspoon at a time, until the pastry comes together. Cover with plastic wrap and chill in the refrigerator for 30 minutes.

2. Heat the caramel with the milk in a heatproof bowl set over a saucepan of simmering water, stirring continuously, until the caramel has completely dissolved. Remove from the heat, stir in the coconut, and let cool.

3. Preheat the oven to 400 °F. Line a baking sheet with greased parchment paper. Roll out the pastry on a lightly floured work surface and use a 3-inch cutter to cut out 14 circles, rerolling the trimmings, if necessary.

4. Place 1 teaspoon of the caramel mixture in the middle of each circle and fold it in half. Seal the edges with a fork. Put the pastries on the prepared baking sheet and brush them with the beaten egg. Bake in the preheated oven for about 10 minutes, until golden brown. Remove from the oven, transfer to a wire rack, and let cool.

Guava Bars

The guava tree is native to South America, but now it is also grown in other tropical regions. Its fruit is soft, juicy, and slightly pitted. Guavas have a sweet and sour flavor and are slightly reminiscent of pears or strawberries. Because they only keep for a few days, they are mainly used for making marmalade, desserts, or juice—the basis for this recipe.

1. To make the guava paste, put the guavas in a saucepan, cover with water, and cook over low heat until tender. Remove the guavas from the pan, mash with a vegetable masher, and strain. Put the guava pulp and granulated sugar into a clean saucepan and simmer. Let it reduce until the mixture is thick enough to pull away from the sides of the pan, then pour into a flat mold and let cool to a firm paste.

2. Preheat the oven to 400 °F. Lightly grease an 8 x 12-inch baking pan.

3. Mix together the flour, sugar, baking soda, salt, and oats. Add the butter and rub in until the mixture resembles bread crumbs. Add the honey and mix well. Press half the crumb mixture into the prepared pan.

4. Cut the guava paste into thin strips and lay them on top of the crumb mixture. Cover with the remaining crumb mixture and lightly press into place using the back of a fork. Bake in the preheated oven for 30 minutes, until golden brown. Remove from the oven and let cool in the pan.

5. Cut into strips about the size of a granola bar and serve. The bars will keep in an airtight container for up to one week.

MAKES 8–10

PREP TIME: 30 minutes, plus time to cool

COOKING TIME: 30 minutes

INGREDIENTS

2 cups all-purpose flour
1½ cups firmly packed light brown sugar
½ teaspoon baking soda
¼ teaspoon salt
1⅔ cups rolled oats
2 cups butter, softened, plus extra for greasing
⅔ cup honey

guava paste

1¼ pound guavas, trimmed and cut into quarters
2 cups granulated sugar
or
1 pound store-bought guava paste, sliced

1.

Mexican

SOPAPILLAS

SERVES 4

PREP TIME: 20 minutes,
plus 2 hours 20 minutes to rise

COOKING TIME: 3–5 minutes

INGREDIENTS

2 teaspoons active dry yeast
3 tablespoons lukewarm water
⅔ cup milk
⅓ cup granulated sugar,
plus extra for sprinkling
1 teaspoon salt
2 tablespoons butter
1 egg, beaten
4 cups all-purpose flour, plus extra
for dusting
oil, for deep-frying

The name of this pastry probably comes from the Spanish word sopai-pa—a term for sweet fried dough. Unlike South American sopapillas, which are a type of tortilla, the Mexican variant puffs up like a donut on account of the special dough. They are also made in savory versions and are an important feature of the local cuisine that developed well over 200 years ago.

1. Put the yeast into a large bowl with the water, stir to dissolve, and let stand in a warm place. Put the milk, sugar, and salt into a saucepan over medium heat, bring to a boil, then add the butter and stir. Remove from the heat and let cool slightly. Stir into the yeast mixture, add the egg, and mix to combine, then gradually mix in the flour. Cover the bowl with a damp dish towel and let rise for 1–2 hours.

2. Turn out the dough onto a lightly floured work surface and punch down into it to knock out the air, then let rise for 20 minutes. Roll out the dough to a thickness of ½ inch, then use a pizza cutter or pastry wheel to cut it into ¼-inch strips.

3. Heat enough oil for deep-frying in a large saucepan or deep fryer to 350–375°F, or until a cube of bread browns in 30 seconds. Drop the dough strips, in small batches, into the oil and fry for 3–5 minutes, until light brown, turning to cook on both sides.

4. Remove from the oil and place on paper towels to drain. Sprinkle with sugar and serve immediately.

1.

2.

3.

Happy Hour

AT THE CEMETERY

Every year in Mexico, on the night of November 1st, the dead are released from their eternal rest for a short time and so begins the Dia de los Muertos … the Day of the Dead.

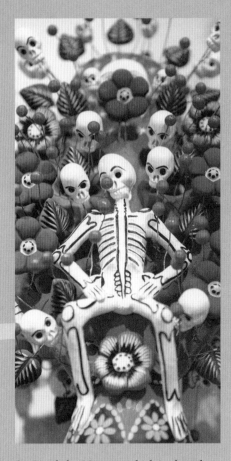

On Dia de los Muertos, which is also celebrated exuberantly by Hispanics in Chicago, Los Angeles, and New York around the same time as Halloween, the cemeteries become a place with strange decorations and special dinner parties for the dead.

On the Day of the Dead, nothing can persuade the dead to stay in their graves and tombs, because, according to an old belief, at the end of the harvest they return to the earth from the afterlife to celebrate a joyful festival with the living. With loud music, lively dancing, and good food, the dead have something to laugh about and the living can remember those who have passed away.

Their souls are long awaited guests and are welcomed with bizarre death symbols. Brightly painted skeletons, glowing plastic bones, and skulls made of sugar and chocolate bearing the name of the deceased on the forehead leave no doubt as to the date: it is Dia de los Muertos (Day of the Dead), one of the most important feast days and liveliest folk festivals in honor of the dead. All the streets are decorated with a welcoming carpet of yellow and orange flowers to guide the dead on the way home from the cemetery. Better safe than sorry, because, after such a long absence, it is easy to lose one's way. The bright orange cempasuchil, also called "flower of the dead," is supposed to be easy to identify, even for the dead with their poor eyesight. The Dia de los Muertos is by no means a mournful occasion. According to ancient Mexican belief, the dead are returned from the afterlife. Spanish missionaries, however, found this somewhat blasphemous. They unsuccessfully tried to abolish the celebration, but eventually had to resign themselves to the fact that Christianity had mingled with Aztec beliefs.

From the point of view of baking history, pan de muerto is nothing more than a bread made from a soft dough, which is similar in consistency to the brioche from France. Pan de muerto probably developed from the empanda, a filled pastry popular throughout South America. Housewives took great pride in their skill in braiding pan de muerto in honor of their deceased ancestors. In Mexico, pan de muerto is such an important product that there are cooking competitions and television programs where professionals and amateurs vie for the title of "Best Pan de Muerto Baker." These loaves try to depict skeletons in as much real-life detail as possible. And no one shies away from the copious use of red icing. Although it had its origins in religious ritual, the pan de muerto, artistically decorated with bones and skeletons, is just the thing to bring along when visiting friends, even when it is not the Day of the Dead. On the night before November 2nd, after the souls have been received at home, there is a farewell ceremony to the dead that takes place in the cemeteries. The pan de meurto is eaten there along with other foods. And, naturally, there is a lot of drinking, music, and dancing. On the stroke of midnight, the dead return to the afterlife. Rest at last, until next year!

CHILEAN
Pineapple Cake

SERVES 8–10

PREP TIME: 50 minutes,
plus 30 minutes to chill

COOKING TIME: 30 minutes

INGREDIENTS

6 eggs
1¼ cups superfine sugar
1¼ cups all-purpose flour, sifted
⅔ cup cornstarch
2 teaspoons baking powder
butter, for greasing
1 cup heavy cream
¾ cup confectioners' sugar
*1 cup canned pineapple chunks
and their can juices*
3 tablespoons pineapple juice
dry unsweetened coconut, to decorate

Pineapple is a much-loved fruit all over the world that has been grown in most tropical regions since the sixteenth century. However, it originally comes from Latin America, where it was already being cultivated before Christopher Columbus brought it to Europe. The pineapple was given to him as a welcome gift in Guadeloupe in 1493. Its sharp taste gives this typical north Chilean cream cake a special kick.

1. Put three of the eggs into a large bowl with the superfine sugar and beat with an electric mixer for 30 minutes. This long beating will ensure that enough air is beaten in to keep the cake light. Sift together the flour, cornstarch, and baking powder into a bowl, then fold into the egg mixture. Separate the remaining eggs and beat the egg whites until they hold stiff peaks. Gently fold into the flour mixture, making sure that it remains light and fluffy. Add the egg yolks, one at a time, stirring gently after each addition.

2. Meanwhile, preheat the oven to 325 °F and grease a 9-inch round cake pan. Pour the batter into the prepared pan and bake in the preheated oven for about 30 minutes. Remove from the oven, transfer to a wire rack, and let cool completely. Cut the cooled cake into two horizontal layers.

3. Meanwhile, whip the cream until it holds stiff peaks, then gently fold in the confectioners' sugar. Transfer to the refrigerator to chill until you are ready to assemble the cake.

4. Mix together the can juices and the pineapple juice and set aside.

5. To assemble the cake, place one cake layer on a plate. Spread with a thick layer of the whipped cream and arrange some of the pineapple chunks on top. Spread a thinner layer of whipped cream over the pineapple.

6. Pour the pineapple juice over the second cake layer and place on top of the whipped cream. Top with the remaining cream, then decorate with the remaining pineapple and the coconut. Chill in the refrigerator for 30 minutes. Serve chilled.

1.

2.

5.

2.

4.

4.

Pan de Muerto

SWEET BREAD

Pan de Muerto is the "bread of the dead": it is baked in Mexico at the end of the harvest season, prior to the "Day of the Dead." This important and popular festival is celebrated every year on November 1st and 2nd. The sweet, soft bread is often decorated with pieces of dough in the shape of bones, which symbolize the loss caused by death.

1. Put the yeast into a large bowl with the water, stir to dissolve, and let stand for about 5 minutes. Meanwhile, put the milk into a saucepan set over medium heat, bring to a boil, then remove from the heat and add the butter, ¼ cup of the sugar and the salt. Stir until dissolved. Add the milk mixture to the yeast mixture.

2. Add one egg and the flour to the liquid ingredients, mix to combine, then knead until a smooth, silky dough forms. Transfer the dough to a clean bowl, cover with plastic wrap, and let rise in a warm place for 2 hours.

3. Turn out the dough onto a lightly floured work surface and divide into four pieces. Set one piece aside. Using the palms of your hands, shape each of the remaining pieces into three ropes of equal length.

4. Line a baking sheet with parchment paper and lightly grease the paper. Weave the three dough ropes into a braid and join the ends to make a round loaf. Take the reserved piece of dough and shape it into two bones and a skull. Arrange these on top of the loaf and press lightly. Put on the prepared baking sheet and let rise for 30 minutes.

5. Meanwhile, preheat the oven to 350 °F. Mix together the anise, cinnamon, and the remaining sugar in a small bowl. Beat the remaining egg and brush it onto the braided dough (do not brush the skull and bones), then sprinkle with the anise mixture.

6. Bake in the bottom of the preheated oven for 20–25 minutes, until golden. If it is browning too quickly, cover with parchment paper or aluminum foil. Remove from the oven and put on a wire rack to cool.

SERVES 8

PREP TIME: 30 minutes,
plus 2 hours 30 minutes to rise

COOKING TIME: 25–30 minutes

INGREDIENTS

1 tablespoon active dry yeast
¼ cup lukewarm water
¼ cup milk
4 tablespoons butter, diced,
plus extra for greasing
⅓ cup granulated sugar
½ teaspoon salt
2 eggs
3⅓ cups all-purpose flour,
plus extra for dusting
½ teaspoon ground star anise
¼ teaspoon ground cinnamon

Brigadeiros

CHOCOLATE CANDIES

MAKES 25

PREP TIME: 35 minutes, plus 4 hours to chill

COOKING TIME: 15 minutes

INGREDIENTS

1¾ cups canned sweetened condensed milk

2 tablespoons butter, plus extra for greasing

2 tablespoons heavy cream

2 teaspoons light corn syrup

2 teaspoons unsweetened cocoa powder

1 cup semisweet chocolate chips

1 cup chocolate sprinkles

During World War II, imported goods were scarce in Brazil. The country drew on its own resources and made the most of being a major producer of cocoa. At the same time, the Swiss manufacturer Nestlé introduced condensed milk to the market there. The combination of the two resulted in these Brazilian chocolate truffles, named after Brigadier Eduardo Gomes, who was a popular military man and politician in Brazil at the time.

1. Pour the condensed milk into a small saucepan and heat over low heat, being careful that it does not boil. Add the butter, cream, and light corn syrup, stirring continuously.

2. When small bubbles start to appear in the mixture, add the cocoa powder and chocolate chips. Simmer for about 10 minutes, until thickened, then remove from the heat.

3. Pour the mixture into a bowl and let cool to room temperature.

4. Meanwhile, put the chocolate sprinkles into a shallow bowl and lightly grease your hands. Roll the cooled mixture into 1-inch balls or other shapes and toss in the sprinkles until completely coated. Place the brigadeiros in paper liners and chill in the refrigerator for 4 hours, or until ready to serve.

1.

2.

4.

Garibaldi COOKIES

MAKES 24–30

PREP TIME: 15 minutes

COOKING TIME: 15 minutes

INGREDIENTS

1¼ cups all-purpose flour

*¾ cup confectioners' sugar,
plus extra for dusting*

1 teaspoon finely grated lime zest

*1 stick butter, softened,
plus extra for greasing*

pinch of salt

Garibaldi cookies, named after the Italian revolutionary, are also popular in Great Britain. In this South American version, the raisins or soft fruit are omitted, and fine lime zest and confectioners' sugar are used instead.

1. Preheat the oven to 350°F. Lightly grease a baking sheet. Put the flour, sugar, and lime zest into a medium bowl and mix to combine. Add the butter and salt and beat to a smooth dough.

2. Turn out onto a lightly floured work surface, roll out into a large rectangle, and cut the dough into about three wide strips. Use your hands to roll the strips into tubes, then cut them into ¾-inch pieces. Roll into small balls, then place on the prepared sheet. Pinch with your fingers to create a ridged shape on each cookie, then bake in the preheated oven for about 15 minutes, until golden brown.

3. Remove from the oven, sprinkle with sugar, and serve.

1.

1.

2.

1.

2.

RING
CAKE

Mantecada

This sponge cake is popular in Colombia and Venezuela, and its batter consists mainly of butter, sugar, cornmeal, and eggs—and just a little flour. It is based on a kind of muffin from Spain, and the rum and orange rind are essential ingredients. It is often served with a scoop of ice cream, cream, or fresh fruit.

1. Preheat the oven to 350°F. Grease a cake tube pan. Put the butter, sugar, flour, and baking powder into a bowl and beat with an electric mixer until slightly fluffy. Add the eggs, one at a time, stirring after each addition, then sift the cornmeal into the mixture. Continue to beat until smooth. Add the rum and the orange zest, stirring well.

2. Pour the batter into the prepared pan and bake in the middle of the preheated oven for 30–40 minutes.

3. Remove the cake from the oven and carefully turn out of the pan. Serve hot or at room temperature.

SERVES 6–8

PREP TIME: 15 minutes

COOKING TIME: 30–40 minutes

INGREDIENTS

4 sticks butter, plus extra for greasing
2¼ cups granulated sugar
¾ cup all-purpose flour
1 tablespoon baking powder
10 eggs
3 cups fine yellow cornmeal
2 teaspoons rum
finely grated zest of 1 orange

AMARANTH
Alegrias
COOKIES

2.

MAKES 10–15

PREP TIME: 15 minutes

COOKING TIME: 15 minutes

INGREDIENTS

2 cups water
3⅔ cups firmly packed dark brown sugar
3 tablespoons honey
juice of 2 lemons
⅔ cup amaranth, toasted
(available in health-food stores)
½ cup raisins
⅓ cup skinned, unroasted peanuts

Amaranth has been considered sacred for a long time, and the Incas believed the plant to be a source of great power. In fact, this grain is highly nutritious and easily outshines European cereals. The seeds usually grow on inflorescences that can be up to a yard long.

1. Put the water into a large saucepan and bring to a boil. Add the sugar, honey, and lemon juice, bring back to a boil, and cook until a thick syrup forms.

2. Remove from the heat, then add the amaranth to the syrup and mix to combine. Add the raisins and peanuts and mix again. Let cool slightly, then press into 10–15 small molds or shape into pyramids. Turn out of the molds and serve.

Polvorones

COOKIES

2.

MAKES 20–25

PREP TIME: 15 minutes

COOKING TIME: 10 minutes

INGREDIENTS

2 sticks butter, plus extra for greasing

1 cup granulated sugar

⅓ cup confectioners' sugar

2 eggs

1 teaspoon vanilla extract or 1 vanilla bean, scraped

4⅓ cups all-purpose flour, sifted, plus extra for dusting

1 teaspoon baking powder

½ teaspoon salt

½ cup cinnamon sugar (available online)

Polvorones comes from the Spanish word for "dust": these heavy, crumbly cookies are eaten in various forms in Latin America and Spain and are particularly popular during the Christmas season. The cinnamon and vanilla flavor is also appropriate for the festive season.

1. Preheat the oven to 375 °F. Line a baking sheet with greased parchment paper. Put the butter, granulated sugar, and confectioners' sugar into a large bowl and beat with an electric mixer until light and fluffy. Add the eggs, one at a time, gently stirring after each addition, then stir in the vanilla extract. Add the flour, baking powder, and salt and stir to combine.

2. Turn out the dough onto a lightly floured work surface and roll out to a thickness of ¼ inch. Use a 2-inch fluted cutter to cut out 20–25 cookies, rerolling the trimmings, if necessary. Place on the prepared baking sheet and bake in the preheated oven for 8–10 minutes, until golden brown.

3. Remove the polvorones from the oven and sprinkle with the cinnamon sugar while they are still hot. Transfer to a wire rack to cool. The polvorones will keep for up to one week in an airtight container.

CARAMEL COOKIES

Alfajores

MAKES 24

PREP TIME: 20 minutes, plus 30 minutes to chill

COOKING TIME: 15 minutes

INGREDIENTS

2 cups all-purpose flour, sifted, plus extra for dusting

3 tablespoons confectioners' sugar, sifted, plus extra for sprinkling

½ teaspoon salt

2 sticks butter, softened, diced

¾ cup dulce de leche (caramel sauce)

¼ teaspoon ground cinnamon

¼ teaspoon ground cloves

¼ teaspoon grated nutmeg

Alfajores consist of two (or even three) filled layers of fine pastry. This sweet pastry has its origins in Arabia and then spread via Spain to South America as early as 1870. Nowadays, it is particularly popular in Argentina. This recipe with dulce de leche, in which the cookies are sprinkled with sugar, is only one of many versions.

1. Preheat the oven to 350°F. Line a large baking sheet with parchment paper. Put the flour, sugar, salt, and butter into the bowl of an electric mixer and mix until a smooth dough forms. Wrap in plastic wrap and chill in the refrigerator for 30 minutes.

2. Turn out the dough onto a lightly floured work surface and roll out to a thickness of ¼ inch. Use a 2-inch cutter to cut out 48 circles, rerolling the trimmings, if necessary. Place the circles on the prepared baking sheet. Use a toothpick to make three holes in 24 of the circles. Bake in the preheated oven for about 15 minutes, until golden brown.

3. Meanwhile, put the dulce de leche, cinnamon, cloves, and nutmeg into a bowl and mix to combine.

4. Spread 1 teaspoon of this mixture on the flat side of the 24 solid cookies, then top with the remaining cookies. Sprinkle with confectioners' sugar and serve.

4.

Coconut Kisses

2.

3.

There is a huge variety of recipes for coconut macarons throughout the world. But this sweet cookie in combination with coconut always provides a tropical thrill. Crispy on the outside and slightly sticky on the inside, these kisses are irresistible!

1. Preheat the oven to 350 °F. Line a baking sheet with parchment paper and grease the paper.

2. Put all the ingredients into a large bowl and mix to a firm dough. Divide the dough into 24 pieces and roll each piece into a ball.

3. Place the balls on the prepared baking sheet, brush with egg white, and bake in the preheated oven for 15 minutes, until the tops are golden brown. Remove from the oven and transfer to a wire rack to cool. Decorate with the cherries and serve.

MAKES 24

PREP TIME: 10 minutes

COOKING TIME: 15 minutes

INGREDIENTS

butter, for greasing
3 cups dry unsweetened coconut
½ cup all-purpose flour
4 egg yolks
1 egg white, plus extra for brushing
2 tablespoons coconut milk
1 cup firmly packed light brown sugar
1 teaspoon vanilla extract or 1 vanilla bean, scraped
candied cherries, to decorate

3.

1.

2.

3.

MEXICAN
Corncake

SERVES 6

PREP TIME: 15 minutes

COOKING TIME: 40 minutes

INGREDIENTS

*4 tablespoons butter,
plus extra for greasing*
2 tablespoons vegetable shortening
⅓ cup cornmeal
⅓ cup cold water, plus extra if needed
*2 cups fresh corn kernels or drained,
canned corn kernels*
3 tablespoons heavy cream
3 tablespoons cornstarch
¼ cup granulated sugar
¼ teaspoon baking powder
¼ teaspoon salt

Corn has been cultivated for thousands of years in Mexico and the work involved has made it one of the outstanding achievements of prehistoric times. In Latin America (and Africa), corn is still the most important staple food. Of course, it also makes a versatile cake all year round: the fresh, juicy corn kernels give it a coarse and pleasing texture.

1. Preheat the oven to 350°F. Grease a 14-inch loaf pan. Cream the butter with the vegetable shortening until light and fluffy. Fold in the cornmeal. Add the water, a little at a time, mixing after each addition until a firm but pliable dough forms. Add the corn kernels and mix well.

2. Mix together the cream, cornstarch, sugar, baking powder, and salt in a large bowl. Add the corn-and-butter mixture and mix together until combined.

3. Transfer the batter to the prepared pan and bake in the preheated oven for 40 minutes. If the cake is browning too quickly, cover it with aluminum foil. Remove from the oven and let cool in the pan for 1–2 minutes, then remove from the pan and transfer to a wire rack to cool completely. Serve cut into slices or squares.

1.

2.

3.

Arepas
FLATBREADS

MAKES 16

PREP TIME: 20 minutes,
plus 30 minutes to rest

COOKING TIME: 15–20 minutes

In Colombia and Venezuela, this round, flat corn bread is traditionally eaten for almost every meal. In the Andes, large, flat arepas are baked, while on the coast thick, small ones are fried. They are always freshly made and served hot. They sometimes have a filling. The thick ones are also cut open and filled with meat, fish, cheese, and vegetables.

1. Mix together the flour and salt in a large bowl and pour the hot water over the mixture to cover. Add the butter and mix well until a firm dough forms, then wrap in plastic wrap and let rest for 30 minutes.

2. Divide the dough into 16 equal pieces and shape each piece into a 4-inch circle, about ½ inch thick. Place on a sheet of parchment paper and cover with plastic wrap.

3. Heat some oil in a skillet, add the arepas in small batches, and cook over medium heat on both sides until golden brown. If the arepas are browning too quickly, reduce the heat. The arepas are cooked when they are crisp outside but soft in the middle.

4. Serve straight from the pan with salad greens, cheese, and ham.

INGREDIENTS

*2 cups arepa flour or
instant polenta*
1 teaspoon salt
3 cups hot water
2 tablespoons butter, melted
vegetable oil, for frying

to serve
salad greens
shredded American or cheddar cheese
sliced cooked ham

Spicy Jalapeño

CORN BREAD

Jalapeños are small, hot peppers named after the Mexican city of Xalapa (formerly Jalapa). Today, this type of chile is still mainly grown in that region as well as in the neighboring state of Texas. It gives this hearty, tasty corn pancake its characteristic flavor.

SERVES 6

PREP TIME: 20 minutes

COOKING TIME: 35 minutes

INGREDIENTS

1 tablespoon vegetable oil

4 fresh jalapeño chiles, halved, seeded, and thinly sliced

1 scallion, finely chopped

1 tablespoon finely chopped flat-leaf parsley

2 cups cornmeal

1½ cups all-purpose flour

2 tablespoons sugar

1 tablespoon baking powder

1 teaspoon salt

3 eggs

2 cups light cream

1 stick butter, melted, plus extra for greasing

1. Heat the oil in a small skillet, add the chiles, scallion, and parsley, and sauté for 2 minutes, until translucent. Remove from the heat and set aside.

2. Preheat the oven to 375 °F. Grease or line a 10-inch square cake pan with parchment paper. Mix together the cornmeal, flour, sugar, baking powder, and salt in a large bowl. Put the eggs, cream, butter, and chile mixture into a separate large bowl and stir to combine. Add the cornmeal mixture and mix together to form a firm batter.

3. Pour the batter into the prepared pan and bake in the preheated oven for 30 minutes, or until a toothpick inserted into the center comes out clean. Remove from the oven and let cool in the pan for 5 minutes. Turn out of the pan and carefully remove the parchment paper, brushing it with water if it sticks to the bread. Put the bread on a wire rack to cool completely, then cut into small rectangles and serve.

1.

2.

3.

3.

Out of AFRICA

It is a little known fact that the art of baking bread had its origins in Africa. About 5,000 years ago, the Egyptians discovered the effects of yeast and made the first leavened breads. In fact, there were more than 30 different types of bread in Egypt. So it is hardly suprising that the Egyptians were known to the Romans as "bread eaters." However, very early on, people in other parts of Africa had also started experimenting with bread making. The Bedouin, for example, invented an oven in the ground, where dough could be baked into bread using the hot Sahara sand and heated coals. Africans mainly used cassava, millet, and other grains to make their early breads.

If you want to learn about how ovens worked 5,000 years ago when baking was invented by Egyptians, then watch some African tribes. They still bake bread in holes in the ground, naturally heated by the sun.

AFRICAN
Ginger Cookies

MAKES 25

PREP TIME: 10 minutes

COOKING TIME: 20 minutes

INGREDIENTS

*2 cups all-purpose flour,
plus extra for dusting*

⅓ cup granulated sugar

3 teaspoons ground ginger

½ teaspoon freshly ground cayenne pepper

*1 stick butter, softened,
plus extra for greasing*

½ cup water

Originating from South Asia, ginger was initially mainly valued by Europeans for its positive effects on health. However, from the Middle Ages onward, they also began to use it as a spice in foods. It was then introduced to the African colonies. These delicious spicy cookies are still popular in Africa today.

1. Preheat the oven to 350 °F. Line a baking sheet with parchment paper, then grease the paper. Sift together the flour, sugar, ginger, and cayenne pepper into a large bowl.

2. Thoroughly rub in the butter until the mixture resembles coarse crumbs. Add the water and mix to a firm dough.

3. Roll out the dough on a floured work surface to a thickness of about ½ inch. Use a 2-inch round cutter to cut out 25 circles. Place the circles on the prepared sheet and bake in the preheated oven for 15–20 minutes, or until pale golden. Remove from the oven, transfer to a wire rack, and let cool. The cookies can be stored in an airtight container for up to one week.

2.

3.

2.

3.

3.

3.

SOUTH AFRICAN
Milk
Tarts

MAKES 12

PREP TIME: 45 minutes,
plus 1 hour to chill

COOKING TIME: 25 minutes

INGREDIENTS

3 tablespoons butter, melted

1 cup granulated sugar

3 egg yolks

1¼ cups all-purpose flour

1 teaspoon baking powder

¼ teaspoon salt

1 vanilla bean, scraped, or 1 teaspoon vanilla extract

4 cups milk

3 egg whites

1 tablespoon cinnamon sugar (available online)

halved fresh strawberries and confectioners' sugar, to decorate

pastry dough

2 sticks butter, plus extra for greasing

¼ cup granulated sugar

2 egg yolks

2 tablespoons heavy cream

2⅓ cups all-purpose flour, plus extra for dusting

In contrast to the traditional English custard tart, the milk tart has a higher proportion of milk and egg. This creates a lighter texture and stronger milk flavor. These tarts are one of the most popular pastries in South Africa.

1. Preheat the oven to 350 °F. Lightly grease the cups in a 12-cup muffin pan and dust with flour. To make the dough, put the butter and sugar into a bowl and cream together. Add the egg yolks and mix to incorporate, then add the cream and mix until combined. Using a spatula, carefully fold in the flour to form a dough. Let chill for 1 hour.

2. Roll out the dough on a floured work surface, then use a 2-inch round cutter to cut out 12 circles. Use the circles to line the cups in the prepared pan, then line with parchment paper, fill with pie weights or dried beans, and bake in the preheated oven for 10 minutes. Remove from the oven and increase the oven temperature to 375 °F. Remove the paper and weights.

3. Put the butter and sugar into a large bowl and beat together until smooth. Add the egg yolks, one at a time, and beat until smooth. Sift in the flour, baking powder, and salt and stir until well mixed. Add the vanilla seeds or vanilla extract and milk and stir. Put the egg whites into a separate bowl and beat until they hold stiff peaks. Carefully fold into the butter-and-sugar mixture, then pour into the pastry shells and sprinkle with the cinnamon sugar.

4. Bake for 25 minutes, then remove from oven and let cool. Place a halved strawberry on each tart, dust with confectioners' sugar, and serve.

Moroccan
COUNTRY BREAD

1.

1.

MAKES 3 LOAVES

PREP TIME: 25 minutes,
plus 1 hour to rise

COOKING TIME: 30 minutes

INGREDIENTS

1 tablespoon active dry yeast
2 cups lukewarm water
2 teaspoons salt
6¾ cups all-purpose flour,
plus extra for dusting
1 tablespoon olive oil

Many Moroccans still bake their own bread. Families in rural areas use small dome-shape, wood-burning ovens, adding different ingredients to give their bread its own unique character. This rustic bread is a great accompaniment to stews or even with a salad. They deliberately avoid kneading the dough to give the bread its characteristic coarse texture.

1. Preheat the oven to 350°F. Lightly dust a baking sheet with flour. Put the yeast into a large bowl with the water and stir until dissolved. Add the salt and gradually stir in the flour, about 1 cup at a time. Knead until the dough forms a ball. Turn out the dough onto a lightly floured work surface and shape it into a 10-inch log. Divide the dough into three equal pieces and shape each piece into a 4-inch dome-shape loaf.

2. Place the loaves on the prepared baking sheet. Cover with a dish towel and let rise in a warm place for 1 hour, or until doubled in size.

3. Brush each loaf with 1 teaspoon of the oil. Bake in the bottom of the preheated oven for 30 minutes. Remove from the oven and transfer to wire racks to cool.

The Home
of Afternoon Tea

Afternoon tea is as important to the British as spaghetti to the Italians or baguettes to the French. In the UK, the importance of cakes and pastries is especially apparent during the ritual of afternoon tea. Of course, the visual impact must not be neglected at such an important time of the day. Whether it's home bakers trying to make elaborate fondant decorations or creating seasonal specialities, such as Christmas cakes, the British love show-stopping baking. However, there are also the simpler baked goods of Chelsea buns, crumpets, sausage rolls, and muffins. These and similar plain and savory goodies can be found in bakeries on almost every street in the UK. But, when possible, the British love to bake at home and to serve their own home-made cakes and cookies at tea time, just like their mothers and grandmothers before them.

Queen Elizabeth II entertains those of her subjects who have contributed to society by holding large garden tea parties in the summer, at Buckingham Palace and in Edinburgh at Holyrood House.

DORSET
Apple Cake

SERVES 12

PREP TIME: 25–30 minutes

COOKING TIME: 40 minutes

INGREDIENTS

2 Pippin apples
1¾ cups all-purpose flour
1 teaspoon baking powder
1 stick chilled butter, diced,
plus extra for greasing
⅔ cup granulated sugar,
plus extra for sprinkling
finely grated zest of 1 lemon
2 eggs, beaten
whipped cream, to serve (optional)

The Romans brought the apple from Turkey to Central Europe. Dozens of new varieties were produced. Apple trees flourished in the mild, slightly damp climate in the south of England, such as the counties of Dorset and Kent.

1. Preheat the oven to 375 °F. Lightly grease an 8-inch round, springform cake pan. Peel and core the apples, cut one apple into quarters lengthwise, then thinly slice the quarters vertically and set aside. Dice the remaining apple and set aside.

2. Sift together the flour and baking powder into a large bowl. Add the butter and rub it in with your fingertips until the mixture resembles bread crumbs.

3. Add the sugar, diced apple, lemon zest, and eggs to the flour mixture and mix to a firm dough. Pour the batter into the prepared pan and prick several times with a fork. Decorate the top of the cake with the apple slices.

4. Bake the cake in the preheated oven for 40 minutes. Remove from the oven and let cool for 1–2 minutes. Unclip and remove the springform, leaving the cake on the bottom of the pan, then transfer to a wire rack to cool completely. Sprinkle with granulated sugar and serve with whipped cream, if using.

1.

3.

3.

1.

2.

3.

Strawberry & Cream Cheesecake

SERVES 12

PREP TIME: 45 minutes,
plus time to cool

COOKING TIME: 1 hour

This British cheesecake is made with a crust of crushed graham crackers, and the layer of fruit provides a sharp, fresh contrast to the rich, creamy cheese filling. It makes a colorful and mouthwatering dessert.

1. Preheat the oven to 350 °F. Grease a 10-inch round springform cake pan and chill in the refrigerator. Mix the crushed cookies with the butter, then press the mixture into the bottom of the prepared pan. Bake in the middle of the preheated oven for 10 minutes. Remove from the oven and let cool. Do not turn off the oven.

2. Meanwhile, put the cream cheese and mascarpone cheese into a large bowl and beat until combined. Whip together the cream, sugar, and vanilla extract until frothy, then pour into the cheese mixture. Add the eggs and the egg yolks, one at a time, beating after each addition until combined.

3. Pour the cheesecake mixture onto the crust, then bake for 50 minutes. Remove from the oven and let cool.

4. Unclip and release the springform, leaving the cheesecake on the bottom of the pan. Arrange the strawberry slices decoratively on top of the cooled cheesecake, then chill in the refrigerator until ready to serve.

INGREDIENTS

2 cups crushed graham crackers or butter cookies

1 stick butter, plus extra for greasing

1¼ cups cream cheese

1 cup mascarpone cheese

1 cup heavy cream

1 cup granulated sugar

1 teaspoon vanilla extract or 1 vanilla bean, scraped

4 eggs

2 egg yolks

fresh strawberries, sliced, to decorate

Sally Lunn *Bun*

SERVES 10–12

PREP TIME: 35 minutes,
plus 2 hours to rise

COOKING TIME: 20 minutes

INGREDIENTS

*1½ sticks butter,
plus extra for greasing*

4 eggs

1 cup milk

*1½ ounces fresh yeast (available in bakeries
or online)*

*4 cups all-purpose flour,
plus extra for dusting*

¼ cup granulated sugar

2 teaspoons salt

1 egg yolk, beaten, for brushing

This recipe for large, round, soft buns is said to have been first brought to the English city of Bath by the Huguenot Sally Lunn on her flight from France in 1680. Since then, this sweet bun has been closely associated with this spa town in the West of England. The yeast dough for the bun is unusually rich in egg and butter.

1. Melt the butter in a small saucepan. Beat the eggs in a large bowl, then gradually add the melted butter, beating continuously.

2. Heat the milk in a small saucepan, then remove from the heat and crumble in the yeast. Sift together the flour, sugar, and salt into a separate bowl, then beat in the egg-and-butter mixture. Add the yeast mixture and mix to a smooth dough.

3. Put the dough into a bowl, cover with plastic wrap, and let rise in a warm place for about 90 minutes, until doubled in size.

4. Grease an 8-inch round springform cake pan and dust with flour, shaking off any excess. Punch down the dough to knock out the air, knead for 1–2 minutes, then place in the prepared pan. Cover with a damp dish towel and let rise for 30 minutes. Preheat the oven to 375 °F.

5. Brush the top of the dough with the egg yolk. Bake in the preheated oven for 15–20 minutes, until golden brown. Let cool slightly, then slice and serve.

1.

2.

3.

Teatime

A SWEET TEMPTATION IN THE AFTERNOON

The baking world owes a debt of gratitude to Anna Maria Russell, Duchess of Bedford, for such delights as scones with clotted cream and little tarts so sweet and colorful they make your stomach rumble just looking at them.

Fancy individual little cakes that are painstakingly decorated with fondant icing, candies, and even ribbons make any afternoon tea a special occasion.

In the middle of the nineteenth century, tea time was invented as a late afternoon repast for the Duchess of Bedford, who found the time between lunch and dinner too long. The story goes that all she asked for was a little cup of tea. Actually, the duchess just needed an excuse to calm her growling stomach.

The custom of afternoon tea has never really disappeared in Great Britain but has developed a variety of styles over the years. At one time, it offered a respectable opportunity for ladies to enter hotels unaccompanied by a male relative to meet with their friends to gossip over tea and cakes. In recent years, the pastry chefs in the best London hotels started to vie with each other to produce the most attractive and exquisite little cakes and "fancies" for afternoon tea. This was soon noticed and reported in the press. It quickly caught on with the public and nowadays, at certain hotels, it is sensible to book in advance, especially if it is for a special occasion. These little afternoon intervals are not inexpensive and, like the Duchess, the hotels realized this was a way of filling in vacant time, but for them at a profit.

Whether the Duchess is truly the creator of this tradition is doubtful from a historical perspective. In reality, Charles II and his wife, Catherine of Braganza, were the ones who brought the tea ceremony to the court when they returned from exile in 1662. As a new-fangled drink from China, tea was all the rage in London and it was only polite to offer a dainty cookie to nibble on while one sipped tea and gossiped.

However, the concept of an afternoon meal was by no means restricted to the privileged—it served a practical purpose for the entire population. With the advent of the Industrial Revolution, people would go off to work in factories for long days with minimal breaks and would need a quick meal immediately upon their return home. "High tea," not to be confused with "afternoon tea," was more of a meal for the working classes that happened late in the afternoon. Before the Industrial Revolution, most of the population had their main meal at midday, but this was now delayed until the workers arrived home late in the afternoon. Once home, a substantial meal was dished up as soon as possible. The first reference to "high tea" was in 1825.

Restaurant staff around the world owe the tip or gratuity to the tradition of drinking a cup of tea in the afternoon. The gentry relied upon quick service to make sure they got properly hot tea. To encourage this, there was a box on each table for a "voluntary" contribution to speed up service, which evolved into what we know as tipping today.

1.

2.

4.

4.

7.

8.

Lemon Meringue *Pie*

The crucial ingredient of lemon meringue pie is lemon curd. The intensely aromatic lemon cream, made with egg yolks and sugar, as well as lemon juice and zest, is a classic of English cuisine that can also be spread on bread. For the right consistency of the meringue topping, only the peaks should be allowed to brown. Underneath, the meringue should still retain its creamy consistency.

1. To make the dough, sift the flour into a bowl. Rub in the butter with your fingertips until the mixture resembles fine bread crumbs.

2. Mix in the remaining dough ingredients. Turn out onto a lightly floured board and knead briefly. Wrap in plastic wrap and chill in the refrigerator for 30 minutes.

3. Preheat the oven to 350 °F. Grease an 8-inch round tart pan. Roll out the dough on a lightly floured work surface to a thickness of ¼ inch, then use it to line the pan.

4. Prick all over with a fork, line with parchment paper, and fill with pie weights or dried beans. Bake in the preheated oven for 15 minutes.

5. Remove from the oven and take out the paper and weights. Reduce the oven temperature to 300 °F.

6. Mix the cornstarch with a little of the water to form a paste. Put the remaining water into a saucepan. Stir in the lemon juice and rind and the cornstarch paste.

7. Bring to a boil, stirring, and cook for an additional 2 minutes. Let cool slightly. Stir in ⅓ cup of the sugar and the egg yolks. Pour the filling into the pastry shell.

8. Beat the egg whites until stiff. Gradually beat in the remaining sugar and spread over the pie. Return to the oven and bake for 40 minutes. Remove from the oven and let cool before serving.

SERVES 6–8

PREP TIME: 45 minutes, plus 30 minutes to chill

COOKING TIME: 1 hour

INGREDIENTS

3 tablespoons cornstarch

1¼ cups water

juice and grated rind of 2 lemons

¾ cup granulated sugar

2 egg yolks, beaten

2 egg whites

pastry dough

1¼ cups all-purpose flour, plus extra for dusting

6 tablespoons butter, cut into small pieces, plus extra for greasing

1¼ cup confectioners' sugar, sifted

finely grated rind of ½ lemon

½ egg yolk, beaten

1½ tablespoons milk

Victoria

SPONGE CAKE

SERVES 8

PREP TIME: 30 minutes,
plus time to cool

COOKING TIME: 25–30 minutes

INGREDIENTS

1⅓ cups all-purpose flour
2¼ teaspoons baking powder
*1½ sticks butter, softened,
plus extra for greasing*
¾ cup granulated sugar
3 eggs
confectioners' sugar, for dusting

filling

3 tablespoons raspberry preserves
1¼ cups heavy cream, whipped
16 fresh strawberries, halved

This traditional sponge cake, which is basically a layer cake, owes its name to Queen Victoria of England (1819–1901). She liked to enjoy a slice for afternoon tea. Because its light batter is sensitive to cooking times and temperatures, oven manufacturers use this recipe to test their ovens.

1. Preheat the oven to 350 °F. Grease two 8-inch cake pans and line with parchment paper.

2. Sift the flour and baking powder into a bowl and add the butter, sugar, and eggs. Mix together, then beat well until smooth.

3. Divide the batter evenly between the prepared pans and smooth the surfaces. Bake in the preheated oven for 25–30 minutes, or until well risen and golden brown and the cakes feel springy when lightly pressed.

4. Let cool in the pan for 5 minutes, then turn out and peel off the parchment paper. Transfer to wire racks to cool completely. Sandwich the cakes together with the raspberry preserves, whipped cream, and strawberry halves. Dust with confectioners' sugar and serve.

2.

3.

4.

2.

3.

5.

White Chocolate & Rose Cupcakes

MAKES 12

PREP TIME: 25 minutes,
plus 30 minutes to cool
and 1 hour to chill

COOKING TIME: 15–20 minutes

These pretty, delicate cupcakes are ideal for a young girl's birthday party. This cupcake, with its white, artistically swirled frosting, is easy to decorate, for example, with colored fondant shapes or edible rose petals. These small cakes can be served at wedding receptions or on Valentine's Day.

1. Preheat the oven to 350 °F. Place 12 paper liners in a muffin pan.

2. Put the butter, sugar, and rose water into a bowl and beat until pale and creamy. Gradually beat in the eggs. Sift in the flour and baking powder and fold in gently. Fold in the white chocolate. Divide the batter among the paper liners.

3. Bake the cupcakes in the preheated oven for 15–20 minutes, or until risen, golden, and firm to the touch. Transfer to a wire rack and let cool.

4. To make the frosting, put the chocolate and milk into a heatproof bowl set over a saucepan of barely simmering water and heat until the chocolate is melted. Remove from the heat and stir until smooth. Let cool for 30 minutes. Put the cream cheese and confectioners' sugar into a bowl and beat until smooth and creamy. Fold in the chocolate. Chill in the refrigerator for 1 hour.

5. Meanwhile, make the decoration. Put the sugar into a shallow bowl. Gently brush each side of the rose petals with egg white. Dip in the sugar, gently turning to coat, then place on a sheet of parchment paper to dry.

6. Swirl the frosting over the top of the cupcakes. Decorate with the sugar-frosted rose petals and serve.

INGREDIENTS

1 stick unsalted butter, softened
½ cup granulated sugar
1 teaspoon rose water
2 eggs, beaten
1 cup all-purpose flour
1 teaspoon baking powder
2 ounces white chocolate, grated

frosting
*4 ounces white chocolate,
broken into pieces*
2 tablespoons milk
¾ cup cream cheese
3 tablespoons confectioners' sugar, sifted

to decorate
½ cup superfine sugar
24 pink rose petals
1 egg white, beaten

Cherry Bakewell
TARTS

4.

MAKES 10

PREP TIME: 40 minutes,
plus 1 hour 15 minutes to chill

COOKING TIME: 30 minutes

INGREDIENTS

*1 stick unsalted butter, softened,
plus extra for greasing*
1 cup confectioners' sugar
3 eggs
1¼ cups ground almonds
¼ cup all-purpose flour
1 tablespoon rum
¾ cup cherry preserves

pastry dough
*2⅓ cups all-purpose flour,
plus extra for dusting*
¼ cup granulated sugar
pinch of salt
1 egg yolk
1¼ sticks chilled unsalted butter, diced
2–3 tablespoons cold water

In the hills of the central English county of Derbyshire, in the little town of Bakewell, there are several shops selling the "original" pastry that bears its name. And yet, although it has spread throughout Britain, the origin of the Bakewell tart with cherry preserves is uncertain. Recipes for it have been found in different areas since the nineteenth century.

1. To make the dough, sift together the flour, sugar, and salt into a large bowl. Add the egg yolk, butter, and water and mix using the dough hook of a food processor. Turn out onto a lightly floured work surface and knead to a smooth dough. Wrap in plastic wrap and chill in the refrigerator for 1 hour.

2. Meanwhile, put the butter and the confectioners' sugar into a bowl and beat with an electric mixer until pale and fluffy. Add the eggs, one at a time, beating after each addition until combined. Add the ground almonds and the flour. Mix to combine, then stir in the rum.

3. Grease ten 3-inch tart pans. Remove the dough from the refrigerator and roll out to a thickness of ⅛ inch. Cut out 10 circles and press them into the pans, rerolling the trimmings, if necessary. Chill the tart shells in the refrigerator for 15 minutes.

4. Meanwhile, preheat the oven to 400°F. Spread a thin layer of cherry preserves in the bottom of the tart shells, then spread the almond mixture evenly over the top. Bake in the middle of the preheated oven for 30 minutes, or until golden brown. Remove from the oven and transfer to a wire rack to cool completely. Carefully turn out of the pans and serve.

Hot Cross Buns

4.

MAKES 14

PREP TIME: 30 minutes,
plus 2 hours to rise

COOKING TIME: 15–20 minutes

INGREDIENTS

½ cup lukewarm water
1½ ounces fresh yeast (available in bakeries or online)
3¾ cups white bread flour, plus extra for dusting
2 teaspoons milk, plus extra for brushing
2 eggs
⅓ cup granulated sugar
1½ teaspoons salt
6 tablespoons butter, softened, plus extra for greasing
⅔ cup golden raisins
½ teaspoon cinnamon
½ teaspoon allspice
pinch of nutmeg
butter and marmalade, to serve

to decorate

½ cup all-purpose flour
1 teaspoon confectioners' sugar
¼ cup water

Traditionally, Christians eat this spicy-sweet bun on Good Friday. The cross with which it is marked is seen as a symbol of the Crucifixion of Christ. In England, many superstitions surround these buns. Healing effects are attributed to them as well as protection from shipwreck. If a bun is hung in the kitchen, it is supposed to protect the house from fire and ensure successful bread baking.

1. Pour the water into a large bowl, crumble in the yeast, stir in ¾ cup of the flour, then cover the bowl with a dish towel and let stand for 20 minutes.

2. Add the milk, eggs, sugar, salt, and the remaining flour and knead, using the dough hook of a food processor or electric mixer, until smooth. Stir in the butter, golden raisins, cinnamon, allspice, and nutmeg. Cover with a damp dish towel and let rise for about 1 hour, until doubled in size.

3. Meanwhile, to make the decoration, mix together the flour, sugar, and water in a small bowl.

4. Grease two large baking sheets. Turn out the dough onto a lightly floured work surface, punch down to knock out the air, then divide into 14 pieces. Roll each piece into a ball and place the balls on the prepared sheets. Fill a disposable pastry bag with the flour mixture, cut off the tip, and pipe a cross onto each ball, then gently brush some milk over the tops of the buns. Let the buns rise for 40 minutes, then brush with milk again.

5. Meanwhile, preheat the oven to 375 °F. Bake the buns in the preheated oven for 15–20 minutes, until golden. Serve warm with butter and marmalade.

Brandy Snaps

MAKES 20

PREP TIME: 30–35 minutes

COOKING TIME: 20 minutes

INGREDIENTS

6 tablespoons unsalted butter
⅓ cup granulated sugar
3 tablespoons light corn syrup
⅔ cup all-purpose flour
1 teaspoon ground ginger
1 tablespoon brandy
finely grated rind of ½ lemon

filling
⅔ cup heavy cream
1 tablespoon brandy (optional)
1 tablespoon confectioners' sugar

In the Middle Ages, the Belgians and the French used to eat small waffles, especially on market days. The recipe reached England and there it evolved into brandy snaps. The waffles are rolled and filled with whipped cream (and brandy). However, other fillings—chocolate chips or butter-cream—can also be used.

1. Preheat the oven to 325 °F and line three large baking sheets with parchment paper.

2. Put the butter, sugar, and corn syrup into a saucepan and heat gently over low heat, stirring occasionally, until smooth. Remove from the heat and let cool slightly.

3. Sift the flour and ginger into the pan and beat until smooth, then stir in the brandy and lemon rind. Drop 20 small spoonfuls of the batter onto the prepared baking sheets, spaced well apart.

4. Bake in the preheated oven, one sheet at a time, for 10–12 minutes, or until the snaps are golden brown. Remove from the oven, let cool for about 30 seconds, then lift each snap with a spatula and wrap around the handle of a wooden spoon. If the snaps become too firm to wrap, return to the oven for about 30 seconds to soften.

5. When firm, remove the snaps from the spoon handles and transfer to a wire rack to cool completely.

6. To make the filling, whip the cream with the confectioners' sugar and the brandy, if using, until thick. Chill in the refrigerator until required.

7. Just before serving, pipe the cream mixture into both ends of each snap.

4.

5.

6.

2.

3.

4.

Iced Madeira Cake

This traditional Madeira cake has a firm yet light texture, much like pound cake, due to the sponge mixture. The lemon flavor and sugar icing are an integral part of this recipe. The cake originally derives its name from the wine that was imported from the Portuguese island of Madeira and was popular in Britain in around 1800. A slice often accompanied a glass of the wine as a dessert. Nowadays, it is served with tea or liqueur instead of the wine from this Portuguese island.

1. Preheat the oven to 325°F. Grease a 9-inch loaf pan and line with parchment paper.

2. Put the butter and granulated sugar into a large bowl and beat together until pale and creamy. Beat in the lemon rind, then gradually beat in the eggs. Sift the all-purpose flour and baking powder into the mixture and fold in gently until thoroughly incorporated. Fold in the milk and lemon juice.

3. Spoon the batter into the prepared pan and bake in the preheated oven for 1–1¼ hours, or until well risen, golden brown and a toothpick inserted into the center comes out clean. Let cool in the pan for 15 minutes, then turn out onto a wire rack to cool completely.

4. To make the icing, sift the confectioners' sugar into a bowl. Add the lemon juice and stir to make a smooth, thick icing. Gently spread over the top of the cake. Drizzle the warmed lemon curd over the icing and drag a toothpick through the two to create a swirled effect.

SERVES 10

PREP TIME: 30 minutes, plus cooling

COOKING TIME: 1–1¼ hours

INGREDIENTS

1½ sticks unsalted butter, softened, plus extra for greasing
¾ cup granulated sugar
finely grated rind of 1 lemon
3 eggs, lightly beaten
2¼ cups all-purpose flour
1¼ teaspoons baking powder
2 tablespoons milk
1 tablespoon lemon juice

icing
1⅓ cups confectioners' sugar
2–3 tablespoons lemon juice
2 teaspoons lemon curd, warmed

Strawberry
SHORTCAKE

SERVES 6–8

PREP TIME: 25 minutes

COOKING TIME: 15–20 minutes

INGREDIENTS

2 cups all-purpose flour
2 teaspoons baking powder
4 tablespoons butter, diced,
    plus extra for greasing
¼ cup granulated sugar
½–⅔ cup milk

topping
¼ cup milk
2 cups mascarpone cheese
5 tablespoons superfine sugar
3 cups hulled and quartered strawberries
finely grated rind of 1 orange

The shortbreadlike cake is covered with a tasty cream cheese layer with lovely fresh strawberries. Strawberries and cream are the epitome of summer for many people. In Britain, the heart-shape fruits have been enjoyed since the Middle Ages and have long been a symbol of purity, passion, and healing.

1. Preheat the oven to 400 °F. Lightly grease an 8-inch loose-bottom round cake pan.

2. Sift the flour and baking powder into a large bowl, add the butter, and rub in with your fingertips until the mixture resembles fine bread crumbs. Add the sugar. Stir in enough of the milk to form a soft but smooth dough. Gently press the dough evenly into the prepared pan. Bake in the preheated oven for 15–20 minutes, until risen, firm to the touch, and golden brown. Let cool for 5 minutes in the pan, then turn out onto a wire rack and let cool completely.

3. To make the topping, put the milk, mascarpone cheese, and 3 tablespoons of the sugar into a bowl and beat until smooth and fluffy. Put the strawberries into a separate bowl and sprinkle with the remaining sugar and the orange rind.

4. Spread the mascarpone mixture over the cake and pile the strawberries on top. Spoon over any juices left over from the strawberries in the bowl, sprinkle with mint leaves, and serve.

RASPBERRY CRUMB *Muffins*

MAKES 12

PREP TIME: 20 minutes,
plus 5 minutes to cool

COOKING TIME: 20 minutes

Their pinkish color makes these muffins attractive. Raspberry pieces peek out from the delicious cake, giving it a fresh fruity aroma. These summer berries grow even in the relatively cool country of Scotland.

1. Preheat the oven to 400°F and grease a 12-cup muffin pan or line with 12 muffin cups.

2. To make the crumb topping, sift the flour into a bowl. Cut the butter into small pieces, add to the bowl with the flour, and rub it in with your fingertips until the mixture resembles fine bread crumbs. Stir in the sugar and set aside.

3. To make the muffins, sift together the flour, baking powder, baking soda, and salt into a large bowl. Stir in the sugar.

4. Lightly beat the eggs in a large bowl, then beat in the yogurt, butter, and vanilla extract. Make a well in the center of the dry ingredients, pour in the beaten liquid ingredients, and add the raspberries. Stir gently until just combined. Do not overmix.

5. Spoon the batter into the prepared pan. Sprinkle the crumb topping over each muffin and press down lightly. Bake in the preheated oven for about 20 minutes, until well risen, golden brown, and firm to the touch.

6. Let the muffins cool in the pan for 5 minutes, then serve warm or transfer to a wire rack to cool completely.

INGREDIENTS

2¼ cups all-purpose flour
1 tablespoon baking powder
½ teaspoon baking soda
pinch of salt
½ cup granulated sugar
2 eggs
1 cup plain yogurt
6 tablespoons butter, melted and cooled, plus extra for greasing
1 teaspoon vanilla extract
1¼ cups frozen raspberries

crumb topping

⅓ cup all-purpose flour
2½ tablespoons butter
2 tablespoons granulated sugar

Gingernuts

MAKES 30

PREP TIME: 25 minutes

COOKING TIME: 15–20 minutes

INGREDIENTS

2¾ cups all-purpose flour
2¾ teaspoons baking powder
pinch of salt
1 cup granulated sugar
1 tablespoon ground ginger
1 teaspoon baking soda
1 stick butter, plus extra for greasing
¼ cup light corn syrup
1 egg, beaten
1 teaspoon grated orange rind

In the Middle Ages it was hard to find pepper in Europe, so ginger was used for seasoning instead. The spice gives these hard cookies with a rich syrupy flavor, which we call gingersnaps, a faintly pungent touch.

1. Preheat the oven to 325 °F. Lightly grease several baking sheets.

2. Sift together the flour, baking powder, salt, sugar, ginger, and baking soda into a large mixing bowl.

3. Heat the butter and corn syrup together in a saucepan over low heat until the butter has melted. Remove the pan from the heat and let cool slightly, then pour the contents onto the dry ingredients.

4. Add the egg and orange rind and mix thoroughly with a wooden spoon to form a dough. Using your hands, carefully shape the dough into 30 even balls. Place the balls on the prepared baking sheets, spaced well apart, then flatten them slightly with your fingers.

5. Bake in the preheated oven for 15–20 minutes, then carefully transfer to a wire rack to cool completely.

3.

4.

MILLIONAIRE'S
Shortbread

3.

4.

These pieces of confectionery, popular in the UK with a cup of tea or coffee, are probably found in more than a hundred varieties (including with peanut butter and raisins). They all are made of a cookie base with a layer of caramel and a chocolate coating. They taste a little like a chocolate bar—only much better! A touch of sea salt gives the caramel layer a modern tinge.

1. Preheat the oven to 350 °F. Grease a shallow 8-inch square cake pan.

2. Put the butter and sugar into a bowl and beat together until pale and creamy. Sift in the flour and add the ground almonds. Use clean hands to mix and knead to a crumbly dough. Press into the bottom of the prepared pan and prick the surface all over with a fork. Bake in the preheated oven for 15 minutes, or until pale golden. Let cool.

3. To make the topping, put the butter, sugar, corn syrup, and condensed milk into a saucepan over low heat and heat gently until the sugar has dissolved. Increase the heat to medium, bring to a boil, then simmer for 6–8 minutes, stirring continuously, until the mixture becomes thick. Stir in half the salt, then quickly pour the caramel over the shortbread layer. Sprinkle with the remaining salt.

4. Spoon the chocolate into a paper pastry bag and snip off the end. Pipe the chocolate over the caramel and swirl with the tip of a knife. Let cool, then chill for 2 hours, or until firm. Cut into 16 squares.

MAKES 16

PREP TIME: 30 minutes, plus 2 hours to chill

COOKING TIME: 15 minutes

INGREDIENTS

1 stick butter, softened, plus extra for greasing
¼ cup granulated sugar
1⅓ cups all-purpose flour
½ cup ground almonds

topping
1½ sticks butter
½ cup granulated sugar
3 tablespoons light corn syrup
1¾ cups canned condensed milk
¼ teaspoon sea salt crystals
6 ounces semisweet chocolate, melted

Scones

MAKES 9

PREP TIME: 15 minutes

COOKING TIME: 10–12 minutes

INGREDIENTS

3⅔ cups all-purpose flour, plus extra for dusting

½ teaspoon salt

2 teaspoons baking powder

4 tablespoons butter

2 tablespoons granulated sugar

1 cup milk, plus extra for glazing

strawberry jam or preserves and clotted cream, crème fraîche, or Greek yogurt, to serve

1.

2.

Rich, salty-sweet scones are widely popular in the British Isles—but they originate in Scotland. Here, before baking powder was invented, they were prepared in a skillet, like pancakes. Baking powder and a careful mixing of ingredients ensure the unusual consistency of this soft, crustless pastry that is eaten for afternoon tea.

1. Preheat the oven to 425 °F. Sift together the flour, salt, and baking powder into a bowl. Rub in the butter using your fingertips until the mixture resembles fine bread crumbs.

2. Stir in the sugar. Make a well in the center and pour in the milk. Stir in, using a spatula, and bring together to make a soft dough.

3. Turn out the dough onto a floured surface and lightly flatten it until it is ½ inch thick. Cut out scones, using a 2½-inch cookie cutter, and place on a lined baking sheet.

4. Brush with a little milk and bake in the preheated oven for 10–12 minutes, until golden and well risen. Let cool on a wire rack. Serve freshly baked with strawberry jam or preserves and clotted cream, crème fraîche, or Greek yogurt.

3.

4.

3.

3.

3.

Chelsea Buns

MAKES 6

PREP TIME: 40 minutes,
plus about 35 minutes to rise

COOKING TIME: 20 minutes

INGREDIENTS

½ teaspoon active dry yeast
⅔ cup lukewarm milk
4½ tablespoons granulated sugar
2¼ cups all-purpose flour,
plus extra for dusting
¼ teaspoon salt
2 tablespoons butter,
plus extra for greasing
½ teaspoon allspice
¼ cup golden raisins
2½ tablespoons candied peel
1 egg, beaten

An English baker created these sweet buns in Chelsea, London, in the early eighteenth century. The Bun House there was so popular that even English kings used to shop there. According to legend, in 1829, more than 50,000 people waited outside the shop on Good Friday—and 240,000 warm buns were sold over the counter.

1. Preheat the oven to 400 °F. Lightly grease a baking sheet. Combine the yeast in a bowl with the milk and ½ tablespoon of the granulated sugar and set aside for 10 minutes.

2. Meanwhile, sift together the flour and salt into a mixing bowl, add the butter, and rub in, then add the yeast mixture and beat well. Cover and set aside until the mixture doubles in size.

3. Turn out the dough onto a lightly floured work surface, lightly knead, and roll out to a 10-inch square. Sprinkle with 2 tablespoons of the granulated sugar, the allspice, golden raisins, and candied peel and roll into a log shape. Cut into six slices and lay the slices flat on the prepared sheet. Let stand until doubled in size. Brush with the beaten egg, then bake in the preheated oven for 20 minutes, or until golden.

4. Sprinkle with the remaining 2 tablespoons of granulated sugar and serve.

CHOCOLATE
Shortbread

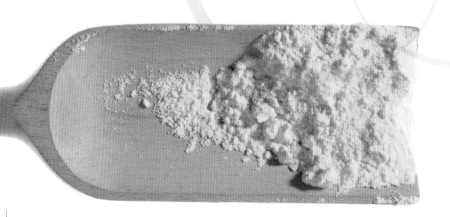

MAKES 22

PREP TIME: 25 minutes,
plus 20–25 minutes to chill

COOKING TIME: 15–20 minutes

INGREDIENTS

1¾ cups all-purpose flour

⅔ cup cornstarch,
plus extra for dusting

2 sticks butter, softened,
plus extra for greasing

½ cup granulated sugar

4 ounces milk chocolate
or semisweet chocolate,
chopped into small chunks

Shortbread is a sweet pastry from Scotland. The large, firm but brittle cookies, which—due to the high-butter content—crumble easily when bitten into, are an afternoon tea classic. The cookies are baked at a low temperature so that they keep their light color and the delicious chocolate pieces can stand out.

1. Preheat the oven to 350 °F. Lightly grease two baking sheets. Sift together the flour and cornstarch into a bowl and set aside.

2. Put the butter and sugar into a bowl and beat with a wooden spoon until pale and creamy. Gradually stir in the flour and cornstarch and three-quarters of the chocolate chunks and mix to a soft dough. Divide the dough into two pieces, then shape each piece into a ball and wrap in plastic wrap. Chill in the refrigerator for 20–25 minutes.

3. Lightly dust a work surface with a little cornstarch and gently roll out the dough to a thickness of ½ inch. Using a 2¼-inch round cutter, stamp out 22 circles, rerolling the trimmings, if necessary. Place the circles on the prepared baking sheets and top with the remaining chocolate chunks, lightly pressing them into the dough. Bake in the preheated oven for 15–20 minutes, or until pale golden. Let cool on the baking sheets for 10 minutes, then transfer to a wire rack to cool completely.

1.

2.

3.

1.

4.

4.

Fruitcake

SERVES 16

PREP TIME: 30 minutes,
plus several hours or overnight
to soak and 2 months to store

COOKING TIME: 2¼–2¾ hours

The Romans were already using candied and dried fruits for their cakes. With the fall of the price of sugar in the sixteenth century, a rich range of candied fruit became available. Since then, many different versions of fruitcakes have been popular, especially in the UK, where this rich, juicy cake is baked especially for weddings and Christmas.

1. Put the golden raisins, raisins, apricots, and dates in a large bowl and stir in the rum, if using, orange rind, and orange juice. Cover and let soak for several hours or overnight.

2. Preheat the oven to 300 °F. Grease an 8-inch round springform cake pan and line with parchment paper.

3. Beat together the butter and sugar until pale and creamy. Gradually beat in the eggs, beating hard after each addition. Stir in the soaked fruits, candied peel, candied cherries, candied ginger, and blanched almonds.

4. Sift together the flour and allspice, then fold lightly and evenly into the mixture. Spoon into the prepared pan and smooth the surface, making a slight depression in the center with the back of the spoon.

5. Bake in the preheated oven for 2¼–2¾ hours, or until the cake is beginning to shrink away from the sides and a toothpick inserted into the center comes out clean. Let cool completely in the pan.

6. Unclip and release the springform, turn out the cake, and remove the parchment paper. Wrap in some wax paper and aluminum foil, and store for at least two months. To add a richer flavor, prick the cake with a toothpick and spoon 1–2 tablespoons of rum or brandy over the top, if using, before storing.

INGREDIENTS

2⅓ cups golden raisins

1½ cups raisins

1 cup chopped dried apricots

½ cup chopped pitted dates

*¼ cup dark rum or brandy,
plus extra for flavoring (optional)*

*finely grated rind and
juice of 1 orange*

*2 sticks unsalted butter, softened,
plus extra for greasing*

1 cup firmly packed light brown sugar

4 eggs, beaten

⅓ cup chopped candied peel

⅓ cup quartered candied cherries

*⅓ cup chopped candied ginger or
preserved ginger*

⅓ cup blanched almonds, chopped

1⅔ cups all-purpose flour

1 teaspoon allspice

Cherry Cake

SERVES 8

PREP TIME: 20 minutes

COOKING TIME: 1–1¼ hours

INGREDIENTS

1¼ cups candied cherries, quartered
¾ cup ground almonds
1⅔ cups all-purpose flour
1 teaspoon baking powder
1¾ sticks unsalted butter,
plus extra for greasing
1 cup granulated sugar
3 extra-large eggs
finely grated rind and juice
of 1 lemon
6 sugar cubes, crushed

King Henry VIII of England brought the cherry to England in the sixteenth century, assisted by his gardener Richard Harrys. He had previously tasted cherries in Flanders. The first cherry trees were planted in Teynham. This village in the county of Kent became a center for cherry cultivation. Since then, cherry cake has become a British classic—with a good portion of sugar and almonds.

1. Preheat the oven to 350 °F. Grease an 8-inch round cake pan and line with parchment paper.

2. Stir together the cherries, almonds, and 1 tablespoon of the flour. Sift together the remaining flour and the baking powder into a separate bowl.

3. Cream together the butter and sugar until light and fluffy. Gradually add the eggs, beating hard, until evenly mixed.

4. Add the flour mixture and fold lightly and evenly into the creamed mixture with a metal spoon. Add the cherry mixture, fold in evenly, then fold in the lemon rind and juice.

5. Spoon the batter into the prepared pan and sprinkle with the crushed sugar cubes. Bake in the preheated oven for 1–1¼ hours, or until risen and golden brown and shrinking from the sides of the pan.

6. Let cool in the pan for about 15 minutes, then turn out onto a wire rack to cool completely.

1.
2.
3.

4.
5.
6.

British Pies

LIVE AND LET PIE

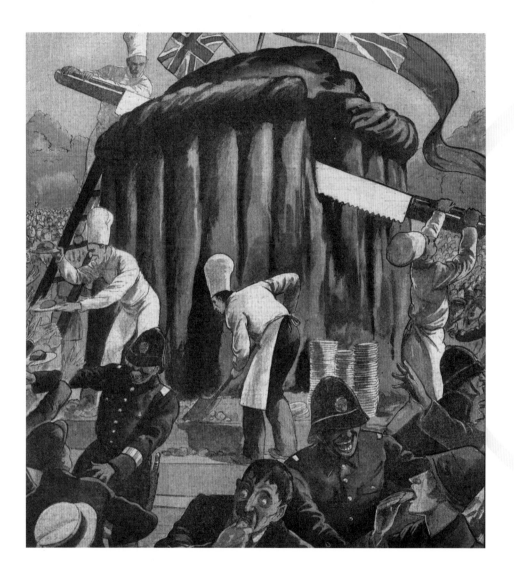

In terms of their pies, when it comes to this culinary feat, there is no joking with the British. There is a long tradition of pie making in Britain and there are many variations on recipes for pastries and fillings.

A good pie is a magnificent dish—sweet or savory, it may have different ingredients. For centuries, pies have been known for being nutritious and durable. Today, fruit pies have made their triumphal procession in the baking world.

Denby Dale, a modest town in the English county of Yorkshire, has only rarely been a talking point during its unremarkable history. The first time was in 1788, at the celebration of the recovery of King George III from a mental breakdown. In honor of this special event, the owners of the White Hart pub baked an oversized pie, which they themselves demolished—and washed down with decent ale, of course. If you believe the chroniclers, the pie filling was as large as two sheep. With Wellington's victory over Napoleon in 1815, the time had finally come for the name of the town to be carved in stone as the ultimate Pie Village. A certain George Wilby, who had been at the battle, celebrated it accordingly. The Golden Jubilee of Queen Victoria in 1887 and the end of World War I in 1918 also justified the continuation of the giant pie tradition in Denby, as did the anticipated four Royal births in 1964. The 20-foot-long, 6½-foot-wide, and 20-inch-high pie provided 30,000 servings. However, this was surpassed in 1988 when Denby Dale duly celebrated its two-hundred-year pie-baking tradition anniversary. The most recent pie in 2000 holds the current record: about 14 yards long, nearly 10 feet wide, and filled with 5 tons of ground beef.

Pies are integral to British food culture, even if they weren't actually invented there. Evidence of pie baking goes back to the time of the Egyptian pharaohs, where the pastries were so popular that they were included in grave goods to provide the deceased with sustenance "for the long journey to eternity." Dried flatbreads filled with honey were found in the tomb of Ramses II. In fact, we still think of pies as being perfect to take on long journeys. It was for this reason that they were so popular with the Royal Navy and in the mining industry. After all, they combine several practical features, but most importantly are nutritious and durable. In the days of the Cornish mining industry, miners would take a special version of the treat with them as they descended into the darkness below: a single pie, one half sweet, one half savoury. It was a main course and dessert rolled into one piece of dough.

The first time "pye" made its official debut with the English public was at the luncheon following the coronation of King Henry VI (1422–61). The "Partryche and Pecock enhackyll" pie contained whole peacocks that had been cooked and then baked in the crust. This later developed into the tradition of decorating pie crusts with pastry chickens or pheasants to indicate the meat contained within. This eventually evolved into the pre-Victorian practice of putting a porcelain bird under the pastry lid of every pie to "let the steam escape and to draw attention to the quality of the content."

For Denby Dale, such adaptations are probably somewhat superfluous given the size of its pies. All that remains to be seen is just what happy event will soon be found in Yorkshire to be worthy of honoring with an even bigger pie.

DATE & WALNUT
LOAF

MAKES 1 LOAF

PREP TIME: 20 minutes

COOKING TIME: 35–40 minutes

INGREDIENTS

⅔ cup chopped, pitted dried dates
½ teaspoon baking soda
finely grated rind of ½ lemon
½ cup hot tea
3 tablespoons unsalted butter,
plus extra for greasing
⅓ cup firmly packed light brown sugar
1 medium egg
1 cup all-purpose flour
1 teaspoon baking powder
¼ cup chopped walnuts
walnut halves, to decorate

When it's raining or snowing outside, and warm and cozy inside—that's just the right time for some rich date and walnut loaf. The nuts give it a touch of winter and the sticky fruit of the date palm provide a high sugar concentration. And although this is really a cake—the cut slices may be spread with butter, like bread.

1. Preheat the oven to 350°F. Grease an 8½-inch loaf pan and line with parchment paper.

2. Put the dates, baking soda, and lemon rind into a bowl and add the hot tea. Let soak for 10 minutes, until soft.

3. Meanwhile, cream together the butter and sugar until light and fluffy, then beat in the egg. Stir in the date mixture.

4. Fold in the flour and baking powder, using a large metal spoon, then fold in the walnuts. Spoon the batter into the prepared pan and smooth the surface. Top with the walnut halves.

5. Bake in the preheated oven for 35–40 minutes, or until risen, firm, and golden brown. Let cool in the pan for 10 minutes, then turn out onto a wire rack to cool completely.

2.

3.

4.

1.

2.

3.

Crumpets

MAKES 10

PREP TIME: 20 minutes,
plus 1 hour to rest

COOKING TIME: 6 minutes

INGREDIENTS

1¾ cups white bread flour
1 teaspoon baking powder
½ teaspoon salt
1 cup lukewarm milk
⅔ cup lukewarm water
1 teaspoon active dry yeast
oil, for oiling and frying

The English crumpet has a chewy, spongy texture—crispy on the outside and juicy inside—and is typically eaten hot: with butter, cheese, or egg, but also with jam. It probably evolved in the nineteenth century from the Scottish crumpet, which looks like a pancake and is made with baking powder.

1. Sift together the flour, baking powder, and salt into a large bowl. Gradually add the milk and water, adding the yeast halfway through. Beat vigorously until the mixture is the consistency of heavy cream.

2. Cover the bowl with plastic wrap and let rest for 1 hour at room temperature, until the mixture has expanded and bubbles have formed in it.

3. Oil four individual 3¼-inch pastry rings and heat some oil in a heavy skillet. Place the rings in the skillet and pour 2–3 tablespoons of the batter into each ring. Gently cook until the tops are dry or have developed small holes.

4. Turn out the crumpets, using a blunt knife, and transfer to a warm plate. Repeat until all the mixture has been used, oiling the rings and skillet when necessary.

CRUSTY

White Loaf

MAKES 1 LOAF

PREP TIME: 20 minutes,
plus 1 hour 30 minutes to rise

COOKING TIME: 30 minutes

INGREDIENTS

1 egg

1 egg yolk

⅔–1 cup lukewarm water

*3¾ cups white bread flour,
plus extra for dusting*

1½ teaspoon salt

2 teaspoons sugar

1 teaspoon active dry yeast

2 tablespoons butter, diced

sunflower oil, for greasing

This loaf is easy to make with just a few ingredients. This good old-fashioned bread, tender on the inside and crisp on the outside, is a wonderful choice for divine toast or a sandwich. This bread keeps well, due to the white flour, and can be found almost everywhere in Britain.

1. Brush a bowl with oil. Put the egg and egg yolk into a bowl and lightly beat to mix. Add enough lukewarm water to make up to 1¼ cups. Stir well.

2. Put the flour, salt, sugar, and yeast into a large bowl. Add the butter and rub it in with your fingertips until the mixture resembles bread crumbs. Make a well in the center, add the egg mixture, and work to a smooth dough.

3. Turn out onto a lightly floured work surface and knead well for about 10 minutes, or until smooth. Shape the dough into a ball, place it in the prepared bowl, and cover with a damp dish towel. Let rise in a warm place for 1 hour, or until the dough has doubled in size.

4. Oil a 9-inch loaf pan. Turn out the dough onto a lightly floured work surface and knead for 1 minute, or until smooth. Shape the dough the length of the pan and three times the width. Fold the dough in three lengthwise and place it in the pan with the seam underneath. Cover and let stand in a warm place for 30 minutes, or until it has risen above the pan. Preheat the oven to 425 °F.

5. Bake in the preheated oven for 30 minutes, or until firm and golden brown. Test that the loaf is cooked by tapping on the bottom with your knuckles—it should sound hollow. Transfer to a wire rack to cool.

2.

3.

4.

1.

2.

3.

ENGLISH Muffins

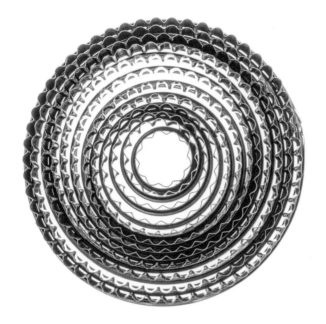

MAKES 8–10

PREP TIME: 15 minutes, plus
2 hours to rise and 1 hour to rest

COOKING TIME: 8–10 minutes

English muffins are nourishing, savory pan-baked breads. They are flat and are freshly toasted just before eating. In Central Europe, they are also called "toasties." In the nineteenth century, they were popular at tea time and were sold on the street by loud, yelling "muffin men."

1. Mix together the whole-wheat flour, all-purpose flour, yeast, salt, and baking soda in a large bowl. Add the buttermilk and water and mix to combine. Turn out onto a floured work surface and knead until a smooth dough forms. If it is too wet, add a little flour. Transfer to a clean bowl, cover with a damp dish towel, and let rise for about 2 hours.

2. Turn out the dough onto a lightly floured work surface and roll out to thickness of ½ inch. Use a 3-inch round cutter to cut out 8–10 circles, rerolling the trimmings, if necessary. Do not overwork the dough. Sprinkle the circles with fine cornmeal and let rest for 1 hour.

3. Put some oil into a flat griddle pan or heavy skillet and heat over medium heat. Add the muffins to the pan, in batches, and cook on one side for 4–5 minutes, until golden brown. Turn and cook on the other side for 4–5 minutes, until golden brown. Place the cooked muffins on some paper towels and let cool before serving.

INGREDIENTS

1 cup whole-wheat flour
1 cup all-purpose flour,
plus extra for dusting
2 teaspoons active dry yeast
1 teaspoon salt
¾ teaspoon baking soda
¾ cup low-fat buttermilk
1–2 tablespoons water
fine cornmeal or polenta, for dusting
vegetable oil, for frying

1.

2.

2.

Sausage Rolls

MAKES 12

PREP TIME: 20 minutes

COOKING TIME: 20–25 minutes

INGREDIENTS

2 teaspoons milk, plus extra for brushing
¾ slice white bread, crusts removed and diced
1 pound bulk sausage or sausage meat with the casing removed
1 onion, finely chopped
1 egg
1 egg yolk
1½ teapoons ground cumin
1 teaspoon paprika
flour, for dusting
1 pound store-bought puff pastry
beaten egg white, for brushing
salt and pepper, to taste

These puff pastry rolls with a sausage filling are a typically British pastry and a popular savory party snack. You can enjoy them hot or cold, but they must be fresh! For this reason, sausage rolls are best made at home and eaten with friends and family.

1. Preheat the oven to 350 °F. Line a baking sheet with parchment paper. Put the milk into a large bowl, add the bread, and let soak until soft. Add the sausage meat, onions, egg, egg yolk, cumin, and paprika and season with salt and pepper, and mix to combine.

2. Roll out the pastry on a lightly floured work surface and cut out twelve 5-inch squares, reserving the trimmings. Brush the pastry squares with the egg white. Spread the sausage meat mixture evenly down the center of each square, then roll up the pastry to enclose the filling.

3. Transfer the sausage rolls to the prepared sheet with the seam underneath. Reroll the pastry trimmings and use a shaped cutter to cut out 12 decorative shapes.

4. Brush the sausage rolls with milk and decorate each one with a pastry shape. Brush the shapes with milk, then bake the sausage rolls in the middle of the preheated oven for 20–25 minutes, until golden.

MIXED SEED

Bread

MAKES 1 LOAF

PREP TIME: 25–30 minutes, plus 1 hour 30 minutes to rise

COOKING TIME: 30 minutes

INGREDIENTS

2¾ cups white bread flour, plus extra for dusting

1 cup rye flour

1½ tablespoons instant nonfat dry milk

1½ teaspoons salt

1 tablespoon packed light brown sugar

1 teaspoon active dry yeast

1½ tablespoons sunflower oil, plus extra for greasing and brushing

2 teaspoons lemon juice

1¼ cups lukewarm water

1 teaspoon caraway seeds

½ teaspoon poppy seeds

½ teaspoon sesame seeds

topping

1 egg, beaten with 1 tablespoon water

1 tablespoon sunflower seeds

Compared with traditional British white bread, this wheat bread contains seeds that give it a much greater depth of flavor—while still being a light wheat bread. It does not need toasting and also tastes good eaten fresh with a little butter.

1. Put the white flour, rye flour, instant milk, salt, sugar, and yeast into a large bowl. Pour in the oil and add the lemon juice and water.

2. Stir in the seeds and mix well until smooth. Turn out onto a lightly floured surface and knead well for about 10 minutes.

3. Brush a bowl with oil. Shape the dough into a ball, place in the bowl, and cover with a damp dish towel. Let rise in a warm place for 1 hour, until the dough has doubled in volume.

4. Oil a 9-inch loaf pan. Turn out the dough onto a lightly floured surface and knead for 1 minute, until smooth. Shape into a loaf the length of the pan and three times the width. Fold the dough in three lengthwise and place in the pan with the seam underneath. Cover and let stand in a warm place for 30 minutes, until it has risen above the pan.

5. Preheat the oven to 425 °F. Brush the egg and water glaze over the loaf, then gently press the sunflower seeds all over the top.

6. Bake in the preheated oven for 30 minutes, or until golden brown and hollow on the bottom when tapped. Transfer to a wire rack to cool.

1.

2.

4.

4.

4.

6.

A Long &

Rich Tradition

Many of the recipes that are popular in the United States actually have their roots in Ireland, and it is completely wrong to think that cooking on the Green Island of Europe is limited to just Irish stew or some substantial pies and cakes. For example, sourdough bread has long belonged to the Irish classics, and with the current trend for natural ingredients, sourdough bread has recently gained in popularity. Over the last few years, the gourmet scene in Ireland has developed considerably, but without forgetting old traditions such as "blaa," a white and soft bread that is famous in the south of Ireland. Or "boxty," the famous potato pancake that's often been served for Irish breakfast. And at any time of the day, a fruity tea cake is an absolute must.

IRISH SODA *Bread*

4.

This bread is made with baking soda and is popular throughout Ireland. It's quick and easy to make and works every time—its consistency just can't go wrong. On the Emerald Isle, several versions of this light and tasty bread are served at every possible occasion: in the morning with scrambled eggs, at lunchtime with Irish cheeses, or with an Irish Stew in the evening for dinner.

1. Preheat the oven to 425 °F. Lightly grease a baking sheet.

2. Sift the dry ingredients into a mixing bowl. Make a well in the center, pour in most of the buttermilk, and mix well, using your hands. The dough should be soft but not too wet. If necessary, add the remaining buttermilk.

3. Turn out the dough onto a floured work surface and knead for about 10 minutes. Shape into an 8-inch circle.

4. Place the bread on the prepared baking sheet, cut a cross in the top, and bake in the preheated oven for 25–30 minutes.

5. Serve sliced with butter and a sweet or savory topping.

MAKES 1 LOAF

PREP TIME: 10–15 minutes

COOKING TIME: 25–30 minutes

INGREDIENTS

3 tablespoons butter, melted, for greasing
3⅔ cups all-purpose flour,
plus extra for dusting
1 teaspoon salt
1 teaspoon baking soda
1¾ cups buttermilk

Irish

TEA CAKE

SERVES 8–10

PREP TIME: 25 minutes

COOKING TIME: 1 hour

INGREDIENTS

*1½ sticks butter, softened,
plus extra for greasing*

1 cup granulated sugar

*1 teaspoon vanilla extract or
1 vanilla bean, scraped*

2 eggs

⅓ cup cream cheese

*1¾ cups all-purpose flour
plus extra for dusting*

1 teaspoon baking powder

¼ teaspoon salt

¾ cup golden raisins

⅔ cup buttermilk

glaze

⅓ cup confectioners' sugar, sifted

2 teaspoons fresh lemon juice

This cake is simple yet delicious, and it can be served with fresh fruit or whipped cream as a dessert or just enjoyed on its own with a cup of tea.

1. Preheat the oven to 325 °F. Grease a 9-inch loaf pan. Dust with flour and line the bottom with parchment paper.

2. Put the butter, sugar, and vanilla extract into a large mixing bowl and beat with an electric mixer until fluffy. Add the eggs, one at a time, beating after each addition until combined.

3. Add the cream cheese and beat until well combined. Sift together the flour, baking powder, and salt into a separate bowl. Put the golden raisins into a small bowl. Add 3 tablespoons of the flour mixture to the golden raisins and stir until they are well coated. Gradually add the remaining flour mixture to the butter mixture, alternating with the buttermilk, and mix until smooth. Add the golden raisins and stir with a wooden spoon until well combined.

4. Transfer the batter to the prepared pan, smoothing the surface with a spatula. Bake in the middle of the preheated oven for about 1 hour until golden, and a toothpick inserted into the center comes out clean. Remove from the oven and let cool in the pan for 10 minutes. Using a spatula, separate the cake from the sides of the pan and transfer to a wire rack to cool.

5. Meanwhile, to make the glaze, combine the sugar and lemon juice in a small bowl and stir until smooth. Spread the icing over the warm cake and let cool completely. Cut into slices and serve.

2.

3.

4.

THE WONDERS of FRENCH BAKING

Fine pastries are just as much a symbol of France as the Eiffel Tower or the Louvre museum in Paris. Consequently, whether you are in a big French city or a small village, one sight is common: the streets are peppered with people enjoying a nice cup of coffee with a crispy croissant and a newspaper. Fruit tarts, petits fours, and the lavishly colorful macarons that are currently enjoying something of a revival are of the same cultural importance as the classy fashion and shoe boutiques. However, all those sweet treats are still overshadowed by the baguette, which is a staple part of the daily diet for all French people. A small piece of this bread greets the new day in France when served for breakfast with preserves; later on in the day, it turns into a welcome companion during lunch and dinner. A meal without a baguette would be just as unthinkable for a French person as a meal that is not graced with an exquisite tart to round it off.

The baguette is a politically sensitive product. Any party who tried to change the price of this bread provoked major discussions. In France, as with coffee and milk, the price of bread is controled by the government.

Croissants

MAKES 12

PREP TIME: 30 minutes,
plus rising and chilling

COOKING TIME: 15–20 minutes

INGREDIENTS

*3⅔ cups white bread flour,
plus extra for dusting*

¼ cup granulated sugar

1 teaspoon salt

2¼ teaspoons active dry yeast

*1¼ cups lukewarm milk,
plus extra if needed*

*2½ sticks butter, softened,
plus extra for greasing*

*1 egg, lightly beaten with
1 tablespoon milk, for glazing*

Croissants are a classic breakfast item in France and are made with puff dough. Cold butter is worked into a yeast dough in several folding and rolling operations. Croissants are a fairly recent recipe. The first one was baked in the nineteenth century. Its crescent moon shape is mentioned for the first time in 1863. The French term croissant de lune means "crescent moon" in English.

1. Stir the dry ingredients into a large bowl, make a well in the center, and add the milk. Mix to a soft dough, adding more milk, if too dry. Knead on a lightly floured work surface for 5–10 minutes, or until smooth and elastic. Let rise in a large greased bowl covered in plastic wrap in a warm place until doubled in size. Meanwhile, flatten the butter with a rolling pin between two sheets of wax paper to form a rectangle about ¼ inch thick, then chill in the refrigerator. Preheat the oven to 400 °F.

2. Knead the dough for 1 minute. Remove the butter from the refrigerator and let soften slightly. Roll out the dough on a well-floured work surface to 18 x 6 inches. Place the butter in the center, fold up the sides, and squeeze the edges together gently. With the short end of the dough toward you, fold the top third down toward the center, then fold the bottom third up. Rotate 90 degrees clockwise so that the fold is to your left and the top flap opens toward your right. Roll out to a rectangle and fold again. If the butter feels soft, wrap the dough in plastic wrap and chill. Repeat the rolling process two times. Cut the dough in half. Roll out one half into a triangle ¼ inch thick (keep the other half refrigerated). Use a cardboard triangular template with a base of 7 inches and sides of 8 inches to cut out the croissants. Repeat with the refrigerated dough.

3. Brush the triangles lightly with the egg glaze. Roll into croissant shapes, starting at the bottom and tucking the point under to prevent them from unrolling while cooking. Brush again with the glaze. Place on an ungreased baking sheet and let double in size. Bake in the preheated oven for 15–20 minutes, or until golden brown.

1.

1.

3.

3.

4.

5.

VANILLA
Macarons

MAKES 16

PREP TIME: 20 minutes,
plus cooling

COOKING TIME: 10–15 minutes

In France, a pastry chef is only considered a real artist if he is able to make high-quality macarons. The French patisserie Ladurée claims to have invented macarons in 1791, but in fact they first appeared during a royal wedding in 1533, served with foie gras pâté.

1. Place the ground almonds and confectioners' sugar in a food processor and process for 15 seconds. Sift the mixture into a bowl. Line two baking sheets with parchment paper.

2. Place the egg whites in a clean, grease-free bowl and beat until holding soft peaks. Gradually beat in the granulated sugar to make a firm, glossy meringue. Beat in the vanilla extract.

3. Using a spatula, fold the almond mixture into the egg mixture, one-third at a time. When all the dry ingredients are thoroughly incorporated, continue to cut and fold the mixture until it forms a shiny batter with a thick, ribbonlike consistency.

4. Pour the batter into a pastry bag fitted with a ½-inch plain tip. Pipe 32 small circles onto the prepared baking sheets. Tap the baking sheets firmly onto a work surface to remove air bubbles. Let stand at room temperature for 30 minutes. Preheat the oven to 325°F.

5. Bake in the preheated oven for 10–15 minutes. Let cool for 10 minutes, then carefully peel the macarons off the parchment paper and let cool completely.

6. To make the filling, beat the butter and vanilla extract in a bowl until pale and fluffy. Gradually beat in the confectioners' sugar until smooth and creamy. Use to sandwich together pairs of macarons.

INGREDIENTS

1 cup ground almonds
1 cup confectioners' sugar
2 extra-large egg whites
¼ cup granulated sugar
½ teaspoon vanilla extract

filling
4 tablespoons unsalted butter, softened
½ teaspoon vanilla extract
¼ cup confectioners' sugar, sifted

Tarte Tatin

SERVES 6

PREP TIME: 25–30 minutes,
plus resting

COOKING TIME: 45–50 minutes

INGREDIENTS

1 cup granulated sugar
1¼ sticks unsalted butter
7 Pippin, Golden Delicious, or other sweet crisp apples (about 1¾ pounds), peeled, cored, and sliced
1 sheet store-bought puff pastry
all-purpose flour, for dusting
vanilla ice cream, to serve (optional)

The principal feature of this apple pie is the layer of caramel that covers the fruit when you turn the cake out. According to legend, the Tatin sisters invented the tart by accident. They ran a hotel in Lamotte-Beuvron in central France in 1900. Amid the hustle and bustle of the establishment, a cake fell out of its baking sheet. They put it back with the apples underneath, covered it with fresh dough, and baked it again.

1. Put an 8-inch ovenproof skillet over low heat and add the sugar. Melt the sugar until it starts to caramelize, but do not let it burn, then add the butter and stir it in to make a light toffee sauce. Remove from the heat.

2. Place the apple slices in the skillet on top of the toffee sauce. The apples should fill the pan. Put the pan over medium heat and cover. Simmer, without stirring, for about 5–10 minutes, or until the apples have soaked up some of the sauce, then remove from the heat.

3. Preheat the oven to 375 °F. Roll out the pastry on a lightly floured surface until the dough is large enough to thickly cover the skillet with extra space on the sides. Lay it on top of the apples and tuck the edges down inside between the fruit and the skillet until it is sealed. Don't worry about making it look too neat—it will be turned over before eating.

4. Put the skillet into the preheated oven and bake for 25–35 minutes, checking to make sure the pastry doesn't burn. The pastry should be puffed and golden. Remove from the oven and let rest for 30–60 minutes.

5. When you're ready to eat, make sure the tart is still a little warm (reheat it on the stove, if necessary) and place a plate on top. Carefully turn it over and remove the skillet. Serve with some vanilla ice cream, if using.

VANILLA
Millefeuille

SERVES 6

PREP TIME: 1½–1¾ hours

COOKING TIME: 45 minutes

INGREDIENTS

3 sheets store-bought puff pastry
flour, for dusting

crème pâtissière
2 tablespoons cornstarch
⅔ cup granulated sugar
2 teaspoons vanilla sugar (to make your own, beat a drop vanilla extract into sugar)
2 cups milk
2 egg yolks

icing
2 egg whites
2¾ cups confectioners' sugar
4 ounces semisweet chocolate, broken into pieces

Fans of puff pastry cannot pass over this classic from France. The millefeuille (thousand leaves) consists of layers of puff pastry with a vanilla cream in between. The confectioner adds a decorative icing to the top of the cake. Nowadays, there are also savory millefeuilles, some filled with cheese and spinach.

1. Preheat the oven to 425 °F. Line a baking sheet with parchment paper. Roll out one sheet of pastry on a work surface lightly dusted with flour to a ¼-inch-thick square. Transfer to the prepared baking sheet, prick all over with a fork, then place another baking sheet on top to prevent the pastry from rising.

2. Bake in the preheated oven for 10 minutes. Remove the top baking sheet, then return the pastry to the oven and bake for an additional 5 minutes, until golden brown. Repeat with the remaining pastry. Let cool, then cut each pastry square in half to make two rectangles.

3. To make the crème pâtissière, put the cornstarch, granulated sugar, and vanilla sugar into a saucepan over medium heat. Add the milk and egg yolks and cook, stirring, until the mixture comes to a boil and thickens. Remove from the heat and let cool completely.

4. Put a piece of pastry on a wire rack, spread with one-fifth of the crème pâtissière, then place another piece of pastry on top. Spread with one-fifth of the crème pâtissière and top with another piece of pastry. Repeat until you have used all the crème pâtissière, then top with the final piece of pastry.

5. To make the icing, put the egg whites and confectioners' sugar into a bowl over a saucepan of gently simmering water and beat with an electric mixer for 5 minutes, until thick. Reserve and pour over the top sheet of pastry.

6. Put the chocolate into a bowl over a saucepan of gently simmering water and heat until melted, then pour it into a pastry bag fitted with a fine tip and use to draw wavy lines on the icing.

7. Using the tip of a knife, draw perpendicular lines through the chocolate, from bottom to top and from top to bottom to make the pattern. Use a sharp knife to trim the edges of the millefeuille.

8. Cut the millefeuille into 6 rectangles, chill in the refrigerator, and serve cold.

1.

3.

4.

1.

2.

3.

4.

5.

6.

7.

8.

STRAWBERRY
Éclairs

MAKES 16–18

PREP TIME: 25 minutes

COOKING TIME: 20–25 minutes

French éclairs are usually filled or topped with cream, cream cheese, strawberries, or even chocolate. This oblong dough has been produced since about 1850. It is made from choux dough, a classic French dough.

1. Preheat the oven to 425 °F. Grease two baking sheets. To make the filling, heat the butter and water in a saucepan until boiling.

2. Remove from the heat, quickly tip in the flour, and beat until smooth. Transfer to a bowl.

3. Gradually beat in the eggs with an electric mixer until glossy.

4. Spoon into a pastry bag with a large plain tip and pipe up to eighteen 3½-inch fingers on the baking sheets.

5. Bake in the preheated oven for 12–15 minutes, until golden brown. Cut a slit down the side of each éclair to release steam. Bake for an additional 2 minutes. Cool on a wire rack.

6. Puree half the strawberries with the confectioners' sugar.

7. Finely chop the remaining strawberries and stir into the mascarpone.

8. Pipe or spoon the mascarpone mixture into the éclairs. Serve the éclairs with the strawberry puree spooned over the top. The éclairs are best served within an hour of filling.

INGREDIENTS

pastry dough
4 tablespoons unsalted butter, plus extra for greasing
⅔ cup water
½ cup all-purpose flour, sifted
2 eggs, beaten

filling
8 ounces hulled strawberries
2 tablespoons confectioners' sugar
⅔ cup mascarpone cheese

Crème Brûlée
TARTLETS

MAKES 6

PREP TIME: 35 minutes,
plus 8 hours to chill

COOKING TIME: 20 minutes

INGREDIENTS

pastry dough
*1⅓ cups all-purpose flour,
plus extra for dusting*
¼ cup granulated sugar
pinch of salt
1¼ sticks butter, plus extra for greasing
1–2 teaspoons cold water

4 egg yolks
¼ cup granulated sugar
1¾ cups light cream
*1 teaspoon vanilla extract or 1 vanilla
bean, scraped*
raw brown sugar, for sprinkling

Crème brûlée is a flavored egg custard with a caramel crust created by using a blowtorch at the end. The "burned cream" is the queen of desserts because of its unique taste and crunch. It is often on the menu in French bistros and it has been adapted here so the brûlée is in a tart shell.

1. To make the dough, sift together the flour, sugar, and salt into a bowl. Gradually add the butter, then add the water and mix to a smooth dough using the dough hook of an electric mixer. Wrap the dough in plastic wrap and chill in the refrigerator for at least 1 hour.

2. Preheat the oven to 350 °F. Grease six 4-inch tart pans. Turn out the dough onto a work surface lightly dusted with flour and roll out to a thickness of ¼ inch, then use to line the prepared pans. Reroll and cut out the trimmings, if necessary.

3. Ease the dough into the prepared pans, pressing it up the sides of the pans. Trim the excess, then prick the dough several times with a fork.

4. Line the pastry shells with parchment paper and fill them with pie weights or dried beans. Bake in the middle of the preheated oven for 10 minutes, then remove the weights and paper and bake for an additional 10 minutes, until golden brown, being careful that they don't burn.

5. Meanwhile, put the egg yolks and the sugar into a bowl and beat until foaming. Heat the cream with the vanilla extract in a saucepan over medium heat, but do not let it boil. Beat in the egg-and-sugar mixture and continue to cook without boiling until thickened.

6. Remove from the heat and let cool, then pour into the pastry shells. Let cool completely, then chill in the refrigerator overnight.

7. Sprinkle a generous layer of raw brown sugar over the chilled tarts and heat with a kitchen blowtorch until the surface has caramelized. Alternatively, place the tarts under a hot broiler until the surface has caramelized. Serve immediately.

4.

5.

7.

THE PAINT BOX OF THE
SUN KING

Macarons are a little taste of sugary heaven! Unlike most other foods, the colorful meringue cookies have attained cult status. Like foie gras from Gascony, oysters from Arcachon, and wine from Provençe, they are French culinary classics.

Available in an array of colors, macarons have become not only an export trend, but also an extremely expensive treat. A dozen of the colorful pastries could cost more than a bottle of a good quality red wine.

Macarons, along with the Eiffel Tower and the Arc de Triomphe, are now thought of as a classic French icon. Although, depending on which historic source you consult, they have been turning the heads of people from all walks of life for many centuries, it is only in recent years that they have become really popular. At every major railroad station or airport, these colorful cookies appear like gems or fashion accessories, often at fantastic prices. And yet, they neither travel well, nor keep well. It seems that macarons occupy a curious position in this age of short-lived pleasures. Within a few years, they have turned into a sweet export hit, which has made certain Parisian elite patisseries claim to be the "true inventors" of the macaron. However, although Ladurée and Pierre Hermé are luxury stores that sell a medium box of macarons at the price of perfume, they actually have nothing to do with the original recipe. According to the Larousse Gastronomique culinary encyclopedia, its origins can be traced back to the French monastery of Cormery. The monks there, who were fond of sweet things, are supposed to have invented this type of cookie as early as 1791. However, Catherine de Medici was also served fine almond cookies from Florence at her wedding to the Duke of Orleans in 1533. And the writer François Rabelais heaped such praise on the recipe in his day that even Louis XIV enjoyed macarons at his various weddings. In the mid-17th century, these cookies formed part of the standard repertoire of the "Officiers de Bouche," the chefs at Versailles. The Benedictine Order of Nancy also boasts of having breathed eternal life into macarons. As the nuns were forbidden to eat meat, they specialized in making different types of baked goods. Since 1792, the "macarons of the holy sisters" have been popular creations by the nuns of Nancy.

2.

3.

4.

Lemon TARTE

SERVES 8–10

PREP TIME: 35 minutes, plus chilling

COOKING TIME: 25 minutes

INGREDIENTS

pastry dough
3 tablespoons water
1 tablespoon sugar
⅛ teaspoon salt
1 tablespoon vegetable oil
6 tablespoons unsalted butter, diced
1¼ cups all-purpose flour, plus extra for dusting

2 eggs
2 egg yolks
½ cup freshly squeezed lemon juice
grated zest of 1 lemon
½ cup granulated sugar
6 tablespoons unsalted butter, diced

The lemon has been growing in France for several centuries. One of the strongholds of its cultivation is the town of Menton on the French Riviera; a Lemon Festival has been celebrated there since 1934.

1. Preheat the oven to 400 °F. To make the dough, mix together the water, sugar, salt, oil, and butter with the flour. Refrigerate for 20 minutes.

2. Roll the dough on a lightly floured surface to a thickness of ¼ inch. Place in a 9-inch round tart pan, trimming the edge. Prick with a fork and bake for 15 minutes, until golden brown. Remove from the oven and let cool in the pan. Do not turn off the oven.

3. Meanwhile, beat together the eggs and egg yolks and set aside. Put the lemon juice, lemon zest, sugar, and butter into a saucepan over medium heat and heat until the butter has melted. Reduce the heat, add the beaten egg, and cook, stirring continuously, until the mixture has thickened and bubbles are beginning to form.

4. Pour the lemon-and-egg mixture through a strainer set over the pastry shell, evenly spreading the filling with the back of a spoon. Return to the oven for 5 minutes. Remove from the oven and let cool. Serve cold.

CINNAMON SPICED

Orange Beignets

4.

MAKES 8

PREP TIME: 20 minutes,
plus time to rise

COOKING TIME: 5–10 minutes

INGREDIENTS

2 cups all-purpose flour
1 teaspoon active dry yeast
1½ tablespoons granulated sugar
½ cup lukewarm milk
1 egg, beaten
finely grated rind of 1 small orange
1 teaspoon orange flower water
(available online)
1½ oz butter, melted
sunflower oil, for deep frying
cinnamon sugar (available online),
for dusting
orange slices or segments,
to serve

In France most types of pastries that are baked in fat are known as beignets. They can be filled with fruit, meat, vegetables, or even not have a filling at all. With orange slices, they create an intense, sweet taste experience.

1. Sift the flour into a bowl and stir in the yeast and sugar.

2. Add the milk, egg, orange rind, flower water, and butter and mix to a soft dough, kneading until smooth.

3. Cover and leave in a warm place until doubled in volume. Roll out on a lightly floured surface to ½ inch in thickness and cut into eight 3-inch squares.

4. Heat the oil to 350 °F or until a cube of bread browns in 30 seconds. Fry the beignets in batches until golden brown. Remove with a slotted spoon and drain on paper towels.

5. Sprinkle with cinnamon sugar and serve hot with orange slices or segments.

APRICOT & ALMOND Tarte

Apricot and almond trees are botanical cousins and are found in the South of France. These trees have been cultivated in this region for a long time, and they provide the fruit for this aromatic, but not overly juicy tart. The kernels of apricots harvested in warm regions are often so sweet that they may be used instead of almonds.

1. Preheat the oven to 375 °F. To make the dough, put the flour, butter, and confectioners' sugar into a food processor and process to fine crumbs. Mix together the egg yolk and orange juice and stir into the flour mixture to make a soft dough.

2. Turn out the dough onto a lightly floured work surface and roll out to a circle large enough to line a 9-inch loose-bottom tart pan. Prick the bottom with a fork, cover with a sheet of wax paper, and fill with pie weights or dried beans. Bake in the preheated oven for 10 minutes. Remove from the oven and take out the paper and weights.

3. Put the butter, sugar, egg, almonds, flour, and almond extract into a food processor and process to a smooth paste.

4. Spread the almond filling over the bottom of the pastry shell and arrange the apricots, cut side up, on top.

5. Reduce the oven temperature to 350 °F and bake for 35–40 minutes, until the filling is set and golden brown.

6. Put the apricot preserves into a small saucepan with the water and heat gently until melted. Brush over the apricots and serve the tart.

SERVES 6–8

PREP TIME: 30 minutes

COOKING TIME: 45–50 minutes

INGREDIENTS

6 tablespoons unsalted butter, softened
⅓ cup granulated sugar
1 extra-large egg, beaten
1½ cups ground almonds
⅓ cup all-purpose flour
½ teaspoon almond extract
10–12 apricots, pitted and quartered
¼ cup apricot preserves
1 tablespoon water

pastry dough
1⅓ cups all-purpose flour,
plus extra for dusting
1 stick cold unsalted butter
2 tablespoons confectioners' sugar
1 egg yolk
2 tablespoons orange juicee

Brioche

INGREDIENTS

*2½ cups white bread flour,
plus extra for dusting*

2¼ teaspoons active dry yeast

1 tablespoon granulated sugar

½ teaspoon salt

2 eggs, beaten

*3 tablespoons milk mixed with
1 tablespoon lukewarm water*

*6 tablespoons butter, softened,
plus extra for greasing*

*1 egg yolk beaten with 1½ teaspoons milk,
for glazing*

Normandy in the North of France is probably the home of brioche, which was first mentioned in the fifteenth century. High-quality butter is important for this yeast dough, which is rich in egg and fat. Its ribbed neck and the round dough head on top first appeared in Paris in the nineteenth century.

1. Begin this recipe the day before you want to serve the brioche. Mix together 2¼ cups of the flour, the yeast, sugar, and salt in a large bowl and make a well in the center. Add the eggs and the milk mixture and mix, then gradually stir in the remaining flour until a sticky, flaky dough forms. Add the butter and knead it into the dough. Continue kneading until all the butter is incorporated.

2. Lightly dust a work surface with flour. Turn out the dough and knead for 5–10 minutes, or until all the flour is incorporated and the dough is smooth. Lightly grease a bowl with butter. Shape the dough into a ball and roll it around in the bowl. Cover with plastic wrap and set aside in a warm place until the dough doubles in volume, which can take up to several hours. Punch down the dough to knock out the air and reroll it into a ball. Cover the bowl with plastic wrap and chill for at least 4 hours, up to 20 hours. Generously grease a 1-quart brioche mold and set aside.

3. Lightly dust a work surface with flour. Turn out the dough and lightly knead it. Cut off a piece of dough about the size of an extra-large egg and set aside. Roll the remaining dough into a smooth ball and place it in the mold, pressing down lightly. Use floured fingers to make a wide hole in the center of the dough to the mold's bottom. Shape the remaining dough into a rounded teardrop and drop it, pointed end down, into the hole.

4. Lightly glaze the dough by brushing with the egg-yolk mixture, being careful not to let it drip between the dough and the mold. Cover with a clean dish towel and let rise until the dough is puffy and risen.

5. Meanwhile, preheat the oven to 400°F. Lightly glaze the brioche again. Use scissors dipped in water to make eight snips from the edge of the mold to the edge of the teardrop. Place the mold in the preheated oven and bake for 35–40 minutes, or until well risen, golden brown, and the brioche sounds hollow when tapped on the bottom. Transfer to a wire rack to cool. Serve warm or at room temperature.

1.

2.

3.

2.

3.

4.

MOUSSE-AU-CHOCOLAT
TARTLETS

MAKES 6

PREP TIME: 45 minutes,
plus 2½–3½ hours to chill

COOKING TIME: 45 minutes

INGREDIENTS

pastry dough
2 cups all-purpose flour, plus extra for dusting
pinch of salt
¼ cup granulated sugar
1¼ sticks butter
1 egg
finely grated rind of 1 lemon

filling
1⅔ cups single cream
12 ounces semisweet chocolate, at least 70 percent cocoa solids, broken into pieces
5 egg yolks
¼ cup granulated sugar
2½ tablespoons water
chocolate, to decorate

Chocolate mousse is the most popular dessert in France and is produced here in a tart version. Fine chocolate mousse is wonderfully creamy because plenty of air gets in when it is beaten. The flavor depends on the quality of the chocolate, so buy the best quality chocolate that you can.

1. Preheat the oven to 350 °F. To make the dough, put all the ingredients into a bowl and mix together. Roll the dough into into a ball, wrap in plastic wrap, and chill for 30 minutes in the refrigerator.

2. Roll out the dough on a lightly floured work surface and ease it into six 4-inch tart pans, line them with parchment paper, and fill with pie weights or dried beans. Bake in the preheated oven for 15 minutes, then remove the weights and paper and bake for an additional 10 minutes.

3. To make the filling, heat the cream in a heatproof bowl set over a saucepan of simmering water, then add the chocolate and heat until melted. Remove from the heat and let cool to room temperature. Put the egg yolks, sugar, and water into a separate heatproof bowl set over a saucepan of simmering water and heat, beating continuously, for 8–10 minutes, until the mixture thickens. Remove from the heat, stir into the chocolate mixture, and beat with an electric mixer for 5–6 minutes.

4. Pour the filling into the pastry shells. Carefully transfer to the refrigerator and chill for 2–3 hours, or until the filling is firm. Serve chilled, decorated with chocolate.

RASPBERRY
Charlotte

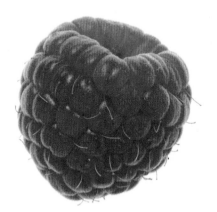

SERVES 8–10

PREP TIME: 40 minutes,
plus 4 hours to chill

COOKING TIME: 10 minutes

INGREDIENTS

*6½ cups fresh raspberries
(about 1¾ pounds),
plus extra to decorate*

9 sheets of gelatin

¾ cup granulated sugar

*3–4 tablespoons water,
plus extra for soaking*

grated rind of ½ unwaxed lemon

25–30 ladyfingers

1¾ cups heavy cream

confectioners' sugar, to decorate

whipped cream, to serve (optional)

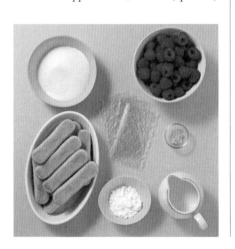

The colorful cake is rumored to be named after Princess Charlotte of England—the only daughter of King George IV—who died while giving birth in 1817 when she was only 21. At the time, the French chef Marie-Antoine Carême was working for the king. Originally, stale bread was used for the shell, but ladyfingers are a perfect replacement. Different fruit can be used for the filling.

1. Puree the raspberries in a food processor, then pass them through a strainer to remove the seeds. Soak the gelatin in a bowl of cold water. Heat the sugar in a small saucepan with the water, stirring until the sugar crystals have dissolved. Remove the sugar syrup from the stove, squeeze the excess water out of the soaked gelatin, add to the syrup, and stir to dissolve. Stir in the raspberry puree and lemon rind. Cover and chill in the refrigerator until the mixture begins to set.

2. Put a 10½-inch cake ring on a plate. Cover the plate completely with tightly packed ladyfingers. Completely line the ring with ladyfingers arranged vertically, leaving no gaps.

3. Whip the cream until it holds stiff peaks, then fold it into the raspberry mixture. Carefully fill the cake ring with the raspberry mixture, making sure that the ladyfingers do not slip out of place, then smooth the top. Let set slightly.

4. Carefully remove the cake ring. Decorate with raspberries and dust with confectioners' sugar. Serve chilled, with dollops of whipped cream, if desired.

1.

2.

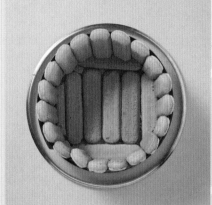

3.

3.

2.

3.

5.

CHOCOLATE
Petits Fours

MAKES 18

PREP TIME: 40 minutes,
plus 30 minutes to chill

COOKING TIME: 25 minutes

INGREDIENTS

4 eggs
¼ cup granulated sugar
⅔ cup all-purpose flour
⅓ cup unsweetened cocoa powder
2½ tablespoons cornstarch
⅔ cup cherry preserves
3 tablespoons kirsch

icing
½ cup heavy cream
⅔ cup confectioners' sugar
3 tablespoons butter
6 ounces semisweet chocolate, at least 70 percent cocoa solids, broken into pieces
18 sour cherries or maraschino cherries, to decorate

There are numerous varieties of petits fours. Literally, it means "small oven," as, at one time, after completing their daily production, bakers took advantage of the residual heat of the wood or coal ovens to bake this French confection. The petits fours are cut out of cake, filled with preserves, glazed with cream, and elaborately decorated.

1. Preheat the oven to 350 °F. Line a baking sheet with parchment paper. Put the eggs and sugar into a large bowl and beat with an electric mixer until light and fluffy. Mix together the flour, unsweetened cocoa powder, and cornstarch in a separate bowl, then fold into the egg mixture.

2. Spread the mixture evenly on the prepared baking sheet and bake in the preheated oven for 20 minutes. Remove from the oven, then lay a clean dish towel over the cake and quickly turn out. Remove the baking sheet and carefully peel off the parchment paper.

3. Heat the preserves in a small saucepan and stir in the kirsch. Cut the chocolate cake in half horizontally. On one half, spread the prepared preserves evenly over the entire surface. Stack the remaining half on top. Chill in the refrigerator for 30 minutes.

4. To make the icing, heat the cream in a saucepan with the confectioners' sugar. Stir in the butter, then add the chocolate, piece by piece. Remove from the heat and let cool until thick but still liquid.

5. Meanwhile, cut the chilled cake into 18 equal pieces and transfer to a wire rack set over a sheet of parchment paper. Pour the icing over the cakes, then place a sour cherry on each petit four and serve.

LEMON POPPY SEED

Madeleines

MAKES 36

PREP TIME: 20 minutes

COOKING TIME: 10 minutes

INGREDIENTS

oil, for oiling
3 eggs
1 egg yolk
finely grated rind of
1 lemon
¾ cup granulated sugar
1¼ cups all-purpose flour
1 teaspoon baking powder
1¼ sticks unsalted butter,
melted and cooled
1 tablespoon poppy seeds

The madeleine is a pastry that originated in around 1750 in the kitchens of the Polish aristocrat Stanislas Leszczynski. After his death, one of his pastry chefs settled in the town of Commercy in the Lorraine region and offered madeleines for sale. In the nineteenth century, several madeleine factories were built, but the cake has only been manufactured industrially since 1939.

1. Preheat the oven to 375 °F. Lightly grease three 12-cup madeleine pans.

2. Beat the eggs, yolk, lemon rind, and sugar in a large bowl until pale and thick.

3. Sift the flour and baking powder over the mixture and fold in lightly, using a metal spoon. Fold in the melted butter and poppy seeds.

4. Spoon the batter into the pans and bake in the preheated oven for about 10 minutes, until well risen.

5. Turn out the cakes and cool on a wire rack, then serve while the cakes are still fresh.

1.

2.

3.

4.

1.

3.

4.

Summer Fruit *Tartlets*

MAKES 12

PREP TIME: 30 minutes,
plus 30 minutes chilling time

COOKING TIME: 20 minutes

The combination of fresh fruit and cream in a slightly crumbly pastry shell is a wonderful summer dessert, and there are countless variations. French patisseries also offer the tarts with a lemon, strawberry, or chocolate filling.

1. Sift the flour and confectioners' sugar into a bowl. Stir in the almonds. Add the butter, rubbing in until the mixture resembles bread crumbs. Add the egg yolk and milk and work in until the dough binds together. Wrap in plastic wrap and chill for 30 minutes. Meanwhile, preheat the oven to 400 °F.

2. Roll out the dough on a lightly floured surface and use it to line 12 deep tart pans. Prick the bottoms with a fork and press a piece of aluminum foil into each.

3. Bake in the preheated oven for 10–15 minutes, or until light golden brown. Remove the foil and bake for an additional 2–3 minutes. Transfer to a wire rack to cool.

4. To make the filling, place the cream cheese and confectioners' sugar in a bowl and mix together. Place a spoonful of filling in each tart and arrange the berries on top.

5. Dust with sifted confectioners' sugar and serve.

INGREDIENTS

⅔ cups all-purpose flour, plus extra for dusting
⅔ cup confectioners' sugar, sifted
½ cup ground almonds
1 stick butter
1 egg yolk
1 tablespoon milk

filling
1 cup cream cheese
confectioners' sugar, to taste, plus extra, sifted, for dusting
3 cups fresh summer berries, such as hulled and quartered strawberries, raspberries, and blueberries

3.

5.

7.

Fraisier

SERVES 8

PREP TIME: 40 minutes,
plus 1 hour to chill

COOKING TIME: 40 minutes

INGREDIENTS

1 stick unsalted butter,
softened, plus extra for greasing

1¼ cups granulated sugar

1 teaspoon vanilla extract
or 1 vanilla bean, scraped

2 eggs

3 cups all-purpose flour

2 teaspoons baking powder

pinch of salt

¾ cup milk

12 ounces fresh strawberries, hulled

confectioners' sugar, for dusting

4 ounces marzipan

buttercream

2¼ sticks unsalted butter, softened

2 cups confectioners' sugar

1 teaspoon vanilla extract
or 1 vanilla bean, scraped

Fraisier is the French word for strawberry cake made from sponge and cream, which really showcases this fruit. The French naval officer and botanist Amédée-François Frézier first brought a strawberry plant with large berries to Europe in 1714. He had discovered it on the Chilean coast.

1. Preheat the oven to 350°F. Grease and line an 8 x 4-inch loaf pan. Put the butter, sugar, and vanilla extract into a bowl and beat with an electric mixer until light and fluffy. Add the eggs, one at a time, beating after each addition until combined.

2. Sift together the flour, baking powder, and salt into a separate bowl. Gradually beat in the butter mixture, alternating with the milk.

3. Pour the batter into the prepared pan and bake in the middle of the preheated oven for about 40 minutes, or until a toothpick inserted into the center of the cake comes out clean.

4. Turn the cake out of the pan onto a wire rack and let cool. Trim the top of the cake to make it flat, if necessary, then cut in two horizontally.

5. To make the buttercream, put the butter, sugar, and vanilla extract into a large bowl and beat with an electric mixer until creamy. Spread half the buttercream on top of one cake half and cover with the strawberries standing upright. Cover with the remaining buttercream, filling in any gaps. Place the other cake half on top, pressing down firmly but gently.

6. Dust a work surface with confectioners' sugar. Roll out the marzipan into a rectangle. Place on top of the cake, covering both the top and the sides.

7. Use a sharp knife to trim the edges of the marzipan. Chill in the refrigerator for at least 1 hour before serving.

Baguette

PAIN DE PARIS

When thinking about France, the mind immediately conjures up images: Paris and the Eiffel Tower, of course, with a glass of red wine and the obligatory cheese alongside it, most certainly. Perhaps one or two automobile relics are also making their way along the coils of the memory as we cast our minds back to the days when we still had dreams. Our first car, rusty and old, on its last legs during that first vacation together on the Côte. It was still fun though. French cuisine and wines are highly praised, and rightly so. French culture, literature, art, and architecture were turned into icons and placed on a pedestal long ago and now serve to reinforce all of the common clichés.

However, the humble baguette, one of the greatest of all French inventions, is not even worthy of a line in the Larousse Gastronomique, a classic work in the French gastronomic world. It doesn't even mention the baguette's history. Born as the illegitimate offshoot of a coarse, round bread, the baguette was invented in the mid-eighteenth century, when the Parisian nobility ignored the famine that was plaguing their own people, abandoning themselves to increasingly decadent culinary delights. The slender, delicate bread made from wheat was just right for the noble palate as it did not offend with its coarseness. It is difficult to tell exactly when the supposed descent of the baguette from luxury gourmet item to staple food for all began, but the likelihood is that myth and reality came together at the end of the nineteenth century. The global triumph of the baguette could no longer be stopped; be it on the harbor wall in the Vieux Port of La Rochelle or in New York's Times Square—the baguette has now found its place in global cuisine.

Goose liver from Gascony, truffles from Périgord, ham from Bayonne. Or even sea salt from the Atlantic, oysters from Normandy, escargots from Burgundy—the list of regional French culinary delights goes and on. But where does the baguette actually come from? Where exactly is the home of the greatest national culinary treasure? A simple bread that has accomplished the enormous feat of being considered both a blueprint for all fast foods and an indispensable accompaniment to cultured dining. A simple loaf of bread that has long since attained iconic status and is mentioned in the same breath as the Eiffel Tower and Concorde: where does it come from? While those icons embody

Every year in February, the World Champion-ship of Baguette Making is held in Paris. More than 250 bakers from all over the world try to win the crown of French baking. The baking result is always the same because the traditional baguette is 28 inches long and weighs 7 ounces.

technique and myth, the baguette is undoubtedly the minimalist among other French icons, which have long been confined to spending the autumn of their lives in museums or as tourist attractions.

The baguette, however, is still on everyone's lips. Baked using the minimum of ingredients, energy, and activity, it represents a return to basics and the bare essentials in the form of bread. By remaining both pure and original, the baguette has gained a sacrosanct status for itself. The baguette is wholesome, unadulterated, and simply a purist. Any attempt to find decorative elements in this icon will be in vain. The baguette is everywhere because it has made itself an indispensable part of everyday life. No one dares put a regional stamp on it; a baguette from Paris is as much of an original as its counterpart from Nice, Bordeaux, or Lyon. Even its foreign siblings have been standardized, probably because they carry the same label; be it in Polish (bagetka), Italian (baguette), German (baguette), or Portuguese (baguete), the language always adapts itself to the bread.

When the baguette first began its triumph in noble palaces around 300 years ago, its task was to protect the palates of connoisseurs and save them from coarse and sharp-edge crusts. Nowadays, for many, the baguette is the first taste of continental living for visitors to Europe. The baguette's popularity in so many countries has created a bread-making industry that produces a vast range of bakes in all shapes, sizes, grains, textures, and flavors. The current desire for locally produced fresh bread, free from artificial ingredients, has its roots in people's experience of buying daily baguettes from bakeries while in France.

Porteuse de pain

Baguettes

MAKES 4

PREP TIME: 20 minutes,
plus 1 hour to rise

COOKING TIME: 20–25 minutes

INGREDIENTS

*3⅔ cups white bread flour,
plus extra for dusting*

2 teaspoons sugar

2 teaspoons salt

*4½ ounce fresh yeast (available in
bakeries or online)*

1⅔ cups lukewarm water

The baguette is the classic white bread from France. Gluten-rich flour, yeast, and cool dough processing make for the typical rough, uneven pores. A high proportion of crust creates the strong flavor.

1. Mix together the flour, sugar, and salt in a bowl. Make a well in the center and crumble the yeast into it. Pour the water into the well and mix in the yeast and flour to make a smooth dough.

2. Divide the dough into four pieces, cover with plastic wrap, and let rise for 30 minutes.

3. Transfer the dough pieces to a work surface lightly dusted with flour, punch down to knock out the air, and shape each piece into a 2-inch-thick roll.

4. Place the uncooked baguettes on a dish towel dusted with flour. Make folds in the towel to separate each baguette from the next. It is important that the loaves are not too close together so that they have room to rise. Cover with plastic wrap and let rise in a warm place for about 30 minutes.

5. Preheat the oven to 475 °F and place a bowl of water in the bottom of the oven. Line a baking sheet with parchment paper. Put the baguettes on the prepared sheet and make five diagonal cuts in each, using a sharp knife.

6. Dust the baguettes with flour and bake in the middle of the preheated oven for 20–25 minutes, until golden brown.

1.

3.

4.

Quiche

LORRAINE

SERVES 4–6

PREP TIME: 30 minutes,
plus 30 minutes to chill

COOKING TIME: 45–50 minutes

INGREDIENTS

1 tablespoon butter
1 small onion, finely chopped
2 cups sliced button mushrooms
18 strips bacon, diced and cooked
2 eggs, beaten
1 cup light cream
½ cup shredded Gruyère or Swiss cheese
salt and pepper

pastry dough

1⅔ cups all-purpose flour,
plus extra for dusting
1 stick butter
2–3 tablespoons cold water

This classic quiche from Alsace Lorraine is also known as bacon tart. Around 1850, the recipe spread throughout the rest of France. This savory tart, baked in a tart pan, is eaten warm as an appetizer or as a main dish. Originally, it was made from bread dough, but today pastry dough is used. Onions, bacon, cheese, eggs, and cream should definitely be in the filling.

1. To make the dough, sift the flour into a bowl and rub in the butter with your fingertips until the mixture resembles fine bread crumbs. Stir in just enough water to bind to a soft dough.

2. Roll out the dough on a lightly floured work surface and use to line a 9-inch tart pan. Press into the edges, trim the excess. Chill in the refrigerator for 15 minutes.

3. Preheat the oven to 400 °F. Prick the bottom with a fork, cover with a piece of wax paper, and fill with pie weights or dried beans, then bake the pastry shell in the preheated oven for 10 minutes, until lightly browned. Remove from the oven and take out the paper and weights, then bake for an additional 10 minutes.

4. Melt the butter in a skillet, add the onion, and sauté for 2 minutes, then add the mushrooms and sauté, stirring, for an additional 3–5 minutes. Add the bacon, then spread the filling evenly in the pastry shell.

5. Put the eggs into a bowl with the cream and beat together, then season to taste with salt and pepper. Pour into the pastry shell and sprinkle with the cheese. Bake for 20–25 minutes, until golden brown and just set.

FOUGASSE
OLIVE BREAD

MAKES 2 LOAVES

PREP TIME: 20–25 minutes, plus rising

COOKING TIME: 25–30 minutes

INGREDIENTS

2½ cups white bread flour, plus extra for kneading

⅓ cup semolina flour, plus extra for dusting

2¼ teaspoons active dry yeast

1½ teaspoons sugar

2 teaspoons salt

1 cup lukewarm water

olive oil, for oiling and brushing

1 cup pitted ripe black olives, finely chopped

1½ tablespoons herbes de Provence (optional)

tapenade or olive oil, to serve (optional)

Fougasse is usually associated with Provence, but the bread also exists in different variations in other regions of the country. The classic version is shaped or slit like an ear of wheat and contains olives and herbs—typical ingredients from the French Mediterranean region.

1. Mix together the white bread flour, semolina flour, yeast, sugar, and salt in a bowl and make a well in the center. Gradually stir the water into the well, drawing in flour from the side until a soft, sticky dough forms. You might not need all the water, depending on the flour. Turn out the dough onto a lightly floured work surface and knead for 5–10 minutes, or until it becomes smooth. Shape the dough into a ball, place it in an oiled bowl, and roll it around so it is coated in oil. Cover the bowl with plastic wrap and set aside in a warm place until the dough has doubled in volume.

2. Preheat the oven to 450°F. Dust two baking sheets with semolina flour and set aside. Turn out the dough onto a lightly floured work surface. Add the olives and herbs, if using, and quickly knead until they are evenly distributed. Divide the dough into two equal portions.

3. Using an oiled rolling pin, roll one piece of dough into an oval 9–10 inches long. Dust a sharp knife with semolina flour and make a long vertical slit in the center of the dough, without cutting through the edges, then make three slits on each side in a herringbone pattern. Transfer the dough to a prepared baking sheet. Shape the remaining dough and place on the other baking sheet. Use oiled fingers to pull the slits apart, if necessary. Lightly brush the fougasses with oil, being careful to brush inside the slits. Place in the preheated oven, reduce the temperature to 400°F, and bake for 25–30 minutes, or until the loaves are golden brown and sound hollow when tapped on the bottom. Transfer to a wire rack to cool. Serve warm, with tapenade or olive oil.

Garlic & Herb
Bread Spirals

SERVES 6–8

PREP TIME: 30 minutes,
plus 2 hours to rise

COOKING TIME: 25 minutes

INGREDIENTS

*3⅔ cups white bread flour,
plus extra for dusting*
2¼ teaspoons active dry yeast
1½ teaspoons salt
1½ cups lukewarm water
2 tablespoons oil, plus extra for greasing
6 tablespoons butter, melted and cooled
3 garlic cloves, crushed
2 tablespoons chopped fresh parsley
2 tablespoons snipped fresh chives
beaten egg, for glazing
sea salt flakes, for sprinkling

Garlic has been used since ancient times as a seasoning, but also as a remedy. Egyptian slaves used it as a tonic and to remove lice. The plant came from the Asian steppes across the Mediterranean Sea to Europe and since then it has been an important part of Southern French cuisine.

1. Brush a large baking sheet with oil. Combine the flour, yeast, and salt in a mixing bowl. Stir in the water and half the oil, mixing to a soft, sticky dough.

2. Turn out the dough onto a lightly floured work surface and knead until smooth and no longer sticky. Return to the bowl, cover, and let stand in a warm place for about 1 hour, until doubled in size.

3. Meanwhile, preheat the oven to 475 °F. Mix together the butter, garlic, herbs, and remaining oil. Roll out the dough to a 13 x 9-inch rectangle and spread the herb mix evenly over the dough to within ½-inch of the edge.

4. Roll up the dough from one long side and place on the prepared baking sheet with the seam underneath. Cut into 12 thick slices and arrange, cut side down, on the baking sheet about ¾ inch apart.

5. Cover and let rise in a warm place until doubled in size and springy to the touch. Brush with the beaten egg and sprinkle with sea salt flakes. Bake in the preheated oven for 20–25 minutes, until golden brown and firm. Let cool on a wire rack.

Baking *in* the SUN

From Portugal, Spain, Italy, and Greece to Turkey—the countries of the Mediterranean have many things in common: a lot of sun and sea and a food culture that helps itself to nature's rich treasures. For this reason, fresh fruit, nuts, and olives find their way into the bakeries. Italy's baking culture, for example, can look back on a long tradition. More than 2,000 years ago, the focaccia we are familiar with today was already one of the favorite foods of the Etruscans living in central Italy. Even today, the Italian art of baking is a celebrated craft and is as creative as ever. Hardly anyone knows that the famous ciabatta was only invented around the end of the twentieth century by Arnaldo Cavallari. Ever since, there has been no stopping its triumphal march into the culinary world. Nowadays, it is difficult to imagine an Italian meal without ciabatta. On the other hand, in contrast to the somewhat neutral-tasting bread common to the Mediterranean region, there is a variety of extremely sweet pastries and desserts. Tuscan Christmas cake, lemon polenta cake, and succulent fig tarts are just a few examples of the creations made possible in Mediterranean households by the fruits of nature.

Many different countries and many different cultures—the baking tradition varies a lot between Portugal and Turkey. However, all countries share a focus on fresh fruit and vegetables.

Spanish
CUSTARD FLAN

SERVES 8

PREP TIME: 40 minutes,
plus 40 minutes to chill

COOKING TIME: 1 hour

INGREDIENTS

2 eggs
¼ cup superfine sugar
2 teaspoons vanilla extract
2 teaspoons cornstarch
1 cup milk
1 cup heavy cream
pinch of ground nutmeg
chopped blanched almonds and
fresh raspberries, to decorate

pastry dough
2¼ cups all-purpose flour,
plus extra for dusting
2 tablespoons superfine sugar
1 stick butter, diced,
plus extra for greasing
2–3 tablespoons water
1 egg yolk
1 tablespoon lemon juice

Different versions of pastry tarts with custard fillings have been known since the Middle Ages, especially in Western Europe. Spaniards love the combination of custard with fresh fruit—the flan in this recipe is enhanced for a special occasion with raspberries, cream, and almonds.

1. To make the pastry dough, sift the flour into a large bowl. Stir in the sugar and rub in the butter until the mixture resembles fine bread crumbs, then gradually add the water, egg yolk, and lemon juice. Mix to a pliable dough.

2. Turn out the dough onto a lightly floured work surface and gently knead. Form into a ball, wrap in plastic wrap, and chill in the refrigerator for 30 minutes.

3. Preheat the oven to 375 °F. Lightly grease a 9-inch round, loose-bottom fluted tart pan. Take the dough from the refrigerator a few minutes before using, then roll out on a lightly floured work surface. Ease the pastry into the prepared pan and trim the edges. Transfer to the refrigerator to chill for 10 minutes. Place a piece of parchment paper, large enough to cover the edges, onto the pastry, fill with pie weights or dried beans, and bake in the preheated oven for 10 minutes.

4. Remove the paper and weights and bake for an additional 5 minutes. Remove from the oven and reduce the oven temperature to 300 °F.

5. Meanwhile, put the eggs, sugar, and vanilla extract into a large bowl and mix together. In a separate bowl, blend the cornstarch with a little of the milk to form a smooth paste. Pour the remaining milk and half the cream into a small saucepan. Add the cornstarch mixture and stir until smooth and combined. Heat gently, stirring, until the milk is hot but not boiling. Gently whisk into the egg mixture until just combined.

6. Strain the mixture into the pastry shell and sprinkle with nutmeg. Carefully transfer to the oven and bake for 35–40 minutes, or until just set. Remove from the oven and let cool completely. Whip the remaining cream until it holds soft peaks, then spread it over the cooled filling. Decorate with chopped almonds and fresh raspberries and serve immediately.

3.

3.

5.

6.

1.

2.

3.

4.

Chocolate

PHYLLO PACKAGES

Phyllo pastry is a popular staple in eastern Mediterranean kitchens. It is similar to central European pastry, but the leaves are thinner and more translucent. They are made singly and used singly by extremely skilled confectioners. Luckily, you can purchase them at the grocery store already made (either chilled or frozen).

1. Preheat the oven to 375 °F. Grease a baking sheet. Mix the nuts, mint, and sour cream in a bowl. Add the apples, stir in the chocolate, and mix well.

2. Cut each pastry sheet into four squares. Brush one square with butter, then place a second square on top and brush with butter.

3. Place 1 tablespoonful of the chocolate mixture in the center, bring up the corners, and twist together. Repeat until all of the pastry and filling have been used.

4. Place the packages on the prepared baking sheet and bake in the preheated oven for about 10 minutes, until crisp and golden. Remove from the oven and let cool slightly.

5. Dust with confectioners' sugar and serve.

MAKES 18

PREP TIME: 15–20 minutes

COOKING TIME: 10 minutes

INGREDIENTS

1 cup ground hazelnuts

1 tablespoon finely chopped fresh mint

½ cup sour cream

2 Pippin apples, peeled and grated

2 ounces semisweet chocolate, melted

4–6 tablespoons butter, melted, plus extra for greasing

9 sheets phyllo pastry, about 6 inches square

confectioners' sugar, sifted, for dusting

2.

2.

3.

Lemon Polenta Cake

SERVES 8

PREP TIME: 20 minutes,
plus 20 minutes to cool

COOKING TIME: 30–35 minutes

In the seventeeth century, polenta, which is made from corn, was a "poor people's food" that was found from Spain to as far as southern Russia. The solid porridge, made from coarsely ground grain, is a regional culinary tradition, especially in Italy, and creates desserts with a wonderful coarse texture.

INGREDIENTS

1¾ sticks unsalted butter,
plus extra for greasing
1 cup superfine sugar
finely grated rind and juice
of 1 large lemon
3 eggs, beaten
1½ cups ground almonds
¾ cup instant polenta
1 teaspoon baking powder
crème fraîche or whipped cream, to serve

syrup
juice of 2 lemons
¼ cup superfine sugar
2 tablespoons water

1. Preheat the oven to 350°F. Grease a deep 8-inch round cake pan and line with parchment paper.

2. Beat together the butter and sugar until pale and fluffy. Beat in the lemon rind, lemon juice, eggs, and ground almonds. Sift in the polenta and baking powder and stir until evenly mixed. Spoon the batter into the prepared pan and smooth the surface. Bake in the preheated oven for 30–35 minutes, or until just firm to the touch and golden brown. Remove the cake from the oven and let cool in the pan for 20 minutes.

3. Meanwhile, to make the syrup, put the lemon juice, sugar, and water into a small saucepan. Heat gently, stirring until the sugar has dissolved, then bring to a boil and simmer for 3–4 minutes, or until slightly reduced and syrupy. Turn out the cake onto a wire rack, then brush half of the syrup evenly over the surface. Let cool completely.

4. Cut the cake into slices, drizzle the extra syrup over the top, and serve with crème fraîche or whipped cream.

CRANBERRY & PINE NUT

Biscotti

MAKES 18–20

PREP TIME: 15–20 minutes

COOKING TIME: 30–35 minutes

INGREDIENTS

butter or oil, for greasing
⅓ cup firmly packed light brown sugar
1 extra-large egg
1¼ cups all-purpose flour, plus extra for dusting
½ teaspoon baking powder
1 teaspoon ground allspice
⅓ cup dried cranberries
⅓ cup pine nuts, toasted

Biscotti are twice-baked cookies of Italian origin, and this recipe is a classic version with cranberries and pine nuts. The name goes back to the medieval word biscoctus, meaning "twice cooked." The Roman scholar Pliny the Elder is said to have boasted they would be edible for centuries. Nonperishable food was especially useful on long journeys.

1. Preheat the oven to 350 °F. Grease a baking sheet and line it with parchment paper.

2. Beat together the sugar and egg in a large bowl until pale and thick enough to form a trail when the beaters are lifted.

3. Sift together the flour, baking powder, and allspice into the bowl and fold into the mixture.

4. Stir in the cranberries and pine nuts and mix lightly to a smooth dough.

5. With lightly floured hands, shape the dough into a long rope, about 11 inches long. Press to flatten slightly.

6. Lift the dough onto the baking sheet and bake in the preheated oven for 20–25 minutes, until golden. (Do not turn off the oven.)

7. Let cool for 3–4 minutes, then cut into ½-inch-thick slices and arrange on the baking sheet.

8. Bake in the oven for 10 minutes, or until golden. Remove from the oven, transfer to a wire rack, and let cool completely.

2.

5.

6.

7.

1.

2.

3.

Mascarpone *Cheesecake*

SERVES 10

PREP TIME: 45 minutes,
plus 3 hours to cool and chill

COOKING TIME:
1 hour–1 hour 10 minutes

INGREDIENTS

crust
6 ounces amaretti cookies
½ cup granulated sugar
3 tablespoons butter
3 tablespoons honey

1¼ cups mascarpone cheese, at room temperature
2½ cups cream cheese, at room temperature
1¼ cups granulated sugar
5 eggs
1 egg yolk
½ cup heavy cream
1 teaspoon vanilla extract or 1 vanilla bean, scraped
finely grated zest of 1 orange

People have been making cheesecakes with curd cheese or sour cream since the time of the ancient Romans. Many different versions have long been found across Europe. In this version, Italian cookies and honey dominate and the filling contains a hefty portion of mascarpone. This mild, Italian soft cheese, made with cream, makes the cake creamier and produces a more intense flavor.

1. Preheat the oven to 325 °F. To make the crust, put the cookies into a food processor with the sugar and pulse until reduced to fine crumbs. Add the butter and honey and process until incorporated. Press the mixture into the bottom of a 10-inch springform cake pan.

2. Put the mascarpone cheese, cream cheese, and sugar into a large bowl and mix to combine. Add the eggs and egg yolk and beat until incorporated. Add the cream, vanilla extract, and orange zest and stir until the mixture is well combined.

3. Pour the batter into the prepared pan and bake in the preheated oven for 1 hour–1 hour 10 minutes, until set but still soft in the middle. Turn off the oven but do not remove the cheesecake. After 1 hour, remove the cheesecake from the oven and transfer to a wire rack to cool completely. Unclip and remove the springform from the pan, leaving the cheesecake on the bottom of the pan, then transfer to the refrigerator to chill for at least 2 hours. Serve chilled.

Torta Caprese

CHOCOLATE CAKE

SERVES 12

PREP TIME: 20 minutes,
plus 20 minutes to soak

COOKING TIME: 40 minutes

INGREDIENTS

⅔ cup raisins

*finely grated rind and juice
of 1 orange*

*1½ sticks butter, diced,
plus extra for greasing*

*4 ounces bittersweet chocolate,
broken into pieces*

4 extra-large eggs, beaten

½ cup superfine sugar

1 teaspoon vanilla extract

⅓ cup all-purpose flour

½ cup ground almonds

½ teaspoon baking powder

pinch of salt

*⅓ cup blanched almonds,
lightly toasted and chopped*

confectioners' sugar, sifted, to decorate

For more than 3,000 years, the inhabitants of what is present-day Mexico have been making use of the cacao tree. In 1528, the Spanish conquistadors brought the fruit to Europe. However, they did not like the taste of unsweetened chocolate. It became popular in Europe only after honey and cane sugar were added. Fine chocolate is the basis for this rich cake, which needs to be topped with only a little confectioners' sugar.

1. Preheat the oven to 350 °F. Line a deep, loose-bottom, 10-inch round cake pan with wax paper. Grease the paper.

2. Put the raisins into a small bowl, add the orange juice, and let soak for 20 minutes.

3. Melt the butter and chocolate together in a small saucepan over medium heat, stirring. Remove from the heat and set aside to cool.

4. Put the eggs, sugar, and vanilla extract into a large bowl and beat with an electric mixer until light and fluffy. Stir in the cooled chocolate mixture.

5. Drain the raisins if they have not absorbed all the orange juice. Sift together the flour, ground almonds, baking powder, and salt into the egg-and-sugar mixture. Add the raisins, orange rind, and blanched almonds, then fold all the ingredients together.

6. Spoon into the prepared pan and smooth the surface. Bake in the preheated oven for 40 minutes, or until a toothpick inserted into the center comes out clean and the cake starts to come away from the side of the pan. Let cool in the pan for 10 minutes, then remove from the pan, transfer to a wire rack, and let cool completely. Dust the surface with confectioners' sugar before serving.

2.

4.

5.

LA COMIDA
de Picasso

Lunchtime. But it's not just an ordinary lunch. None other than Pablo Picasso is sitting in front of an empty plate with a glass before him, staring out at what appears to be nothing.

Every moment in his life, Pablo Picasso enjoyed being an artist—even at lunchtime. The bread loaves are a symbol of his extraordinary abilities.

The mood in the photograph is curiously ordinary; it is only when we take a second glance at the picture, photographed by Robert Doisneau in 1952, that it reveals its true message: Small loaves of bread caricature the genius painter's most important tools as a pair of oversized hands. Fingers as large as the paws of a monster taking a break. They also allude to a French pun, which—at least in the French language—puts the loaves and Picasso's hands on the same level. The loaves (pains) and the hands (mains) are a symbol for superhuman gifts or abilities. In fact, Picasso is obviously enjoying time out from his demanding work as an artist on the Côte d'Azur. What appears to be a humorous finger exercise for both artists, has in more than 60 years become one of the best-selling photo motifs in the entire world. In France and Spain alone—Picasso's two principal places of residence—several million posters have been made from this photo. It may seem that artists chose to depict bread for purely aesthetic reasons, but this kind of bread played a crucial role in the Mediterranean region. The typical long bread, as seen in the photograph, has a long tradition probably going back to the fifteenth century. It was the custom in Spain, as well as in France, to roll the bread out into a long loaf on a work surface sprinkled with ground anise seed. These Mediterranean breads can be traced back to the Late Latin word focacia ("baked dough"), a derivation of the word focus ("hearth/stove," "pan"). The Italian flatbread focaccia, the French fouace (or fouasse or fougasse) and the Spanish hogaza have the same etymological origin.

2.

3.

5

6.

6.

Panforte

CHRISTMAS CAKE

This popular spiced Christmas cake from the Tuscan city of Siena is called panforte and is similar to medieval recipes, such as gingerbread. It developed from a kind of a fruitcake that was a nutritious and non-perishable food in winter. The recipe was later refined using the spices that were traded in Siena and other places.

1. Preheat the oven to 350°F. Line an 8-inch loose-bottom, round cake pan with parchment paper.

2. Spread out the hazelnuts on a baking sheet and toast in the preheated oven for 10 minutes, until golden brown. Transfer to a dish towel and rub off the skins.

3. Meanwhile, spread out the almonds on a baking sheet and toast in the oven for 10 minutes, until golden. Watch them carefully, because they can burn easily.

4. Reduce the oven temperature to 300°F. Chop all the nuts and put into a large bowl. Add the candied peel, apricots, pineapple, and orange rind to the nuts and mix well.

5. Sift together the flour, cocoa, cinnamon, coriander, nutmeg, and cloves into the bowl and mix well.

6. Put the granulated sugar and honey into a saucepan set over low heat and cook, stirring continuously, until the sugar has dissolved. Bring to a boil and cook for an additional 5 minutes, until thickened and beginning to darken. Stir the nut mixture into the saucepan and remove from the heat.

7. Spoon the batter into the prepared cake pan and smooth the surface. Bake in the oven for 1 hour, then remove from the oven and let cool in the pan completely. Carefully turn out of the pan and peel off the parchment paper. Place on a cake plate, dust with confectioners' sugar, and cut into slices to serve.

SERVES 14

PREP TIME: 30 minutes

COOKING TIME: 1½ hours

INGREDIENTS

¾ cup hazelnuts
¾ cup almonds
½ cup chopped candied peel
⅓ cup finely chopped dried apricots
⅓ cup finely chopped candied pineapple
grated rind of 1 orange
⅓ cup all-purpose flour
2 tablespoons unsweetened cocoa powder
1 teaspoon ground cinnamon
¼ teaspoon ground coriander
¼ teaspoon freshly grated nutmeg
¼ teaspoon ground cloves
½ cup granulated sugar
¾ cup honey
confectioners' sugar, for dusting

Cantucci

BISCOTTI

MAKES 25–30

PREP TIME: 20 minutes

COOKING TIME: 20 minutes

INGREDIENTS

butter, for greasing
4 cups all-purpose flour,
plus extra for dusting
1 tablespoon baking powder
2½ cups superfine sugar
pinch of salt
3 eggs
2 egg yolks
2 cups roasted almonds

Cantucci are almond cookies from Tuscany that are twice baked. First they are baked in loaf shapes and then baked as cut slices. This makes them crumbly and they last a long time. The somewhat firm cantucci are enjoyed dunked in a coffee or a dessert wine.

1. Preheat the oven to 325°F. Grease a baking sheet and dust it with flour. Sift together the flour, baking powder, sugar, and salt into a large bowl and make a well in the center. Break two eggs into the well, add the egg yolks, and gently fold into the flour mixture. Add the almonds and mix to combine.

2. Divide the dough into two or three pieces and shape each piece into a 2-inch-high loaf shape. Place on the prepared baking sheet. Beat the remaining egg and brush it over the tops of the loaves, then bake in the preheated oven for 15 minutes.

3. Remove the baked loaves from the oven (do not turn off the oven) and let stand until cool to the touch. Using a knife, cut each loaf into ¾-inch slices. Place on the baking sheet, cut side down, and bake for 5 minutes, or until golden brown. Remove from the oven and let cool. Serve with coffee or dessert wine.

1.

2.

3.

2.

3.

3.

Siphnopitta

CHEESECAKE

Siphnopitta is the Greek version of cheesecake made with honey and slightly stronger tasting cheese. Traditionally, soft, unsalted sheep or goat cheese is used, but you can use Italian ricotta instead. The recipe is from the Cycladic island of Sifnos and is traditionally baked at Easter.

1. Preheat the oven to 350 °F. Lightly grease a 12 x 8-inch rectangular fluted tart pan. Sift together the flour and salt into a large bowl. Beat the butter into the flour mixture, then gradually add the water until the mixture comes together. Shape into a ball, wrap in plastic wrap, and chill in the refrigerator for about 30 minutes.

2. Roll out the pastry on a lightly floured work surface, then ease it into the prepared pan, trimming the edges. Bake in the preheated oven for 10 minutes, then remove from the oven and let cool in the pan. Increase the oven temperature to 375 °F.

3. Put the eggs, ricotta cheese, cinnamon, and honey into a medium bowl and mix to combine. Carefully pour the cheese mixture into the cooled pastry shell and bake for about 30–35 minutes, until firm and golden brown. Dust with cinnamon and let cool. Decorate with the orange slices, orange and lemon rind, and mint sprigs and serve.

SERVES 6–8

PREP TIME: 25 minutes, plus 30 minutes to chill

COOKING TIME: 40–45 minutes

INGREDIENTS

2⅓ cups all-purpose flour, plus extra for dusting

½ teaspoon salt

2 sticks butter, softened, plus extra for greasing

3–4 tablespoons water

4 eggs

2 cups ricotta cheese

1 teaspoon ground cinnamon, plus extra for dusting

⅓ cup honey, or to taste

to decorate
orange slices

chopped fresh orange and lemon rind

fresh mint sprigs

Fig TARTS

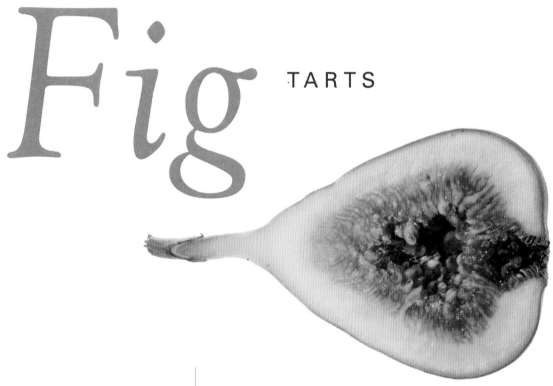

SERVES 4

PREP TIME: 10–15 minutes

COOKING TIME: 15–20 minutes

INGREDIENTS

1 block store-bought puff pastry
all-purpose flour, for dusting
8 fresh ripe figs
1 tablespoon granulated sugar
½ teaspoon ground cinnamon
milk, for brushing
vanilla ice cream, to serve

The fig, which has been cultivated throughout the Mediterranean since ancient times, is one of the oldest domesticated crops. Most figs are traditionally sold dried. Pastries with fresh figs, however, have a real taste of summer. When buying figs, check that they have the right consistency; ripe fruit is soft but not mushy.

1. Preheat the oven to 375 °F. Line a baking sheet with parchment paper. Roll out the pastry on a lightly floured board to a thickness of ¼ inch.

2. Using a saucer as a guide, cut out four 6-inch circles and place on the prepared baking sheet.

3. Use a sharp knife to score a line around each circle, about ½ inch from the edge. Prick the center of each circle all over with a fork.

4. Slice the figs into quarters and arrange eight quarters over the center of each pastry circle.

5. Mix together the sugar and cinnamon and sprinkle it over the figs.

6. Brush the edges of the pastry with milk and bake in the preheated oven for 15–20 minutes, until risen and golden brown. Serve the tarts warm with ice cream.

1.

2.

3.

4.

5.

Honeyed

BAKLAVA PASTRIES

MAKES 30

PREP TIME: 45 minutes

COOKING TIME: 45 minutes

INGREDIENTS

3½ cups finely chopped mixed nuts, such as walnuts, almonds, pistachio nuts
1 pound store-bought phyllo pastry
1½ sticks butter, melted, plus extra for greasing
2 tablespoons granulated sugar
1 teaspoon ground cinnamon

syrup

1⅔ cups granulated sugar
1¼ cups water
1 tablespoon lemon juice
3 tablespoons honey
2 small cinnamon sticks

Baklava is popular in Balkan and Middle Eastern cuisine: a rich, sweet pastry made from phyllo pastry and filled with nuts and sweetened with syrup or honey. This is the recipe for the Turkish version with honey and walnuts. It is popularly served on feast days.

1. Preheat the oven to 350 °F. Grease or line a baking sheet with parchment paper. Spread the nuts in a single layer on the prepared sheet and bake in the preheated oven for 5–10 minutes. Do not turn off the oven.

2. Meanwhile, place one layer of phyllo pastry in a 10 x 14-inch baking pan. (Cover the unused sheets with a damp dish towel to prevent them from drying out.) Brush the pastry with melted butter. Continue layering the pastry and brushing with butter until there are five to seven layers of pastry in the pan.

3. Mix the nuts with the sugar and cinnamon. Sprinkle one-third of the nut mixture over the pastry in the pan, then cover with two or three buttered layers of pastry. Sprinkle half of the remaining nut mixture over the pastry and cover with two to three layers of buttered pastry. Sprinkle the remaining nut mixture over the pastry, cover with five to seven layers of buttered pastry, and fold in all the ovehanging edges. Using a sharp knife, cut the baklava into diamond shapes, cutting right through all the layers, then bake in the preheated oven for 25–30 minutes, until golden brown.

4. Meanwhile, prepare the syrup. Put the sugar and water into a saucepan and heat over low heat until the sugar has dissolved. Bring to a boil, then add the lemon juice, honey, and cinnamon sticks. Reduce the heat and simmer for 10 minutes, then remove from the heat and let cool. Remove the baklava from the oven and immediately pour the syrup over it. Let stand until the pastry has completely absorbed the syrup. The flavor of the baklava will mature after one or two days.

1.

3.

3.

3.

4.

4.

DATE, PISTACHIO & HONEY SLICES

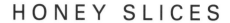

Because of their high sugar content, long shelf life, and the fact that they provide a lot of energy for their size, the fleshy fruit of the date palm is still the ideal food for long journeys. In fact, in the Arab world the date has for centuries been packed as a provision for traveling through the desert. Together with the pithy pistachio and honey, they are also an extremely tasty, nutritious snack.

1. Put the dates, lemon juice, and water into a saucepan and bring to a boil, stirring. Remove from the heat. Stir in the nuts and 1 tablespoon of the honey. Cover and let cool.

2. Preheat the oven to 400°F. To make the pastry, put the flour, sugar, and butter into a food processor and process to fine crumbs. Mix in just enough cold water to bind to a soft, not sticky, dough.

3. Divide the pastry into two pieces, then roll out each piece on a lightly floured work surface to a 12 x 8-inch rectangle. Place one piece on a baking sheet. Spread the date-and-nut mixture to within ½ inch of the edge. Top with the other rectangle of pastry.

4. Firmly press the edges together to seal, then trim the excess and score the top of the pastry to mark out 12 slices. Glaze with the milk. Bake in the preheated oven for 20–25 minutes, or until golden. Brush with the remaining honey and turn out onto a wire rack to cool. Cut into 12 slices and serve.

MAKES 12

PREP TIME: 30 minutes

COOKING TIME: 20–25 minutes

INGREDIENTS

1¾ cups pitted and chopped dried dates
2 tablespoons lemon juice
2 tablespoons water
⅔ cup chopped pistachio nuts
2 tablespoons honey
milk, for glazing

pastry
1¾ cups all-purpose flour, plus extra for dusting
2 tablespoons superfine sugar
1¼ sticks butter
4–5 tablespoons cold water

Ciabatta

BREAD

MAKES 2 LOAVES

PREP TIME: 25 minutes,
plus 2 hours to rest and rise

COOKING TIME: 35 minutes

INGREDIENTS

butter, for greasing
¾ cup lukewarm water
1½ teaspoons active dry yeast
4⅔ cups all-purpose flour
2½ tablespoons olive oil
¾ teaspoon salt

Crispy on the outside, delightfully airy inside, and with a slight taste of olive oil: that's ciabatta. Letting the dough stand for a long time gives the bread its characteristic flavor and the gentle kneading gives the bread its large holes. The Italian bread is now a classic, but it's a recent classic. It was made for the first time only in 1982 by Arnaldo Cavallari in Rovigo in the Veneto region.

1. Grease a baking sheet. Pour the water into a large bowl, add the yeast, and stir to dissolve. Add 1 cup of flour and mix thoroughly. Cover and let rest 30 minutes. Sift the remaining flour into a separate large bowl and make a well in the center. Pour the yeast mixture into the flour, then add the oil.

2. Mix together well, pulling in the flour from the side of the bowl to the center, then knead for about 2 minutes, until a spongy dough forms. Cover with a damp dish towel and let rise for about 1 hour, or until doubled in size.

3. Add the salt and knead for 7–8 minutes, until a smooth dough forms.

4. Divide the dough into two pieces, shape each piece into a loaf, and place on the prepared sheet. Let rise for 30 minutes at room temperature.

5. Meanwhile, preheat the oven to 450°F. Bake the loaves in the preheated oven for 35 minutes, until they are golden brown and sound hollow when tapped on the bottom. Transfer to a wire rack to cool.

1.

3.

4.

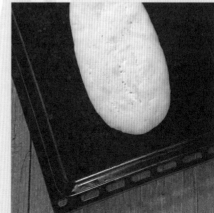

1.

2.

3.

CHERRY TOMATO

Focaccia Bread

Focaccia, baked with yeast dough, is a speciality of Liguria in northern Italy, and its origins date back to the Etruscan era. It can be baked with a little olive oil, herbs, and other ingredients. This flatbread is a forerunner of the pizza and is not eaten as a side dish but as a snack.

1. Mix together 2 tablespoons of the oil and all the garlic. Set aside. Mix together the flour, yeast, table salt, and sugar in a large bowl. Add the remaining oil and the water. Mix to a dough. Turn out onto a lightly floured work surface and knead for 10 minutes, until smooth and elastic, then knead in 1 tablespoon of the garlic-flavored oil.

2. Oil a 6½ x10-inch baking pan at least 1½ inches deep. Press the dough into the bottom of the pan with your hands. Brush with the remaining garlic-flavored oil, then sprinkle with the rosemary. Cover loosely with plastic wrap and set aside in a warm place for about 1 hour, until puffed up and doubled in size.

3. Preheat the oven to 450°F. Sprinkle the tomatoes over the focaccia, squeezing in as many as you can, and press them into the dough. Sprinkle with the sea salt. Put in the preheated oven, then immediately turn down the oven temperature to 400°F. Bake for 25–30 minutes, until golden brown and the bread sounds hollow when tapped on the bottom. Turn out onto a wire rack to cool. Serve warm or cold.

MAKES 1 LOAF

PREP TIME: 20 minutes, plus 1 hour to rise

COOKING TIME: 25–30 minutes

INGREDIENTS

⅓ cup olive oil, plus extra for oiling

2 garlic cloves, crushed

2⅔ cups white bread flour, plus extra for dusting

2¼ teaspoons active dry yeast

2 teaspoons table salt

1 teaspoon granulated sugar

1 cup lukewarm water

2 teaspoons finely chopped fresh rosemary

12–14 ripe red cherry tomatoes

¼ teaspoon sea salt flakes

Feta & Olive Biscuits

MAKES 8

PREP TIME: 12–15 minutes

COOKING TIME: 12–15 minutes

INGREDIENTS

3¼ cups all-purpose flour

1 tablespoon baking powder

¼ teaspoon salt

6 tablespoons butter,
plus extra for greasing

⅓ cup chopped pitted ripe black olives

¼ cup drained and chopped
sun-dried tomatoes in oil

½ cup crumbled feta cheese

¾–1 cup milk, plus extra for glazing

pepper, to taste

Olives have been eaten in Greece for thousands of years and the Greek sheep cheese feta has been around since the days of the Byzantine empire. These biscuits just need a pat of butter and then this savory treat is ready to enjoy.

1. Preheat the oven to 425 °F. Grease a baking sheet.

2. Sift together the flour, baking powder, salt, and pepper into a bowl and rub in the butter evenly with your fingers.

3. Stir in the olives, tomatoes, and cheese, then stir in just enough milk to make a soft, smooth dough.

4. Roll out on a floured surface to a 1¼-inch-thick rectangle. Cut into 2½-inch squares. Place on the baking sheet, brush with milk, and bake in the preheated oven for 12–15 minutes, until golden.

5. Serve the biscuits fresh and warm, with extra butter, if needed.

2.

3.

4.

Pita Bread

SERVES 12

PREP TIME: 30 minutes,
plus 2 hours 10 minutes to rise

COOKING TIME: 10 minutes

INGREDIENTS

1½ teaspoons active dry yeast

1¼ cups lukewarm water

*3⅔ cups all-purpose flour,
plus extra for dusting*

1 teaspoon salt

*1 tablespoon vegetable oil,
plus extra for oiling*

1½ teaspoons sugar

Soft pita flatbread is widespread in the eastern Mediterranean and the Middle East. Freshly baked several times a day, it is served as an accompaniment to many meals. It is a simple, lightly salted dough with a little fat and is traditionally baked directly on the bottom of a stone oven, without a baking sheet.

1. Put the yeast into a large bowl with the water and stir until dissolved. Add the remaining ingredients, mix to combine, then knead until a firm dough forms. Cover with a damp dish towel and let rise for at least 2 hours, until doubled in size.

2. Turn out the dough onto a lightly floured work surface, punch down to knock out the air, then use your hands to roll the dough into a ¾-inch-thick roll. Cut the roll into ½-inch slices. You should have six to eight slices. Roll the slices into balls, cover with a damp dish towel, and let rise for an additional 10 minutes.

3. Preheat the oven to 475°F. Line a baking sheet with parchment paper, then oil the paper and dust it with flour. Roll out the balls on a lightly floured work surface into 6–8-inch circles.

4. Place the circles on the prepared baking sheet and bake in the preheated oven for about 10 minutes, until puffed. Remove from the oven and cover with a damp dish towel to keep the bread soft. The pita breads can be stored in the refrigerator for a few days.

1.

2.

3.

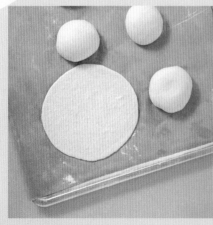

Feta & Spinach Packages

In the Balkans, savory pastry packages are popular, especially stuffed with feta cheese and spinach. In Turkey, they are called borek. It is everyday or festive food, depending on the filling. They taste particularly delicious fresh from the oven. But even when a day old, they are spicier and perfect for a party or a picnic.

1. Preheat the oven to 400 °F. Oil a baking sheet.

2. Heat the oil in a large skillet or wok, add the scallions, and sauté, stirring, for 1–2 minutes. Add the spinach and stir until the leaves are wilted. Cook, stirring occasionally, for 2–3 minutes. Drain off any liquid and let cool slightly.

3. Stir the egg, cheese, and nutmeg into the spinach and season well with salt and pepper.

4. Brush three sheets of pastry with butter. Place another three sheets on top and brush with butter. Cut each sheet down the middle to make six long strips in total. Place 1 tablespoon of the spinach filling on the end of each strip.

5. Lift one corner of phyllo pastry over the filling to the opposite side, then turn over the opposite way to enclose. Continue to fold over along the length of the pastry strip to make a triangular package, finishing with the seam underneath.

6. Place the packages on the prepared baking sheet, brush with butter, and sprinkle with the sesame seeds. Bake in the preheated oven for 12–15 minutes, or until golden brown and crisp. Serve hot.

MAKES 6

PREP TIME: 25 minutes

COOKING TIME: 15–20 minutes

INGREDIENTS

*2 tablespoons olive oil,
plus extra for greasing*
1 bunch scallions, chopped
1 pound spinach leaves, coarsely chopped
1 egg, beaten
¾ cup crumbled feta cheese
½ teaspoon freshly grated nutmeg
6 sheets store-bought phyllo pastry
4 tablespoons butter, melted
1 tablespoon sesame seeds
salt and pepper, to taste

The Home of Traditional BAKING

When it comes to bread, the German-speaking countries are leaders of the pack. Nowhere else will you find so many types of bread. Last year, the German Bakers' Confederation recorded almost 3,000 bread specialities, including some with such whimsical names as "Alpine Loaf", "Cereal King," or "Monk". Bread and its quality are important to the Germans. There are two daily meals in which bread plays an essential role. For breakfast, Germans usually have a soft roll with preserves, and in the evening the family gathers at the table and eats slices of bread topped with sausage or cheese, cucumber or tomato, according to each person's taste. For Germans, bread is the epitome of home, so it is not uncommon to find German emigrants yearning for typical German bread. However, that is not all: A cup of coffee in the afternoon with a delicious piece of cake is part of most German people's daily routine. Here, too, they have a huge range to choose from, including fruitcakes, cream cakes, and pound cakes.

Different regions around Germany have developed completely different bread traditions. The farther you travel to the south of Germany, the more you have big cakes and breads. There are also specialities such as pretzels, a must in Munich's Oktoberfest.

Lebkuchen
COOKIES

MAKES 30

PREP TIME: 30 minutes

COOKING TIME: 15–20 minutes

INGREDIENTS

3 eggs
1 cup granulated sugar
⅓ cup all-purpose flour
2 teaspoons unsweetened cocoa powder
1 teaspoon ground cinnamon
½ teaspoon ground cardamom
¼ teaspoon ground cloves
¼ teaspoon ground nutmeg
1¾ cups ground almonds (almond meal)
¼ cup candied peel, finely chopped

to decorate

4 ounces semisweet chocolate,
broken into pieces
4 ounces white chocolate,
broken into pieces
sugar crystals

The German lebkuchen has evolved over a long period of time from honey cake and various spices. Since the fourteenth century, it has established itself as a traditional Christmas confectionery. It is baked without the use of yeast; its essential ingredients are Asian spices. These had to be imported at a great expense and, therefore, it is mainly merchant towns that can claim a long tradition of lebkuchen baking.

1. Preheat the oven to 350°F. Line several large baking sheets with parchment paper. Place the eggs and sugar in a heatproof bowl set over a saucepan of gently simmering water and beat until thick and foamy. Remove the bowl from the pan and continue to beat for 2 minutes.

2. Sift the flour, cocoa, cinnamon, cardamom, cloves, and nutmeg into the bowl and stir in with the ground almonds and candied peel. Drop heaping teaspoonfuls of the mixture onto the prepared baking sheets, spreading them gently into smooth mounds.

3. Bake in the preheated oven for 15–20 minutes, or until light brown and slightly soft to the touch. Let cool on the baking sheets for 10 minutes, then transfer the cookies to wire racks to cool completely.

4. Place the semisweet and white chocolate in two separate heatproof bowls, set the bowls over two saucepans of gently simmering water, and heat until melted. Dip half the cookies in the melted semisweet chocolate and half in the white chocolate. Sprinkle with sugar crystals and let set.

1.

5.

5.

Plum Cake

SERVES 9

PREP TIME: 40 minutes,
plus 50 minutes to rise

COOKING TIME: 30 minutes

INGREDIENTS

1⅔ cups all-purpose flour

2 tablespoons granulated sugar

1 egg, beaten

½ cup milk

2 tablespoons butter, plus extra for greasing

¼ ounce fresh yeast (available in bakeries or online)

9 plums (about 1¼ pounds), halved and pitted

¼ cup cinnamon sugar (available online)

½ cup chopped hazelnuts (optional), for sprinkling

whipped cream or ice cream, to serve (optional)

Baked with the use of yeast, the plum cake is a light and sweet treat that has an unmistakably fresh taste. It is a Central European confectionery, typical of the late-summer season, when blue-rock plums, a plum sub-species, are ripe and juicy. Some bakeries grace their plum cakes with a crumb topping, which is made out of puff dough.

1. Sift the flour into a bowl, then add the sugar. Make a well in the center, add the egg, and mix to combine, pulling in the flour mixture from the side of the bowl.

2. Put the milk and butter into a small saucepan and heat over low heat until the butter is melted. Remove from the heat and let cool to lukewarm. Crumble the yeast into the mixture, stir to dissolve, and let stand for 5 minutes. Pour the yeast mixture into the flour mixture and knead well.

3. Cover the bowl and let rise for at least 30 minutes, until the dough has doubled in size.

4. Preheat the oven to 350 °F and grease a deep baking pan. Make one or two cuts in each plum half.

5. Rub a little butter on your hands, then punch down the dough to knock out the air and press it into the prepared pan. Firmly press the plum halves, cut side up, into the dough. Sprinkle with the cinnamon sugar and let stand for 15 minutes. Sprinkle the chopped hazelnuts over the plums, if using.

6. Bake in the preheated oven for about 30 minutes, then remove from the oven and let cool slightly. Serve lukewarm with whipped cream or ice cream, if desired.

STOLLEN

SERVES 8

PREP TIME: 1 hour, plus time to soak, rise and rest

COOKING TIME: 1 hour

INGREDIENTS

⅓ cup blanched almonds, coarsely chopped

2 cups raisins

½ cup candied peel

¼ cup dark rum

3 cups white bread flour, plus extra for dusting

1 cup lukewarm milk

1½ ounces fresh yeast (available in bakeries or online), crumbled

3 tablespoons honey

3½ sticks softened butter, diced, plus 1 stick butter, melted

1 teaspoon salt

4 ounces marzipan, grated

2 teaspoons vanilla extract

grated zest of 1 lemon

1¼ cups confectioners' sugar, plus extra for dusting

The shape of the stollen, which is made for Christmas, is a reminder of the Baby Jesus swaddling band. Known traditionally as Christmas bread, stollen was previously eaten for Lent and prepared with canola oil. In 1430, the German nobility complained to the Pope about its unpleasant taste. However, it was not until 1491 that His Excellency allowed for the use of butter in stollen. Later on, the court baker Heinrich Drasdo from Torgau further enhanced it with other richer ingredients, and so the stollen, as we know it today, came into being.

1. Pour boiling water over the almonds and let soak for 10 minutes. Mix the raisins and candied peel with the rum. Drain the almonds and mix with the rum-and-fruit mixture. Let soften overnight.

2. Mix together 1⅔ cups of the flour with the milk, yeast, and honey, knead to a dough, then dust with 1 tablespoon of the remaining flour. Let rise in a warm place for 30 minutes, or until the surface of the dough splits.

3. Mix the remaining flour with the butter, salt, marzipan, vanilla extract, lemon zest, and rum-soaked fruit and nuts, then add the dough and knead for 8 minutes. Cover the dough and let rise in a warm place for about 1 hour, until doubled in size.

4. Meanwhile, preheat the oven to 400°F. Dust a baking sheet with flour. Turn out the dough onto a floured work surface, knead well, and place on the prepared baking sheet.

5. Bake in the middle of the preheated oven for about 1 hour, covering with parchment paper or aluminum foil for the last 20 minutes of cooking if it is browning too quickly. Remove from the oven and brush with the melted butter. Dust with confectioners' sugar, wrap in foil, and let rest for about 2 weeks. Dredge with the confectioners' sugar just before serving.

1.

3.

4.

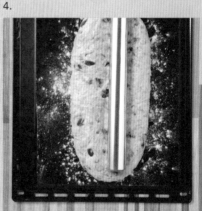

2.

3.

6.

Baumkuchen Small Cakes

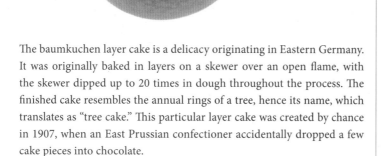

The baumkuchen layer cake is a delicacy originating in Eastern Germany. It was originally baked in layers on a skewer over an open flame, with the skewer dipped up to 20 times in dough throughout the process. The finished cake resembles the annual rings of a tree, hence its name, which translates as "tree cake." This particular layer cake was created by chance in 1907, when an East Prussian confectioner accidentally dropped a few cake pieces into chocolate.

1. Preheat the broiler to medium and grease a 10-inch round springform cake pan.

2. Put the egg yolks, butter, confectioners' sugar, vanilla sugar, flour, and cornstarch into a large bowl and mix to combine. Put the egg whites and salt into a separate bowl and beat, gradually adding the granulated sugar, until they hold soft peaks. Carefully fold into the mixture.

3. Spread a thin layer of the batter on the bottom of the prepared pan and place under the preheated broiler for 1 minute, or until golden brown. Remove from the broiler, spread another thin layer of batter over the first layer, and return to the broiler. Repeat until all the batter has been used.

4. Turn out the cake onto a wire rack and let cool.

5. Meanwhile, to prepare the icing, put the chocolate into a bowl set over a saucepan of gently simmering water, add the vegetable shortening, and stir until melted.

6. Cut the cake into bite-size triangles and use a fork to dip the wider ends in the chocolate mixture. Transfer to a wire rack and let cool.

MAKES 20

PREP TIME: 20 minutes

COOKING TIME: 20 minutes

INGREDIENTS

6 egg yolks

1¾ sticks softened butter, plus extra for greasing

¾ cup confectioners' sugar

1 tablespoon vanilla sugar (to make your own, beat 1–2 drops vanilla extract into sugar)

¾ cup all-purpose flour

⅓ cup cornstarch

6 egg whites

pinch of salt

⅔ cup granulated sugar

icing

8 ounces semisweet chocolate, broken into pieces

1 tablespoon vegetable shortening

HOME OF
3,000 *Breads*

German and Austrian people are well known for being organised, reliable, and economically successful but the culture is less well known for its diversity. However, in German and Austrian baking there are over 3,000 types of bread!

Not only do thousands of bread recipes exist in Germany, but also a lot of regional differences, which may vary from one village to another. Many bread recipes are still kept as family secrets, which often makes it difficult to identify the origin.

So, in terms of baking diversity, no other part of the world has a greater variety of bread. According to constantly growing statistics, in Germany alone there are around 3,000 different types of bread and more than 1,000 kinds of small bakes. As there were no exact figures available, a "bread register" was established in Germany in 2011 in which experts collect and evaluate different recipes. Whether it's whole-wheat or white bread, this incredibly varied baking culture has a longstanding historical background. In the High Middle Ages, Germany and Austria were divided into hundreds of small duchies. These were all different from each other. This conglomerate of small states contrasted with countries such as France and England, which were centrally governed. The fragmentation of Germany and its German neighbors meant that not only the bread, but also its forms varied considerably from one region to another. Sometimes, even neighboring cities used completely different mixtures of ingredients, and their individual compositions were well guarded in secret recipes. Bakers who did not maintain this confidentiality risked severe penalties. All the same, the strict medieval circumstances in Germany turned out to be a godsend for German baking culture. Today, interest in healthy bread with a unique flavor is stronger than ever. Consumption has also increased considerably in recent years. Statistics record an amount of around 155 pounds of bread consumed per capita each year. This is still a long way off from France, which consumes more than 200 pounds per person, although the variety of bread there has increased only in recent years. However, it is a curious fact that of all bread types, whole-wheat bread and whole-grain bread are particularly popular. In the Middle Ages, wealth determined which type of bread you could afford. Only the affluent sectors of the population could afford the expensive white varieties of finely ground wheat flour. This explains why the white wheat baguette, for example, was invented for the French nobility of the seventeenth century: the coarse wholewheat bread might hurt more "sensitive palates." In Germany, too, people mostly ate whole-wheat bread made from coarsely ground whole-grain rye flour because it was cheaper. Today, it is exactly the opposite—the coarser and more natural the bread, the more likely it is to be regarded as a luxury product.

3.

3.

4.

Little *Black Forest* Cakes

MAKES 10

PREP TIME: 40 minutes,
plus 1 hour to chill

COOKING TIME: 45 minutes

INGREDIENTS

3 eggs
½ cup granulated sugar
3½ oz all-purpose flour
1 teaspoon baking powder
2 teaspoons unsweetened cocoa powder
sour cherries or maraschino cherries and grated semisweet chocolate, to decorate

filling

1⅓ cups sour cherries or canned, pitted cherries
½ cup cherry juice
¼ cup granulated sugar
3 sheets of gelatin
3 ounces semisweet chocolate, finely chopped

cream

2 tablespoons kirsch
⅓ cup confectioners' sugar
2 sheets of gelatin
1 cup heavy cream

The Black Forest cherry cake, which enjoys a great popularity throughout Germany (presented here as a sliced version), is still a considerably young invention; this particular cream cake had its first mention in a cookbook in 1934. The recipe quickly captured the interest of the patisseries in Berlin and other major cities in Germany, Austria, and Switzerland. Its origin, however, is unclear. The name is conceivably inspired by the typical Black Forest (Schwarzwald) female costume. The women of this region traditionally wore black dresses with white blouses and red hats.

1. Preheat the oven to 350 °F. Line an 8-inch square baking pan with parchment paper. Beat the eggs with the sugar until foaming. Mix together the flour, baking powder, and cocoa powder, then sift into the egg mixture and mix to combine. Pour into the prepared baking pan and bake in the preheated oven for 30 minutes. Remove from the oven and let cool in the baking pan.

2. To make the filling, puree the cherries with the cherry juice. Add to a saucepan with the sugar, bring to a boil, and cook for 5 minutes. Follow the package directions to dissolve the gelatin sheets, then add to the cherry mixture and let cool until set.

3. Meanwhile, put the chocolate into a heatproof bowl set over a saucepan of gently simmering water and heat until melted. Spread evenly over the cake. Let harden, then spread the cherry jelly evenly on top. Chill in the refrigerator for 1 hour.

4. To make the cream, put the kirsch into a saucepan with the confectioners' sugar and heat over medium heat, then dissolve the sheets of gelatin following the package directions and add to the kirsch mixture. Whip the cream until it holds stiff peaks, then fold into the gelatin mixture. Spread the cream over the cherry jelly.

5. Cut the cake into 10 squares, using a sharp knife. Place a cherry on each piece and sprinkle over some grated chocolate.

Butter
CAKE

MAKES 12

PREP TIME: 20 minutes

COOKING TIME: 30 minutes

INGREDIENTS

*2 cups all-purpose flour,
plus extra for sprinkling*

*1¼ cups granulated sugar,
plus extra for sprinkling*

*5 tablespoons butter, plus extra for
greasing*

1 cup single cream

1 tablespoon baking powder

4 eggs

topping

*¾ cup granulated sugar, plus extra
for sprinkling*

2 cups slivered almonds

2 tablespoons chopped almonds

1 tablespoon milk

1½ sticks butter, melted

This cake is made of a sponge cake with a coating of butter and sugar, to which almonds are usually added. It is, therefore, referred to either as a butter cake or a sugar cake. This delicious treat can be easily produced in large quantities, which is why it is a very welcome and popular addition to all family parties in Germany.

1. Preheat the oven to 350°F. Grease a deep 12 x 8-inch rectangular baking pan and dust with flour, tipping out the excess. Put the flour, sugar, butter, cream, baking powder, and eggs into a large bowl and beat with an electric mixer until combined. Spread evenly in the prepared pan and bake in the preheated oven for 15 minutes. Do not turn off the oven.

2. Meanwhile, make the topping. Put the sugar, slivered almonds, chopped almonds, milk, and two thirds of the melted butter into a medium bowl and mix to combine. Drizzle the remaining butter evenly over the cake.

3. Use a rubber spatula to spread the topping evenly over the cake, then sprinkle with sugar. Return the cake to the oven and bake for an additional 15 minutes. Remove from the oven and let cool in the pan, then cut into squares and serve.

1.

3.

3.

2.

3.

4.

APPLE
Streusel Cake

SERVES 8

PREP TIME: 15 minutes

COOKING TIME: 50 minutes

INGREDIENTS

4 Granny Smith, Cox, or other firm apples, peeled, cored, and diced

2 tablespoons apple juice

⅔ cup firmly packed light brown sugar

1 stick unsalted butter, at room temperature, plus extra for greasing

2 extra-large eggs, beaten

1¾ cups all-purpose flour

1¾ teaspoons baking powder

1½ teaspoons allspice

⅓ cup finely chopped hazelnuts

Apples are particularly widespread across Central Europe and have a long season, so apple cakes are always popular. These classic German treats can be made in umpteen variations with both freshly harvested and stored fruit. Firm and sour apple varieties are used most often to give the already sweet cake a zesty and fresh aroma.

1. Preheat the oven to 375 °F. Grease an 8-inch round springform cake pan and line with parchment paper. Sprinkle the apples with the apple juice.

2. Reserve 1 tablespoon of the sugar, then put the remaining sugar and butter into a mixing bowl and beat until pale and fluffy. Gradually add the eggs, beating thoroughly after each addition. Sift together the flour, baking powder, and spice into the mixture and evenly fold in with a metal spoon.

3. Stir the apples and juice into the mixture, then spoon into the prepared pan and level the surface with a spatula.

4. Mix the hazelnuts with the reserved sugar and sprinkle over the surface of the cake.

5. Bake in the preheated oven for 45–50 minutes, until firm and golden brown. Let cool in the pan for 10 minutes, then turn out onto a wire rack to cool completely.

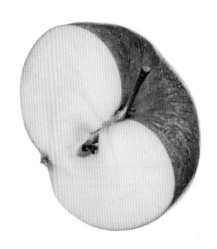

Gugelhupf

TUBE CAKE

SERVES 8

PREP TIME: 25 minutes

COOKING TIME: 1 hour

INGREDIENTS

4 eggs

1¼ sticks butter, plus extra for greasing

¾ cup granulated sugar

2 teaspoons vanilla sugar (available online)

*2⅓ cups all-purpose flour,
plus extra for dusting*

1 tablespoon baking powder

3 tablespoons rum

finely grated rind of 1 lemon

½ cup milk

⅓ cup raisins

confectioners' sugar, for dusting

Essential to the Bundt Cake, or Gugelhupf, is the tall circular structure with an opening in the middle—the bundt pan. It allows the dough to cook evenly. This particular cake style was already known in ancient Roman times. Gugelhupf marble cakes were a popular treat on the tables of the German and Austrian middle classes during the Biedermeier period, even though there was no single standardized recipe for them.

1. Preheat the oven to 350 °F. Grease a bundt pan or tube pan and dust with flour, shaking off the excess.

2. Separate the eggs. Put the butter, sugar, vanilla sugar, and egg yolks into a bowl and beat until creamy. Sift together the flour and baking powder into a separate bowl. Put the egg whites into a clean, grease-free bowl and beat until they hold stiff peaks.

3. Stir the rum, lemon rind, and flour mixture into the butter mixture. Add the milk and stir until bubbles form. Fold in the egg white and raisins.

4. Put the mixture into the prepared pan and bake in the preheated oven for 50–60 minutes. Turn off the oven, open the oven door, and let the cake cool in the oven for 10 minutes. Turn out onto a wire rack and let cool completely. Sift the confectioners' sugar over the cake, cut into slices, and serve.

2.

3.

3.

3.

 3.

5.

Bee Sting *Cake*

SERVES 8

PREP TIME: 45 minutes,
plus time to rise and chill

COOKING TIME: 35 minutes

INGREDIENTS

1½ ounces fresh yeast (available in bakeries or online)
1 cup lukewarm milk
4 cups all-purpose flour, plus extra for sprinkling and dusting
¼ cup granulated sugar
2 eggs
4 tablespoons butter
pinch of salt

almond topping
5 tablespoons butter
2 tablespoons heavy cream
¼ cup granulated sugar
1 cup slivered almonds

filling
2 cups milk
1 vanilla bean
5 egg yolks
⅓ cup granulated sugar
⅓ cup cornstarch
2¼ sticks softened butter

According to a legend, a group of baker apprentices from Andernach on the Rhine used bee nests as weapons to defend their city in 1474, thus causing the attackers to flee. In order to commemorate this victory, they designed a special cake: the bee sting cake.

1. Crumble the yeast into the milk. Stir in 1 tablespoon of the flour and 1 tablespoon of the sugar. Sprinkle with a little flour and let rise in a warm place for 20–30 minutes. Sift the remaining flour into a large mixing bowl and stir in the eggs, the remaining sugar, the butter, and salt. Add the yeast mixture to the flour mixture and knead to a smooth dough. Cover with plastic wrap and let rise in a warm place until doubled in size.

2. Preheat the oven to 350 °F. Line a baking sheet with parchment paper. To make the almond topping, put the butter and cream into a saucepan over low heat. Add the sugar and stir until dissolved, then stir in the almonds. Remove from the heat and let cool.

3. Turn out the dough onto a floured work surface and roll out to a rectangle the size of the baking sheet. Place the dough on the prepared baking sheet and spread with the almond topping. Let rest for 10 minutes, then bake in the middle of the preheated oven for 30–35 minutes.

4. Remove from the oven and let cool. Meanwhile, make the filling. Put the milk into a saucepan with the vanilla bean, bring to a boil, and boil briefly. Remove from the heat, cover, and let stand for about 20 minutes. Meanwhile, put the egg yolks and sugar into a bowl and beat until creamy, then stir in the cornstarch. Strain the cooled vanilla milk into the egg mixture and beat until smooth. Return to the saucepan and heat over low heat until thickened. Transfer to a bowl and stir until cool. Put the butter into a large bowl and beat with an electric mixer until fluffy, then slowly stir into the filling mixture.

5. Cut the cooled cake in half horizontally. Spread the filling on the bottom half and place the other half on top. Chill in the refrigerator for 1–2 hours. Trim the edges of the cake, then cut into slices and serve.

Danube Wave Cake

SERVES 8–10

PREP TIME: 1 hour,
plus 4 hours to chill

COOKING TIME: 40 minutes

INGREDIENTS

*3 sticks softened butter,
plus extra for greasing*
1⅔ cups granulated sugar
8 eggs
2 cups all-purpose flour
2 cups cornstarch
5 teaspoons baking powder
2 cups canned, drained cherries
3 tablespoons unsweetened cocoa powder
⅓ cup milk

crème pâtissière
2 cups milk
*1 teaspoon vanilla extract or 1 vanilla
bean, scraped*
5 egg yolks
⅓ cup superfine sugar
⅓ cup cornstarch

frosting
8 ounces semisweet chocolate
4½ tablespoons butter
½ cup milk

The Danube is one of the widest rivers in Germany. It became the inspiration for this cake, whose sponge consists of a light- and a dark-colored batter. Cherries may also be placed firmly in the dark batter in several places. When sliced, the cake reveals its wavelike structure. The frosting is also often fashioned in such a way that it also resembles waves.

1. Put the butter and sugar into a large bowl and beat with an electric mixer until pale and fluffy. Add the eggs, one at a time, beating after each addition until combined. In a separate bowl, mix together the flour, cornstarch, and baking powder, then sift into the egg-and-butter mixture. Fold in carefully.

2. Preheat the oven to 400°F. Grease a 14 x 8-inch rectangular baking pan. Spread half the batter in the prepared pan. Arrange the cherries evenly on top.

3. Mix the cocoa powder and milk into the remaining batter and spread it over the cherries. Bake in the preheated oven for 20–25 minutes. Remove from the oven and let cool completely.

4. Meanwhile, to make the crème pâtissière, put the milk into a large saucepan and bring to a boil, then stir in the vanilla extract. Remove from the heat and let cool for 20 minutes. Put the egg yolks into a bowl with the sugar and beat with an electric mixer until thick and foaming. Add the cornstarch and cooled milk and mix to combine. Return to the pan and heat over medium heat until thickened. Transfer to a bowl, then place the bowl in a larger bowl filled with ice cubes and chill for 2 hours.

5. Spread the crème pâtissière on the cooled cake. The cake and the crème should be the same temperature. Chill in the refrigerator for 2 hours.

6. For the frosting, put the chocolate, butter, and milk into a heatproof bowl set over a saucepan of barely simmering water and heat until the chocolate is melted. Pour it over the cake and let cool until beginning to set. Use an frosting comb or a fork to make a wavy pattern in the chocolate. Cut the cake into slices and serve chilled.

1.

5.

6.

2.

4.

5.

Cinnamon Stars

Cinnamon stars are a Christmas specialty from Swabia (a region of Württemberg and Bavaria). The stars, sculpted out of dough and covered with icing, are baked at low heat, so that the egg white icing just sets without changing color and the dough remains relatively soft.

1. Beat the egg whites in a clean, grease-free bowl until they hold stiff peaks. Stir in the sugar until thoroughly combined, then continue to beat until thick and glossy.

2. Set aside about one-fourth of this mixture, then fold the hazelnuts and cinnamon into the remaining mixture to make a stiff dough. Chill in the refrigerator for about 1 hour.

3. Preheat the oven to 275 °F. Line two baking sheets with parchment paper. Roll out the dough to a thickness of ½ inch on a work surface heavily dusted with confectioners' sugar.

4. Use a 2-inch star-shape cutter to cut the dough into shapes, frequently dusting the cutter with confectioners' sugar to prevent them from sticking. Reroll the trimmings as necessary until all the dough has been used.

5. Place the cookies on the prepared baking sheets, spaced well apart, and spread the top of each star with the reserved egg white mixture.

6. Bake in the preheated oven for 25 minutes, or until the cookies are still white and crisp on top but slightly soft and moist underneath. Turn off the oven and open the door to release the heat, but leave the cookies in the oven for an additional 10 minutes to dry out. Remove from the oven and transfer to wire racks to cool completely.

MAKES 20

PREP TIME: 25 minutes, plus 1 hour to chill

COOKING TIME: 25 minutes

INGREDIENTS

2 egg whites

1⅓ cups confectioners' sugar, plus extra for dusting

3 cups ground roasted hazelnuts

1 tablespoon ground cinnamon

Red Currant

CAKE

SERVES 10–12

PREP TIME: 45 minutes,
plus 1 hour to chill

COOKING TIME: 30 minutes

INGREDIENTS

9 cups red currants (about 2¼ pounds)
¼ cup granulated sugar
6 egg whites
¾ cup superfine sugar
2 cups ground hazelnuts

dough

2¾ cups all-purpose flour,
plus extra for dusting
¾ cup confectioners' sugar,
plus extra for dusting
pinch of salt
2 eggs
1¼ sticks butter,
plus extra for greasing
3 tablespoons water

The red currant cake is a Central European classic of summertime baking. It is then that the beautiful red fruit of the red currant bush is fully ripe. Their slightly acidy flavor gives this cake an unmistakable kick, which, in this case, is enhanced with a hazelnut aroma.

1. To make the dough, sift together the flour, confectioners' sugar, and salt into a large bowl. Add the eggs, butter, and water, then mix together well. Turn out onto a lightly floured work surface and knead to a smooth dough. Wrap in plastic wrap and chill in the refrigerator for 1 hour.

2. Preheat the oven to 350°F. Grease an 11-inch springform cake pan and dust with flour. Turn out the dough onto a lightly floured work surface and roll out to a thickness of ⅛ inch. Ease into the prepared pan and prick several times with a fork.

3. Put the red currants into a large bowl, add the granulated sugar, and carefully mix together. Put the egg whites into a clean, grease-free bowl and beat until they hold stiff peaks, then add the superfine sugar and gently fold in. Fold the egg whites into the red currants, then fold in the hazelnuts.

4. Spoon the filling into the pastry shell and bake in the preheated oven for 30 minutes. Remove from the oven and let cool. Carefully remove the cake from the pan, dust with confectioners' sugar, and serve.

2.

3.

4.

1.

3.

5.

Berliner
Donuts

MAKES 18–20

PREP TIME: 35 minutes,
plus 3–4 hours to stand and rise

COOKING TIME: 10–15 minutes

INGREDIENTS

1¼ teaspoons active dry yeast

1 cup cold milk

½ teaspoon salt

1 stick butter

2½ tablespoons granulated sugar

*1 teaspoon vanilla sugar (to make your
own, beat 1–2 drops vanilla extract into
sugar)*

1 egg

2 egg yolks

*4 cups all-purpose flour,
plus extra for dusting*

1 tablespoon vinegar

sunflower oil, for deep-frying

*raspberry or strawberry jelly or preserves,
for filling*

confectioners' sugar, for sprinkling

The success of the Berliner donuts—known in Bavaria and Austria as krapfen—dates back to the rise of Berlin as an industrial city and the capital of the German Empire, founded in 1871. This period saw the establishment of steam bakeries in many German towns, which quickly became widespread. Since these times, confectioners have created a great variety of the deep-fried sweet treats.

1. Put the yeast into a bowl with ½ cup of the milk and the salt, stir to dissolve, and let stand for about 1 hour. Put the butter into a bowl with the granulated sugar and vanilla sugar and beat with an electric mixer until pale and fluffy. Add the egg and the egg yolks, one at a time, beating after each addition until incorporated. Sift in the flour, then add the yeast mixture, vinegar, and remaining milk. Beat slowly until a soft dough forms.

2. Cover the dough with a damp dish towel and let rise in a warm place for about 2 hours, until doubled in size.

3. Turn out the dough onto a lightly floured work surface, divide into 18–20 pieces, and shape each piece into a ball. Let rise on the work surface, uncovered, for about 30 minutes, until they develop a skin.

4. Meanwhile, heat enough oil for deep-frying in a large saucepan or deep fryer to 350–375 °F, or until a cube of bread browns in 30 seconds. Carefully slide the donuts into the oil and fry for 1½ minutes, until golden brown. Turn them over and fry for an additional 1½ minutes. Turn them over again and fry the top side for an additional 30 seconds. To maintain the classic white line, do not move the donuts around during frying. Drain on paper towels and let cool.

5. Meanwhile, put some jelly or jam into a pastry bag fitted with a plain tip and pipe into the center of the donuts. Sprinkle with confectioners' sugar and serve.

Spiced Pear & Golden Raisin Strudel

SERVES 6

PREP TIME: 35 minutes

COOKING TIME: 25 minutes

INGREDIENTS

*6 tablespoons unsalted butter,
melted, plus extra for greasing*
3 firm ripe pears, peeled, cored, and diced
finely grated rind and juice of ½ lemon
⅓ cup raw brown sugar
1 teaspoon ground allspice
⅓ cup golden raisins
½ cup ground almonds
6 sheets phyllo dough
confectioners' sugar, sifted, for dusting

The first written Strudel recipe dates back to 1698. A baker named Pueg from Vienna wrote down his "secret," which has now been exposed in the National Library of Austria. The word itself explains the way of baking. "Strudel" was the expression for cooking fruits and nuts inside a dough.

1. Preheat the oven to 400 °F and grease a baking sheet with butter.

2. Mix together the pears, lemon rind and juice, sugar, allspice, golden raisins, and half the almonds.

3. Put two sheets of phyllo dough, slightly overlapping, on a clean dish towel.

4. Brush lightly with melted butter and sprinkle with one-third of the almonds. Top with two more sheets, butter, and almonds. Repeat once more.

5. Spread the pear mixture down one long side to within 1 inch of the edge.

6. Roll the dough over to enclose the filling and roll up, using the dish towel to lift. Tuck the ends under.

7. Brush with a little melted butter and bake in the preheated oven for 20–25 minutes, until golden and crisp.

8. Lightly dust the strudel with confectioners' sugar. Serve the strudel warm or cold, cut into thick slices.

1.

2.

3.

4.

5.

6.

7.

8.

Austrian Sacher Cake

SERVES 12

PREP TIME: 1½ hours

COOKING TIME: 1½ hours

INGREDIENTS

3 ounces semisweet chocolate

2 tablespoons water

6 eggs, separated

pinch of salt

½ cup granulated sugar

1 stick butter, plus extra for greasing

1¼ cups all-purpose flour, sifted, plus extra for dusting

4 teaspoons vanilla extract

3 tablespoons apricot preserves

frosting

½ cup heavy cream

2 tablespoons butter

6 ounces semisweet chocolate, at least 70 percent cocoa solids

⅔ cup confectioners' sugar

2 tablespoons water

In 1832, a 16-year-old Viennese chef's apprentice, Franz Sacher, invented the basic shape of the famed Sachertorte (Sacher cake). One day, the head chef in charge of the kitchen of the emperor's Viennese residence was taken ill, and so Sacher had to step in and create a special dessert for the high-profile guests. But the cake remained unacknowledged until Sacher's son, Eduard, further developed and popularized it during his apprenticeship at the Viennese confectioners Demel.

1. Preheat the oven to 350°F. Grease a 9-inch round springform cake pan and dust with flour. Put the chocolate and water into a heatproof bowl set over a saucepan of barely simmering water and heat until melted. Beat the egg whites with the salt until they hold stiff peaks, then gradually add half the sugar, beating after each addition until combined.

2. Put the butter and the remaining sugar into a separate large bowl and beat with an electric mixer until creamy, then add the egg yolks, one at a time, beating after each addition until combined. Add the flour, vanilla extract, and melted chocolate. Carefully fold in the beaten egg whites.

3. Pour the batter into the prepared pan and bake in the preheated oven for about 1½ hours, or until a toothpick inserted into the center comes out clean. Let cool in the pan, then turn out onto a wire rack to cool completely. Cut the cake in half horizontally.

4. Put the preserves into a small saucepan and heat over low heat until runny, then spread it evenly over the bottom layer of the cake. Place the second layer on top.

5. To make the frosting, put the cream into a saucepan over medium heat and bring to a boil. Remove from the heat and gradually add the butter and chocolate, stirring until melted. Put the sugar and the water into a separate saucepan over medium heat and stir until dissolved. Add the sugar syrup to the chocolate mixture and stir to combine. Let cool slightly, then pour over the cake.

6. Use a spatula to spread the frosting evenly over the top and the sides of the cake. Chill in the refrigerator until firm. Decorate the surface, if desired, before serving.

2.

2.

4.

FOR THE
Love
OF LIFE...

As with most traditional recipes in Europe, the origin of lebkuchen (German gingerbread) can be traced back many centuries. However, in people's minds, historical origins are usually less important than the memories that they associate with lebkuchen.

The unmistakable smell of the mixture of almonds, nuts, ground coriander, ginger, nutmeg, and cardamom triggers childhood memories in most German people. Of a visit to the country fair, where there were beautifully decorated lebkuchen hearts. Or the heavenly gingerbread houses that were the dream palaces of pleasure at Christmastime. What child in Germany wasn't curious to see what was inside? And who wasn't eager to try a small piece of the roof or the iced shutters? Only a tiny bit, where no one would see. Notwithstanding their exotic ingredients, which don't quite fit with the rest of German baking culture, lebkuchen is probably the most mysterious of all baked goods. Although recipes vary between the different regions of Germany, the city of Nuremberg, with its famous Christmas Market, is considered to be the stronghold of lebkuchen production. The quality criteria for typical Nuremberg lebkuchen includes, for example, the fact that no flour is used. This sets Nuremberg bakers apart, because the flour component of most commercial lebkuchen can be up to 50 percent. Where the name lebkuchen comes from is as uncertain as its historical roots. The only certainty is that it has nothing to do with the word for life—"leben." It is possible that the syllable "leb" comes either from the Latin libum for flatbread or the bread used for offerings, or from the old Germanic word for "loaf," which is now a rarely used term that describes the "body" of the bread. The ancient Egyptians already baked spiced honey cakes and placed the loaves in the graves of their dead to take along as provisions for their journey. However, we do not really know how the tradition of this sweet bread came to northern Europe, though there has been evidence of similar recipes in various monasteries in southern Germany. There, the so-called pfefferkuchen (pepper cake) was a dessert. Because rare spices from distant lands were needed to make lebkuchen, it is probable that the monks brought these back from their travels. Later, the spices were ordered from merchants; for this reason, the lebkuchen tradition developed mainly along the major trade routes. In Germany, lebkuchen quickly became a coveted item, which is explained by its long shelf life. In southern Germany and Austria, bakers who specialized in making flat wafers were called zelter. The lebkuchen bakers were, therefore, called lebzelter. Incidentally, a lebzelter is mentioned in the tax records of the City of Munich in 1370.

Houses made from lebkuchen cookies are real artworks and often used as decorations in shop windows, especially in the south of Germany.

1.

3.

4.

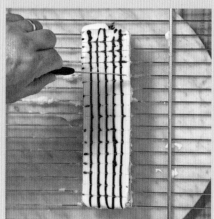

4.

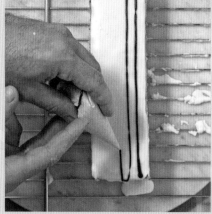

Esterházy SLICES

SERVES 12

PREP TIME: 50 minutes

COOKING TIME: 10 minutes

Esterházy slices are a variation of the Esterházy cake, which was created in the late nineteenth century by a Budapest confectioner for the Hungarian aristocratic Esterházy family, who were renowned for their extravagant entertaining. The cake was named after Prince Paul III, Anton Esterházy, a diplomat and, in 1848, briefly foreign minister of the Austro-Hungarian Empire. The fame of the cake eventually reached Vienna, where it soon became part of that city's legendary confectionery.

1. Preheat the oven to 400°F. Grease a baking sheet and dust it with flour. Beat the egg whites in a clean, grease-free bowl until they hold soft peaks. Fold in the confectioners' sugar, vanilla sugar, and cinnamon and continue beating until the mixture holds stiff peaks. Stir in the ground hazelnuts. Spread the batter evenly on the prepared baking sheet, then bake in the preheated oven for 10 minutes. Remove from the oven, immediately cut the cake into four 3-inch-wide slices, and transfer to a wire rack to cool.

2. Meanwhile, to make the buttercream, put the butter into a large bowl and beat until creamy. Put the egg yolks, sugar, and flour into a medium saucepan and stir together until smooth. Pass through a strainer to remove any lumps, if necessary. Stir in the milk and the rum, put over medium heat, and bring to a boil, stirring continuously. Remove from the heat, cover, and let cool, then stir into the butter.

3. Spread a slice of the cake with the buttercream and top with another slice of cake. Repeat until all the slices are used, ending with a slice of cake.

4. To make the icing, put the egg white, confectioners' sugar, and lemon juice into a bowl and stir to combine. Spread over the top layer of cake. Mix the cocoa powder with the water until smooth. Put into a pastry bag and pipe in long lines on top of the icing. Draw a toothpick through the icing to create a feathered pattern. Cut into slices and serve.

INGREDIENTS

butter, for greasing
all-purpose flour, for dusting
6 egg whites
1 cup confectioners' sugar
½ cup vanilla sugar (to make your own, beat 1–2 drops vanilla extract into sugar)
pinch of ground cinnamon
1¾ cups ground hazelnuts

buttercream
1¾ sticks butter
3 egg yolks
1½ tablespoons granulated sugar
⅓ cup all-purpose flour
1 cup milk
splash of rum or kirsch

icing
½ egg white
1⅔ cups confectioners' sugar
juice of ½ lemon
2 tablespoons unsweetened cocoa powder
1 teaspoon water

Linzer Torte

SERVES 10–12

PREP TIME: 45 minutes,
plus time to rest and mature

COOKING TIME: 30–40 minutes

INGREDIENTS

1¼ sticks butter,
plus extra for greasing
2 eggs
1 tablespoon kirsch or cherry brandy
1¼ cups all-purpose flour,
plus extra for dusting
¾ cup granulated sugar
pinch of salt
pinch of ground cinnamon
¼ teaspoon ground cloves
1½ cups coarsely ground almonds
2 teaspoons unsweetened cocoa powder
¾ cup cherry preserves

The recipe for Linzer torte (a cake named after the city of Linz in Upper Austria) is the oldest cake recipe in the world. It was first published in 1653 in a cookbook of Countess Anna Margarita Sagramosa from Verona. It was popularized by Johann Konrad Vogel, a baker from Franconia in Germany, who emigrated to Linz in 1822. He manufactured this delicacy in large quantities, also shipping his products to other locations.

1. Melt the butter in a small saucepan. Put the eggs into a small bowl with the kirsch and beat together.

2. Mix together the flour, sugar, salt, cinnamon, and cloves in a separate bowl, then add the butter and mix to combine. Add the almonds and the cocoa powder. Slowly add the egg mixture, mixing until a smooth dough forms. Cover the bowl and transfer to the refrigerator to rest for at least 48 hours.

3. Preheat the oven to 325 °F and grease a 10-inch fluted tart pan. Turn out the dough onto a lightly floured work surface. Roll out three-quarters of the dough into a circle with a thickness of ½ inch and place in the prepared pan, working it about 1 inch up the sides of the pan. Spread a ¼-inch layer of preserves on the dough.

4. Roll out the remaining dough and use a pastry wheel to cut it into ½-inch-wide strips. Lay the strips on top of the preserves in a lattice pattern. Bake in the middle of the preheated oven for 30–40 minutes.

5. Remove from the oven and let cool completely, then wrap in aluminum foil and let rest for at least one week. Linzer torte is never served fresh out of the oven and improves with time.

3.

3.

4.

Spiced Fruit Loaf

MAKES 1 LOAF

PREP TIME: 20 minutes,
plus rising

COOKING TIME: 1 hour 10 minutes

INGREDIENTS

3¼ cups white bread flour,
plus extra for dusting

pinch of salt

2 teaspoons allspice

1 stick unsalted butter, diced

2¼ teaspoons active dry yeast

½ cup granulated sugar

¾ cup dried currants

¾ cup raisins

¼ cup chopped candied peel

finely grated rind of 1 orange

1 egg, beaten

⅔ cup milk, warmed

vegetable oil, for oiling

Fruit breads are common in the south of Germany during the weeks of Advent. In some regions in Germany and Austria, it is served to all family members on Christmas Eve after coming back from church. Dried pears and butter are served with the bread.

1. Sift the flour, salt, and allspice into a bowl and rub in the butter until the mixture resembles bread crumbs. Stir in the yeast, sugar, dried fruit, candied peel, and orange rind, then add the egg and warm milk and bring together to form a soft dough.

2. Knead the dough briefly on a lightly floured surface. Dust a clean bowl with flour and add the dough. Cover the bowl and let rise in a warm place for 2 hours.

3. Preheat the oven to 350 °F and oil a 9-inch loaf pan. Knead the dough again briefly, then place it in the prepared pan, cover, and let rise for 20 minutes. Bake in the preheated oven for 1 hour 10 minutes—the loaf should be golden and well risen. Let cool in the pan before slicing and serving.

1.

2.

3.

1.

2.

4.

Onion Tart

SERVES 10–12

PREP TIME: 35 minutes,
plus 1¼ hours to rise

COOKING TIME: 50 minutes

INGREDIENTS

4 mild onions
1 tablespoon butter
2½ ounces smoked pancetta
3 eggs
1½ cups heavy cream
salt and pepper, to taste

pastry dough
2¾ cups all-purpose flour,
plus extra for dusting
½ cup lukewarm milk
¾ ounce fresh yeast (available in
bakeries or online)
1 teaspoon sugar
2 tablespoons butter, melted,
plus extra for greasing

This savory onion tart is typically served in Germany as a snack to go with young wine, also known in German as Federweisser. Vineyard workers and participants of wine festivals especially enjoy eating it warm.

1. To make the dough, put ¾ cup of the flour into a bowl and make a well in the center. Pour the milk into the well and crumble in the yeast. Add the sugar, stir to combine, then cover and let rise for 15 minutes.

2. Add the remaining flour and the butter to the yeast mixture and knead until a smooth dough forms. Cover with a damp dish towel and let rise for 1 hour, until doubled in size. Turn out onto a lightly floured work surface and roll out into a circle.

3. Preheat the oven to 325 °F. Grease an 11-inch fluted tart pan. Ease the dough into the prepared pan.

4. Halve the onions and slice them into thin strips. Melt the butter in a skillet, add the pancetta, and sauté for 1–2 minutes, then add the onions and season with salt and pepper. Sauté for an additional 5–6 minutes, until the onions are translucent, then remove from the heat and let cool. Spread the mixture in the pastry shell.

5. Beat the eggs with the cream, season with salt and pepper, and pour it over the onion-and-pancetta mixture in the pastry shell. Bake in the preheated oven for 50 minutes, until golden brown. If the surface is browning too quickly, cover with aluminum foil. Serve hot or cold.

1.

2.

4.

Scallion & Cheese
TART

SERVES 8

PREP TIME: 35 minutes,
plus 1 hour to rest

COOKING TIME: 50 minutes

The scallion is harvested in the early spring, almost too early, in fact, at a time when the bulb is only beginning to grow. With its crisp, fresh taste, it serves to refine a number of dishes, such as this hearty tart. When contrasted with that of a fully grown common onion, the flavor of a scallion is mild and their stems are characterized by a slight leek flavor.

1. To make the dough, mix together the flour, salt, and butter in a bowl. Add the water, a little at a time, mixing after each addition until a stiff dough forms. Wrap in plastic wrap and let rest for 1 hour.

2. Preheat the oven to 350°F. Oil a 10-inch rectangular fluted tart pan. Put the oil into a skillet over medium heat, add the scallions, and sauté for about 5 minutes, until translucent. Remove from the heat and let cool.

3. Beat the eggs in a large bowl, then add the cheese and ham and mix to combine. Add the cream and scallions and mix together well. Stir in the nutmeg, then season with salt and pepper.

4. Ease the dough into the prepared pan and prick the bottom all over with a fork. Pour the filling into the pastry shell and bake in the bottom of the preheated oven for 45 minutes, until the surface of the tart is golden brown and a toothpick inserted into the center comes out clean. Serve the tart hot or cold.

INGREDIENTS

1 tablespoon oil, plus extra for oiling
3–4 scallions, finely chopped
3 eggs
1⅓ cups Emmenthal or Swiss cheese, grated
6 ounces cooked ham, diced
1 cup heavy cream
pinch of nutmeg
salt and pepper, to taste

pastry dough
1⅔ cups all-purpose flour
pinch of salt
1 stick butter, at room temperature
½ cup water

Baking
in the
SCANDINAVIAN STYLE

Cake, bread, and cookies are an essential part of everyday life in Scandinavia. Undoubtedly, the climate conditions in northern Europe mean that hearty and filling foods are important in the typical Scandinavian diet. A light snack between meals not only helps to boost energy levels but can also lift the spirits, especially during a dark winter. Crispbreads spread with plenty of butter and cakes with the obligatory blueberry topping are a favorite throughout Scandinavia, particularly during the "white nights" around the summer solstice, when the night sky never becomes truly dark. It was once believed that the morning dew at this time of the year had healing powers. The dew would be collected in bottles and used for baking bread, because the bread would rise even higher and taste even better.

The typical Scandinavian way of living is beautiful, but sometimes with rough weather conditions—which is perhaps one reason why many families are enthusiastic about high-quality home baking. A good cake is always an opportunity to assemble friends and family around a table.

Princess Cake

SERVES 12

PREP TIME: 30 minutes,
plus time to chill

COOKING TIME: 40 minutes

INGREDIENTS

butter, for greasing
bread crumbs, for coating
4 eggs
1 cup granulated sugar
½ cup all-purpose flour
¾ cup potato flour
1 teaspoon baking powder
confectioners' sugar, for dusting

filling

1 cup heavy cream
4 egg yolks
3 tablespoons potato flour
or 2 tablespoons cornstarch
2 tablespoons granulated sugar
2 teaspoons vanilla extract
2 cups heavy cream, whipped

topping

10 ounces marzipan
green food coloring
yellow food coloring
pink marzipan rose and
green marzipan leaves, to decorate

This cake was first made by Jenny Åkerström. She was the housekeeping teacher of Princess Margaretha, Princess Martha, and Princess Astrid of Sweden, and she published a cookbook in their honor in 1929. However, the recipe for the princess cake was only published in the 1948 edition of the book, under the name of green cake. It remains unclear why the marzipan is colored green, but the cake certainly looks striking.

1. Preheat the oven to 375 °F. Grease a 9-inch round cake pan, then coat the bottom and side with bread crumbs. Put the eggs and granulated sugar into a mixing bowl and beat with an electric mixer until light and fluffy.

2. Sift together the all-purpose flour, potato flour, and baking powder and carefully fold into the egg mixture until thoroughly combined. Pour the mixture into the prepared pan and bake in the bottom of the preheated oven for 40 minutes, or until golden and a toothpick inserted into the center comes out clean. Transfer to a wire rack to cool.

3. To make the filling, put the heavy cream, egg yolks, potato flour, and sugar into a small saucepan and beat together. Cook over low heat, stirring continuously, until thick. Remove from the heat and stir in the vanilla extract.

4. To make the topping, knead the marzipan until soft, then gradually add the green and yellow food colorings until it is light green in color. Use your hands to flatten the marzipan into a circle, then place between two sheets of parchment paper or on a work surface dusted with confectioners' sugar and roll it out into an ⅛-inch circle with a diameter of 12 inches.

5. Slice the cooled cake into three layers horizontally, cutting the top layer a little thinner than the others. Assemble the cake by spreading half the filling on the bottom layer. Add the second layer of cake and spread with the remaining filling. Top with the whipped cream, then add the final layer of cake, gently forming it into a dome shape. Be careful that not too much cream is hanging over the sides.

6. Lay the marzipan circle on top of the cake, shaping it around the sides until the whole cake is covered. Trim any excess marzipan from the bottom of the cake with a sharp knife. Dust the top with confectioners' sugar and decorate with the marzipan rose and leaves. Chill until ready to serve.

2.

3.

4.

4.

1.

2.

4.

Semla Buns

Semla buns are sweet rolls filled with a marzipan mixture and topped with whipped cream. In Scandinavia, it is a traditional dough on Shrove Tuesday, the day before Lent begins. The Semlor were, therefore, called "Fat Tuesday" and were originally served in dishes with hot milk. Some cafés still serve them this way.

1. Gently heat the milk with the cardamom in a saucepan, then remove from the heat, crumble in the yeast, and stir to dissolve. Break the egg into a bowl and gradually beat in the butter. Add the sugar and salt. Sift the flour into a large bowl and add the egg-and-butter mixture. Add the yeast mixture and knead until a smooth, elastic dough forms. Cover with a damp dish towel and let rise for about 1 hour, until doubled in size.

2. Preheat the oven to 400°F. Dust a baking sheet with flour. Divide the dough into 14–16 pieces, roll each piece into a ball, and put on the prepared baking sheet. Dust with flour, then cover and let rise for an additional 10 minutes.

3. Beat the egg yolk with a little milk and brush over the surface of the rolls. Bake in the middle of the preheated oven for 6–7 minutes. Remove from the oven and let cool.

4. Cut off the top of the rolls horizontally and set aside. Use your fingers to hollow out the rolls, reserving the crumbs. To make the filling, mix the reserved crumbs with the marzipan and milk until a soft paste forms. Spoon the paste into the rolls, pipe over the whipped cream and place a reserved top on each roll. Dust with confectioners' sugar and serve.

MAKES 14–16

PREP TIME: 35 minutes,
plus 1 hour 10 minutes to rise

COOKING TIME: 10 minutes

INGREDIENTS

1¼ cup milk, plus extra for brushing
1 tablespoon ground cardamom
1¾ ounces fresh yeast (available in bakeries or online)
1 egg
1¼ sticks softened butter
¾ cup granulated sugar
½ teaspoon salt
4¾ cups all-purpose flour, plus extra for dusting
1 egg yolk
confectioners' sugar, for dusting

filling
14 ounces marzipan
dash of milk
1¾ cups heavy cream, whipped

Appelkaka
Cake

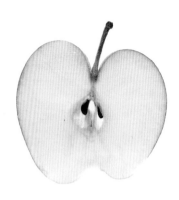

SERVES 12

PREP TIME: 20 minutes

COOKING TIME: 50 minutes

INGREDIENTS

*3 tablespoons biscotti crumbs,
for coating*

*2 sticks softened butter,
plus extra for greasing*

1⅓ cups granulated sugar

4 eggs

1⅓ cups all-purpose flour

1 teaspoon baking powder

4–6 firm crisp apples, cut into wedges

*2 teaspoons ground cinnamon
mixed with 1 tablespoon sugar*

1½ cups chopped almonds

When, after a long summer, it starts to get cool again and the apples are ripe, this juicy Swedish apple cake is simply a must. Fresh apples, cinnamon, and almonds lend it a unique flavor, often crowned with whipped cream or a vanilla sauce.

1. Preheat the oven to 350°F. Grease a 10-inch round springform cake pan and generously coat with biscotti crumbs. Put the butter and sugar into a bowl and beat until smooth and creamy. Add the eggs, one at a time, beating after each addition until combined. Sift together the flour and baking powder into the mixture and stir in.

2. Spread the batter in the prepared pan. Toss the apple wedges with the cinnamon-and-sugar mixture and arrange on the cake batter.

3. Sprinkle with the almonds and bake in the preheated oven for 50 minutes, or until a toothpick inserted in the center comes out clean. Remove from the oven, cut into pieces, and serve warm or cold.

ALMOND STICKS

Almond sticks are a fun and crunchy delight, especially for children—even just a small bite is enough to enjoy the sweet, nutty flavor. It takes a little more of an effort to make than normal snacks, but they're worth it.

1. Preheat the oven to 350°F. Line a large baking sheet with parchment paper. Put the butter and sugar into a bowl and beat until pale and fluffy. Add two eggs and the almond extract and stir until combined. Sift together the flour and the salt into a separate bowl, add to the butter-and-sugar mixture, and knead until a smooth dough forms.

2. Turn out the dough onto a lightly floured work surface and roll out to a thickness of ¾ inch. Using a sharp knife, cut out 25–30 strips, each measuring 1 x 2 inches.

3. Beat the remaining eggs in a shallow bowl. Put the almonds into a separate bowl. Dip the dough strips into the beaten eggs, then into the chopped almonds. Generously sprinkle with sugar and place on the prepared baking sheet.

4. Bake in the preheated oven for 8–10 minutes, then remove from the oven and transfer to a wire rack to cool. The almond sticks can be stored in an airtight container for up to one week.

MAKES 25–30

PREP TIME: 20–25 minutes

COOKING TIME: 8–10 minutes

INGREDIENTS

2 sticks softened butter

½ cup granulated sugar, plus extra for sprinkling

4 eggs

1 teaspoon almond extract

3 cups all-purpose flour, plus extra for dusting

¼ teaspoon salt

2 cups chopped almonds

2.

TIME
for
SEMLOR

Stockholm wouldn't be known as the capital of Scandinavian baking without the semla bun. It has become a tradition to take a break, drink a cup of coffee, and eat a semla bun. In Sweden this sort of break is called "fika".

The people of Stockholm have the greatest respect for the legendary "bun man." Nobody knows his name, what he looks like, or when he will show up in the streets. However, one thing is certain: The "bun man" targets a bakery every day, buys a legendary Swedish semla bun, eats it, and then rates it comprehensively in the newspapers or on his blog on the Internet. A bakery with a good review won't be complaining about a lack of business in the days and weeks that follow. The semla bun, with its cream and marzipan filling, was traditionally only served between Shrove Tuesday and Easter. However, the semla bun is now so popular, that immediately after Christmas all the store windows are so full of them that you'd think there weren't any other specialities in Sweden. Therefore, it was inevitable that someone like the "bun man" should come along and start reviewing this particular treat. This is how the critic describes what makes a particularly good semla bun: "The ingredients must be perfect, the marzipan flavorful but not intrusive, and the cream should look freshly whipped. Everything should be well presented and the proportions must be just right." If these conditions are met, there's nothing to prevent a perfect "fika." You do not know what "fika" is? Fika can be had or held in the late morning and also in the early or late afternoon. In any case, there should always be time for fika, even if the term doesn't actually exist in Scandinavian languages. There is no official translation for "fika," but there is a precise definition for it—as a famous Swedish furniture store once put it in its baking book entitled Fika: "It is a break with coffee and pastries, a cornerstone of Swedish food culture. A moment of relaxation among friends, family, or colleagues. 'Fika' is for any time, any place, anywhere. In Sweden any time is fika time."

Fika is not necessarily a national custom in all Scandinavian countries. However, taking time out for a cup of coffee is a much-loved habit everywhere, be it Denmark, Sweden, or Norway. Taking a short break clearly increases productivity at work—whether it's in the factory, at the office, or at school. And—of course—also at home!

3.

4.

5.

Tosca CAKE

SERVES 8

PREP TIME: 20 minutes

COOKING TIME: 35–40 minutes

INGREDIENTS

1¼ cups all-purpose flour,
plus extra for dusting

1 teaspoon baking powder

½ teaspoon salt

1 stick butter, melted,
plus extra for greasing

1 teaspoon vanilla extract or
1 vanilla bean, scraped

⅓ cup milk

3 eggs

¾ cup granulated sugar

topping

4 tablespoons butter

⅔ cup granulated sugar

⅓ cup heavy cream

2 tablespoons all-purpose flour

pinch of salt

1 cup slivered almonds

¼ teaspoon almond extract

1 teaspoon vanilla extract or bean, scraped

Scandinavia's popular Tosca cake is thought to be named after Giacomo Puccini's opera about the love and suffering of ordinary people, first performed in 1900. The cake is easy to make and so is good to bake for guests. Just put it in the oven as your guests arrive and let them enjoy the smell of the light cake with its caramelized almond topping as it bakes.

1. Preheat the oven to 350 °F. Grease a 9-inch springform cake pan and dust with flour. Line the bottom with parchment paper, then grease the paper.

2. Sift together the flour, baking powder, and salt into a bowl and set aside. Mix together the butter, vanilla extract, and milk in a separate bowl and set aside in a warm place so that the butter remains liquid.

3. Put the eggs and sugar into a large bowl and beat with an electric mixer until pale and thick. Add the flour mixture and the milk mixture alternately, mixing after each addition. Do not overmix. Transfer to the prepared pan and bake in the preheated oven for 20–25 minutes, until the top is just set.

4. Meanwhile, prepare the topping. Combine the butter, sugar, cream, flour, and salt in a saucepan and heat over medium–high heat, stirring, until the butter is melted. Add the almonds, bring to a simmer, and cook for about 1 minute, then remove from the heat. Stir in the almond extract and vanilla extract and set aside.

5. Remove the cake from the oven. Increase the oven temperature to 400 °F. Gently spread the topping on the cake. Return to the oven and bake for an additional 15 minutes, until the topping is golden brown. Let cool, then slice and serve.

Kladdkaka

CHOCOLATE CAKES

MAKES 9

PREP TIME: 15 minutes

COOKING TIME: 15–20 minutes

INGREDIENTS

2 eggs
1⅓ cups granulated sugar
⅓ cup all-purpose flour
pinch of salt
¼ cup unsweetened cocoa powder
1 stick butter, melted,
plus extra for greasing
confectioners' sugar, for dusting
cranberries, to decorate
whipped cream, to serve (optional)

This sticky and sweet chocolate cake is popular in Sweden. It is made with plenty of sugar and just a little flour. These little cakes are similar to brownies, but softer and denser, especially in the middle. Serve with whipped cream or vanilla ice cream.

1. Preheat the oven to 350 °F. Lightly grease nine cups in a muffin pan with fluted cups. Beat together the eggs and sugar in a large bowl, then gradually beat in the flour and salt.

2. Stir the cocoa powder into the butter and carefully mix into the batter.

3. Pour the batter into the prepared holes of the pan and bake in the preheated oven for 15–20 minutes, until slightly crispy on the outside and a toothpick inserted into the center comes out sticky. Remove from the oven and let cool.

4. Dust with confectioners' sugar, decorate with cranberries, and serve with whipped cream, if using.

1.

2.

3.

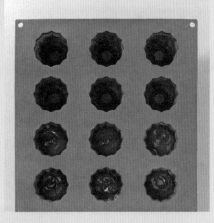

1.

2.

4.

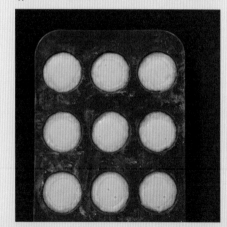

Mazarin

TARTLETS

MAKES 12

PREP TIME: 30 minutes,
plus time to chill

COOKING TIME: 10–15 minutes

INGREDIENTS

1 stick butter
2 eggs
½ cup granulated sugar
*1½ cups slivered almonds,
plus extra to decorate*
*1 teaspoon bitter almond oil
or almond extract*
rose petals, to decorate

pastry dough

*1¼ cups all-purpose flour,
plus extra for dusting*
½ teaspoon baking powder
⅓ cup granulated sugar
1 stick butter, plus extra for greasing
1 egg
1 teaspoon vodka

icing

1¼ cups confectioners' sugar
2 tablespoons milk or water

These tarts, named after the Italian/French cardinal and politician Jules Mazarin (1602–1661), are also simply called mazarins. The cardinal was a gourmet and encouraged an exchange of recipes in Europe. The Swedish mazarins probably evolved from other European almond tarts several decades before. They are considered to be a particular favorite with baking connoisseurs.

1. To make the dough, put the flour, baking powder, sugar, butter, egg, and vodka into a large bowl and mix together until a soft dough forms. Add a little water, if needed, to achieve the correct consistency. Cover with plastic wrap and chill in the refrigerator for several hours.

2. Preheat the oven to 350°F. Grease a 12-cup muffin pan. Turn out the dough onto a lightly floured work surface and roll out to a thickness of ¼ inch. Use a round cutter to cut out 12 circles large enough to line the cups, then gently ease into the prepared pan.

3. Melt the butter in a small saucepan. Put the eggs and sugar into a bowl and beat together, then add the almonds and the almond oil and beat until combined. Stir in the melted butter.

4. Pour the filling into the pastry shells and bake in the preheated oven for 10–15 minutes, until golden brown. Remove from the oven and let cool.

5. Meanwhile, to make the icing, put the confectioners' sugar and milk into a bowl and mix well. Generously coat the cooled tarts with the icing and let set. Decorate with slivered almonds and rose petals.

FROSTED CARROT

Cake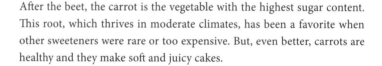

SERVES 16

PREP TIME: 20–25 minutes

COOKING TIME: 40–45 minutes

INGREDIENTS

¾ cup sunflower oil,
plus extra for greasing
¾ cup firmly packed light brown sugar
3 eggs, beaten
1½ cups shredded carrots
½ cup golden raisins
½ cup walnut pieces
grated rind of 1 orange
1⅓ cups all-purpose flour
1 teaspoon baking soda
1¼ teaspoons baking powder
1 teaspoon ground cinnamon
½ teaspoon grated nutmeg
strips of orange zest,
to decorate

frosting
1 cup cream cheese
¾ cup confectioners' sugar
2 teaspoons orange juice

After the beet, the carrot is the vegetable with the highest sugar content. This root, which thrives in moderate climates, has been a favorite when other sweeteners were rare or too expensive. But, even better, carrots are healthy and they make soft and juicy cakes.

1. Preheat the oven to 350 °F. Grease a 9-inch square cake pan and line with parchment paper.

2. Beat together the oil, sugar, and eggs in a large bowl. Stir in the shredded carrots, golden raisins, walnut pieces, and orange rind.

3. Sift together the flour, baking soda, baking powder, cinnamon, and nutmeg into the bowl, then mix evenly into the carrot mixture.

4. Spoon the batter into the prepared pan and bake in the preheated oven for 40–45 minutes, until well risen and firm to the touch.

5. Let cool in the pan for 5 minutes, then turn out onto a wire rack to cool completely.

6. To make the frosting, combine the cheese, sugar, and orange juice in a bowl and beat until smooth. Spread the frosting over the top of the cake and swirl with a spatula.

7. Decorate with strips of orange zest and serve cut into squares.

313

2.

3.

5.

6.

2.

4.

5.

Troika *Cake*

SERVES 8

PREP TIME: 35 minutes

COOKING TIME: 35–40 minutes

This is a Norwegian recipe for rich, dense chocolate cake with raspberry preserves, whipped cream, and marzipan. The name troika means "set of three" in Russia, which reflects the three distinct layers of the cake.

1. Preheat the oven to 350 °F. Line a 12-inch square baking pan with parchment paper, then grease the paper.

2. Mix together the flour, cocoa powder, sugar, baking powder, baking soda, and salt in a large bowl.

3. Add the eggs, vanilla extract, buttermilk, and butter and beat until smooth. Transfer the batter to the prepared pan and bake in the preheated oven for 35–40 minutes, until a toothpick inserted into the center comes out clean. Transfer to a wire rack and let cool completely.

4. Using a large knife, carefully cut the cake in half horizontally. Place one piece on a work surface and spread with the preserves. Whip the cream with the sugar and vanilla extract until it holds stiff peaks. Reserve one-quarter of the cream, then spread the remainder evenly over the preserves. Cover with the second piece of cake and transfer to the refrigerator.

5. Gradually work a few drops of food coloring into the marzipan until it is pale pink in color. Thinly roll it out on a work surface dusted with confectioners' sugar to a 12-inch square. Take the cake out of the refrigerator and spread the remaining cream over the top. Place the marzipan layer on top and press gently. Use a sharp knife to trim any excess. Serve chilled.

INGREDIENTS

2¼ cups all-purpose flour
1⅔ cups unsweetened cocoa powder
1¼ cup granulated sugar
1½ teaspoons baking powder
2½ teaspoons baking soda
½ teaspoon salt
4 eggs
1 teaspoon vanilla extract
⅓ cup buttermilk
*1 stick butter, melted,
plus extra for greasing*

filling and topping
¾ cup raspberry preserves
1 cup heavy cream
2 tablespoons granulated sugar
1 teaspoon vanilla extract
red food coloring
8 ounces marzipan
confectioners' sugar, for dusting

Skoleboller Buns

MAKES 12

PREP TIME: 45 minutes,
plus 1 hour 20 minutes to rise

COOKING TIME: 15–20 minutes

INGREDIENTS

*5 tablespoons butter, melted,
plus extra for greasing*
1¼ cups lukewarm milk
2 teaspoons active dry yeast
¼ cup granulated sugar
½ teaspoon salt
1 teaspoon ground cardamom
4 cups all-purpose flour
*½ cup dry unsweetened coconut,
for sprinkling*

vanilla filling
1 cup milk
2 tablespoons all-purpose flour
*2 tablespoons vanilla sugar (to make your
own, beat 1–2 drops vanilla extract into
sugar)*
2 egg yolks, beaten

icing
¾ cup confectioners' sugar
2 tablespoons lemon juice

The recipe for the Norwegian skoleboller is from the 1950s. At the time people were looking for a simple pastry that schoolchildren could eat in their hands. The flat yeast dough bun gets its special taste from the spice cardamom. It is then filled with vanilla cream and topped with a sugar glaze after baking.

1. Mix together the butter, milk, and yeast in a large bowl. Add the sugar, salt, cardamom, and flour, kneading until a smooth dough forms. Cover with a damp dish towel and let rise for at least 1 hour, until doubled in size.

2. Shape the dough into small balls and use your thumb to make a hollow in the center of each.

3. To make the vanilla filling, put the milk, flour, vanilla sugar, and egg yolks into a saucepan over medium heat, mix to combine, then bring to a boil and cook, stirring continuously, until thickened. Transfer to a bowl and let cool.

4. Meanwhile, preheat the oven to 425 °F. Grease a large baking sheet. Spoon the filling into the hollows in the dough balls. Place the balls on the prepared sheet and bake in the preheated oven for 10–15 minutes until golden brown. Remove from the oven and transfer to a wire rack to cool.

5. Meanwhile, to make the icing, mix together the confectioners' sugar and lemon juice in a small bowl. Coat the buns with the icing, sprinkle with the coconut, and serve.

1.

3.

3.

3.

4.

5.

Sarah Bernhardt Cookies

MAKES 30–35

PREP TIME: 1 hour,
plus 8 hours to cool

COOKING TIME: 15 minutes

These extravagant cookies are named after Sarah Bernhardt (1844–1923), an eccentric French actress absolutely adored by her audiences. One of the first international stars, she performed in Denmark on one of her tours, and the Danes thanked her with this recipe.

1. To make the ganache, put the cream, honey, salt, and vanilla extract into a saucepan. Bring to a boil, then remove from the heat. Add the chocolate and stir with a wooden spoon until melted. Cover with plastic wrap and let cool overnight.

2. Preheat the oven to 325°F. Line two baking sheets with parchment paper. Line a sheet with wax paper.

3. To make the macarons, put the marzipan, sugar, almond extract, and salt into a bowl and mix until well combined. Add the egg whites, one at a time, mixing well after each addition until combined.

4. Put the macaron mixture into a pastry bag fitted with a plain ¼-inch tip and pipe ¾-inch circles on the parchment paper-lined baking sheets. Bake in the preheated oven for 12 minutes.

5. Transfer the macarons to the wax paper-lined baking sheet. Fill a pastry bag with the ganache and pipe a little mound on each macaron. Sandwich pairs of macarons together and chill for about 30 minutes.

6. To make the icing, put the semisweet chocolate into a heatproof bowl set over a saucepan of barely simmering water and heat until melted. Remove from the heat, stir in the oil, and let cool slightly.

7. Remove the macarons from the refrigerator and dip into the glaze. Let cool and set. Finally drizzle melted white chocolate over the semisweet chocolate icing.

8. Store the cookies in the refrigerator and bring to room temperature before serving.

INGREDIENTS

ganache
2 cups heavy cream
3 tablespoons honey
pinch of salt
1 teaspoon vanilla extract
16 ounces semisweet chocolate

almond macarons
9 ounces marzipan paste (available online)
½ cup granulated sugar
1 teaspoon almond extract
½ teaspoon salt
2 egg whites

icing
6 ounces semisweet chocolate, at least 70 percent cocoa solids
2 tablespoons vegetable oil
2 ounces white chocolate, melted

Cinnamon *Swirls*

MAKES 12

PREP TIME: 20 minutes,
plus 1 hour 10 minutes to rise

COOKING TIME: 20–30 minutes

INGREDIENTS

*2 tablespoons butter, cut into small pieces,
plus extra for greasing*
1⅔ cups white bread flour
½ teaspoon salt
2¼ teaspoons active dry yeast
1 egg, lightly beaten
½ cup lukewarm milk
2 tablespoons maple syrup, for glazing

filling
4 tablespoons butter, softened
2 teaspoons ground cinnamon
¼ cup firmly packed light brown sugar
⅓ cup dried currants

These Swedish cinnamon swirls are sold throughout Scandinavia and across the globe. They probably originated between World Wars I and II, as more baking ingredients became available. They are favorites at afternoon coffee parties in Sweden. According to tradition, guests must first eat a filling cinnamon swirl before helping themselves to cakes.

1. Grease a baking sheet and a bowl. Sift the flour and salt into a separate mixing bowl and stir in the yeast. Rub in the chopped butter with your fingertips until the mixture resembles bread crumbs. Add the egg and milk and mix to a dough.

2. Form the dough into a ball, place in the greased bowl, cover, and let stand in a warm place for about 40 minutes, or until doubled in volume. Punch down the dough to knock out the air for 1 minute, then roll out to a 12 x 9-inch rectangle.

3. To make the filling, cream together the butter, cinnamon, and sugar until light and fluffy. Spread the filling over the dough, leaving a 1-inch border. Sprinkle the currants evenly over the top. Roll up the dough from one of the long edges and press down to seal.

4. Preheat the oven to 375°F. Cut the roll into 12 slices and place, cut side down, on the prepared baking sheet. Cover and let stand for 30 minutes.

5. Bake in the preheated oven for 20–30 minutes, or until the swirls are well risen. Brush with maple syrup and let cool slightly before serving.

1.

3.

4.

1.

2.

2.

Seeded Rye
BREAD

MAKES 1 LOAF

PREP TIME: 25 minutes
plus 1–1½ hours to rise

COOKING TIME: 30–35 minutes

Rye is the classic grain used for making bread in northern Europe, where it has been a staple food for centuries and is eaten for most of the meals of the day. Compared with wheat bread, rye bread is darker, has a stronger taste, keeps better, and is much healthier. The rye and wheat bread mixture is seasoned with caraway, also typical of this dark bread.

1. Lightly oil a baking sheet. Mix the rye flour, white flour, salt, caraway seeds, and yeast in a large bowl and make a well in the center. Mix together the butter, honey, and water and pour into the well. Mix with a knife to a soft, sticky dough.

2. Turn out the dough onto a floured work surface and knead for 10 minutes, or until smooth and elastic. Shape into an oval and place on the prepared baking sheet. Slash the top in a diamond pattern, lightly dust with flour, and let stand in a warm place for 1–1½ hours, or until doubled in size.

3. Meanwhile, preheat the oven to 375°F. Bake the loaf in the preheated oven for 30–35 minutes, or until the crust is a rich brown color and the bottom sounds hollow when tapped with your knuckles. Transfer to a wire rack to cool.

INGREDIENTS

*2½ cups rye flour,
plus extra for dusting*
1¾ cups white bread flour
1½ teaspoons salt
1 tablespoon caraway seeds
2¼ teaspoons active dry yeast
2 tablespoons butter, melted
2 tablespoons honey, warmed
1¼ cups lukewarm water
sunflower oil, for oiling

Sweet Treats
from EASTERN EUROPE
& RUSSIA

Eastern European and Russian baking is mainly known for its savory bread and meat pies, but this region also has a flair for delicious, sweet treats, such as the chocolate babka loaf and the vodka coffee cake. Another popular specialty is pierogi, which is a ravioli-like dumpling that is immensely popular in Poland and Russia. These come with different fillings, both sweet as well as savory, and are served either as a main dish or a dessert. A big part of the Eastern European baking tradition dates back to pre-Christian times, when flatbreads and also pancakes were the symbol of the sun, a bountiful harvest, and a happy family.

Bread and salt is a welcome greeting ceremony in many central and eastern European cultures. It is customary to give newcomers bread and salt to wish prosperity and fertility in a settled home. In the nineteenth century, a lot of immigrants brought this tradition to other continents.

Chocolate Babka Loaf

SERVES 8

PREP TIME: 30 minutes, plus 1½ hours to chill and 1 hour to rise

COOKING TIME: 50 minutes

INGREDIENTS

6 egg yolks

1½ sticks butter, melted, plus extra for greasing

1 teaspoon vanilla extract

½ cup granulated sugar

½ teaspoon salt

1 cup milk

5 teaspoons active dry yeast

3¾ cups all-purpose flour, plus extra for dusting

confectioners' sugar, for dusting

chocolate filling

8 ounces semisweet chocolate, at least 70 percent cocoa solids, coarsely chopped

1 tablespoon unsweetened cocoa powder

½ teaspoon ground cinnamon

½ cup granulated sugar

¾ cup coarsely chopped walnuts

This sweet loaf is traditionally baked for Easter in the Christian regions of Eastern Europe. Many Jews living there took the recipe with them when they emigrated to North America and other countries. The Polish and Belarussian word babka means "grandmother," and it is said that the wavy pattern of the dough is reminiscent of her wrinkles.

1. Beat the egg yolks in a bowl, then gradually add the butter and vanilla extract. Add the sugar and salt and stir to combine. Heat the milk in a small saucepan until lukewarm. Add the yeast and stir to dissolve.

2. Sift the flour into a large bowl, then pour in the egg mixture and milk, stirring continuously. Mix until a smooth, elastic dough forms. Transfer to a bowl, cover with plastic wrap, and chill in the refrigerator for 1½ hours.

3. Meanwhile, make the chocolate filling. Put the chocolate, cocoa powder, and cinnamon into a food processor and process until fine crumbs form. Combine the chocolate mixture with the sugar.

4. Grease a 10-inch loaf pan and line a baking sheet with parchment paper. Turn out the dough onto a lightly floured work surface, then roll out to a 10-inch square and place on the prepared sheet. Spread the chocolate mixture evenly on the dough and top with the walnuts, then fold the dough over at two opposite sides of the square and press down. Place in the prepared pan, with the seams at the bottom of the pan, cover with a damp dish towel, and let rise for 1 hour.

5. Meanwhile, preheat the oven to 350 °F. Bake the loaf in the middle of the preheated oven for 40–45 minutes, until golden brown. Remove from the oven, let cool for 10 minutes, then turn out of the pan onto a wire rack and let cool completely. Dust with confectioners' sugar and serve.

2.

4.

4.

1.

5.

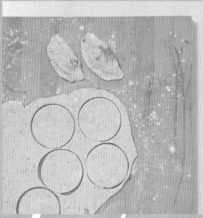

6.

Sweet Pierogi

MAKES 25–30

PREP TIME: 35 minutes,
plus 5 minutes to stand

COOKING TIME: 45–50 minutes

Pierogi are a national dish in Poland. Originally a peasant food, they were later taken up by other parts of society. The dumplings, made from unleavened dumpling dough, are first cooked with the filling and then baked or fried. Either savory or sweet, they can be made in a variety of shapes and flavors and are also found in neighboring countries.

1. Grind the flaxseed in a mortar with a pestle, then add to a small bowl with the water. Beat to combine, then let stand until thick. Sift together the flour and salt into a large bowl. Make a well in the flour and add the oil and the flaxseed mixture. Mix until well combined, then turn out onto a floured work surface and knead until a dough forms.

2. Put the dough into a bowl, cover with a dish towel, and let stand for about 5 minutes.

3. Meanwhile, to make the filling, chop the dried prunes into small pieces. Put them into a saucepan with the water, sugar, and lemon juice and stir until well combined. Add the cinnamon stick and cook over medium heat, stirring frequently, for about 20 minutes, until the water is almost completely absorbed. Remove the cinnamon stick, transfer the filling to a small bowl, and let cool.

4. To make the caramel sauce, mix together the sugar, cream, milk, butter, and salt in a saucepan over medium–low heat. Heat, beating gently, for 5–7 minutes, until thickened. Add the vanilla extract and cook for an additional 1 minute. Remove from the heat and let cool.

5. Roll out the dough on a lightly floured work surface to a thickness of $\frac{1}{8}$ inch, then use a 3-inch round cookie cutter to cut into 25–30 circles, rerolling the trimmings as needed. Put 1–2 tablespoon of filling onto each circle. Fold over the dough and pinch to seal. Meanwhile, bring a large saucepan of water to a boil. Submerge the sealed pierogi, in batches, in the boiling water for 2–3 minutes, until they float. Remove and dry on paper towels.

6. Heat enough oil for deep-frying in a large saucepan to 350–375°F, or until a cube of bread browns in 30 seconds. Add the pierogis, in batches, and deep-fry for 2–3 minutes, until golden brown. Serve hot with the caramel sauce.

INGREDIENTS

1 tablespoon flaxseed
2 tablespoons water
2¼ cups all-purpose flour,
plus extra for dusting
½ teaspoon salt
2 tablespoons oil

filling
2 cups dried prunes
1 cup water
¼ cup granulated sugar
1 tablespoon lemon juice
1 cinnamon stick
vegetable oil, for deep-frying

caramel sauce
1 cup firmly packed light brown sugar
¼ cup heavy cream
¼ cup milk
4 tablespoons butter
pinch of salt
1 tablespoon vanilla extract

Vodka Coffee

CAKE

SERVES 8

PREP TIME: 15 minutes

COOKING TIME: 1 hour

INGREDIENTS

2¼ cups all-purpose flour,
plus extra for dusting

2 teaspoons baking powder

½ teaspoon salt

⅓ cup cornstarch

¼ cup unsweetened cocoa powder

4 tablespoons butter,
plus extra for greasing

1 cup granulated sugar

4 eggs

1 teaspoon vanilla extract

¾ cup milk

½ cup vegetable oil

3 tablespoons vodka

3 tablespoons coffee liqueur

confectioners' sugar and fresh raspberries,
to decorate

icing

2 tablespoons coffee liqueur

3 tablespoons confectioners' sugar

In this cake, as in the drink Russian Coffee, the aromatic coffee has a strong flavor that is beautifully balanced by the sweet and mild vodka. In Poland and Russia, vodka has been traditionally distilled from rye since the fourteenth century and is popular throughout Eastern Europe.

1. Preheat the oven to 350°F. Grease a bundt pan and dust with flour, shaking out any excess.

2. Mix together the flour, baking powder, salt, cornstarch, and cocoa powder in a large bowl. Put the butter and sugar into a separate bowl and beat together, then add the eggs, one at a time, beating after each addition until incorporated. Add the vanilla extract, milk, oil, vodka, and liqueur and mix to combine. Fold in the flour mixture.

3. Pour the batter into the prepared pan and bake in the preheated oven for 1 hour. Let cool in the pan for 5 minutes, then turn out onto a wire rack and let cool completely.

4. To make the icing, mix the liqueur with the sugar and brush onto the top and sides of the cake. Dust with confectioners' sugar, and serve decorated with the raspberries.

2.

3.

4.

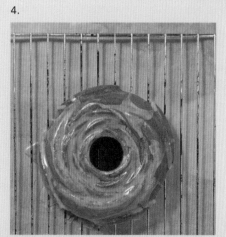

Where Tradition Meets VARIETY

Israel's multicultural society is reflected in its baking culture, which has German, French, Arabic, and Eastern influences, the blend of which accounts for the large variety of flavors. When seeing a rugelach dough for the first time, who would not think of the French croissant? Jerusalem, especially, is considered an important stronghold of the art of baking. Since many immigrants to Israel were no longer able to cook and bake with the foods and fruit typical of their homelands, they were forced to adapt many traditional recipes to suit the local produce.

With so many different people in one country, over the last 50 years Israel's baking culture has evolved a lot in terms of taste and ingredients. The result is a very Mediterranean way of baking, but also with influences from all over the world.

JEWISH HONEY
CAKE

SERVES 8–10

PREP TIME: 25 minutes

COOKING TIME: 45–55 minutes

INGREDIENTS

2¼ cups all-purpose flour

2 teaspoons ground cinnamon

½ teaspoon ground ginger

½ teaspoon ground allspice

1 teaspoon baking powder

½ teaspoon baking soda

2 eggs

¾ cup firmly packed light brown sugar

1 cup honey

½ cup vegetable oil,
plus extra for greasing

½ cup dark rum

¾ cup walnut pieces

This honey cake is the traditional cake for the Jewish New Year, marking a sweet start to the New Year. This cake is also popular throughout the Middle East in a variety of different forms. Honey, as we know it, has existed since Roman times, when it was considered a valuable medicine and was reserved for holidays and special occasions.

1. Preheat the oven to 350°F. Lightly grease a bundt pan. Set aside 1 table-spoon of the flour, then sift together the remaining flour, the cinnamon, ginger, allspice, baking powder, and baking soda into a bowl.

2. Put the eggs and the sugar into a separate bowl and stir to combine. Beat in the honey, oil, and rum. Carefully beat in the flour mixture and mix until the dough is thick and smooth.

3. Toss the walnuts in the reserved flour and stir into the batter. Pour the batter into the prepared pan and bake in the preheated oven for about 45–55 minutes, until a toothpick inserted into the center of the cake comes out clean. Let cool in the pan for about 10 minutes, then remove from the pan and transfer to a wire rack to cool for an additional 30 minutes. Cut into slices and serve.

2.

Hamantaschen

This pastry is an integral part of Jewish culture. It is traditionally eaten for the Feast of Purim and evokes the deliverance of the Jewish people. Haman, the highest Persian official at the time, wanted to kill all the Jews in the country. However, he didn't succeed and was instead executed. The pastry, also called "Haman's ears," alludes to the fact that he lost his ears before the execution.

MAKES 40

PREP TIME: 40 minutes, plus 1½ hours to chill

COOKING TIME: 35–40 minutes

INGREDIENTS

1 cup poppy seeds
½ cup milk
⅓ cup honey
½ cup apricot preserves, chilled

pastry dough

2¼ sticks butter, softened
1⅔ cups granulated sugar
2 teaspoons orange zest
2 tablespoons freshly squeezed orange juice
1 teaspoon vanilla extract
or 1 vanilla bean, scraped
3 eggs
4⅓ cups all-purpose flour,
plus extra for dusting
4 teaspoons baking powder
½ teaspoon salt

1. Line two large baking sheets with nonstick parchment paper. Put the butter and sugar into a bowl and beat with an electric mixer until light and fluffy. Add the orange zest, orange juice, and vanilla extract, then add two of the eggs, one at a time, beating after each addition until incorporated.

2. Sift together the flour, baking powder, and salt into a separate bowl. Gradually add the flour mixture to the butter mixture, mixing on low speed until just combined. Wrap the dough in plastic wrap and chill in the refrigerator for at least 1 hour.

3. Roll out the dough on a floured work surface to a thickness of ⅛ inch. Using a round 3-inch fluted cutter, cut out 40 circles, rerolling the trimmings as necessary, and place on the prepared baking sheets. Chill in the refrigerator for about 30 minutes, until firm. Preheat the oven to 350°F.

4. Meanwhile, grind the poppy seeds in a mortar with a pestle and put them into a medium saucepan. Add the milk and honey and cook over medium–low heat for about 20 minutes, stirring occasionally, until thickened. Remove from the heat and let cool completely.

5. Remove the chilled circles and the apricot preserves from the refrigerator. Pipe either 2 teaspoons of poppy-seed filling or preserves into the center of each circle. Beat the remaining egg with 1 teaspoon of water. Brush the edges of the circles with the egg wash, then fold in the sides to form a triangle. Pinch the dough to enclose the filling.

6. Place the pastries on the prepared sheets and bake in the middle of the preheated oven for 12–15 minutes, until golden. Let cool on the sheets for 5 minutes, then transfer to wire racks to cool completely. The pastries can be stored in an airtight container for up to one week.

Rugelach

MAKES 48

PREP TIME: 45 minutes,
plus 8 hours to chill

COOKING TIME: 20–25 minutes

INGREDIENTS

½ cup granulated sugar
1 teaspoon cinnamon
¾ cup raspberry preserves
1¼ cups finely chopped walnuts
milk, for brushing

pastry dough

2¼ stick softened butter,
plus extra for greasing
1 cup cream cheese
2 cups all-purpose flour,
plus extra for dusting
½ teaspoon salt

The crescent-shape rugelach is of Ashkenazic origin: its Yiddish name and a similar Polish pastry suggest it has Eastern European origins. Although it is a year-round treat in Jewish cuisine, it is most popular in November/December for the Hanukkah festival. It is fun and easy to make and there are many possible variations for the filling.

1. To make the dough, put the butter and cream cheese into a bowl and beat with an electric mixer. Mix together the flour and salt and slowly add to the mixture until a smooth dough forms. It will be sticky. Wrap in plastic wrap and chill in the refrigerator overnight.

2. Preheat the oven to 350°F and lightly grease two or three baking sheets. Divide the dough into three, and return two pieces to the refrigerator.

3. Using a floured rolling pin, roll out the dough on a lightly floured work surface to a ⅛-inch-thick circle with a diameter of about 11 inches.

4. Mix three-quarters of the sugar with the cinnamon in a small bowl. Using a spatula, spread one-third of the preserves on the dough circle, then sprinkle with one-third each of the chopped nuts and cinnamon sugar. Cut each circle into 16 wedges.

5. Starting at the wide end, roll each wedge around the filling, then bend into a crescent shape. Place the crescents on one of the prepared baking sheets, spaced about 1 inch apart, with the ends tucked underneath.

6. Repeat with the remaining two pieces of dough.

7. Brush the crescents with milk and sprinkle with the remaining sugar. Bake in the preheated oven for 20–25 minutes, until golden. Remove from the oven and transfer to a wire rack to cool. The rugelach can be stored in an airtight container for up to three days.

3.

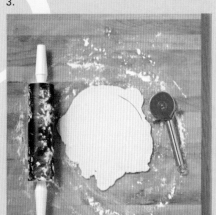

3.

4.

A Taste OF Asia

Asia is not the first region that springs to mind when you think about baking, but this vast area does have a wide and varied baking history. The Chinese are fond of cakes made of rice, such as the nian gao cake, which is eaten during the Chinese New Year and is similar to the Japanese mochi cake. It is served as a sweet or savory cake and is sometimes flavored with cream and cinnamon. So those who think Asian baking is not diverse are very much mistaken, and there is now a growing tradition of varied, interesting baking and in many parts of Asia, Western-style traditional baking with flour is becoming more common.

Wheat flour is used in many Asian cuisines, producing a successful combination of Western-inspired Asian baked goods.

Mango & Rice
TART

SERVES 6

PREP TIME: 1 hour,
plus 4 hours to chill and rest

COOKING TIME: 30 minutes

INGREDIENTS

1 cup jasmine rice
¾ cup sugar
1½ cups water
½ cup coconut milk
1 teaspoon salt
2–3 ripe mangos, peeled and thinly sliced

pastry dough

1⅔ cups all-purpose flour, plus extra for dusting
⅓ cup granulated sugar
1 teaspoon vanilla extract
2 egg yolks
1 stick butter, diced, plus extra for greasing
2 tablespoons water

At home in the tropical rain forests, the mango tree can grow to be more than 130 feet high and its fruits can weigh up to 4½ pounds. The fruit has a unique and sweet aromatic fragrance, which is why the Hindus have been offering it to the gods for thousands of years. In Thailand, mango with sweet rice and coconut is a popular dessert. Here, we offer it as a tart inspired by the tropics.

1. To make the dough, sift together the flour and sugar into a large bowl and add the vanilla extract and the egg yolks. Add the butter and water and knead until a dough forms. Turn out the dough onto a lightly floured work surface and knead until smooth. Wrap in plastic wrap and chill in the refrigerator for 1 hour.

2. Preheat the oven to 350°F. Grease a 10½-inch round, fluted tart pan. Roll out the dough on a lightly floured work surface and ease it into the tart pan. Line with parchment paper, fill with pie weights or dried beans and bake in the preheated oven for 12 minutes. Take out of the oven, remove the paper and weights, and return to the oven for an additional 10 minutes. Remove from the oven and let cool.

3. Meanwhile, place the rice in a saucepan of boiling water and cook for 10–12 minutes or according to package directions, until soft. Drain the rice thoroughly and set aside, cover, and keep warm. Put the sugar and water into a saucepan and heat until a syrup forms. Pour the syrup into a baking pan and stir in the coconut milk and salt. Add the hot rice to the coconut mixture—this will cause the mixture to become quite liquid. Let the rice mixture stand in the pan for about 3 hours to absorb the coconut milk.

4. Pour the rice mixture into the pastry shell and spread evenly. Arrange the sliced mangos decoratively on top of the tart and chill in the refrigerator until ready to serve.

2.

3.

4.

2.

2.

3.

Fortune

COOKIES

MAKES 20

PREP TIME: 10 minutes

COOKING TIME: 10–15 minutes

Traditionally, these crunchy, sweet fortune cookies contain a slip of paper with an inspirational phrase or prophecy inside. Their origins lie in Japan, where a similar dough was mentioned in records there from the nineteenth century. Before World War I, Japanese caterers on the American West Coast gave them away to their guests; however, they became more popular in Chinese-American restaurants.

INGREDIENTS

2 egg whites
½ teaspoon vanilla extract or 1 vanilla bean, scraped
½ teaspoon almond extract
3 tablespoons vegetable oil
1 cup all-purpose flour
1½ teaspoons cornstarch
pinch of salt
⅔ cup granulated sugar
3 teaspoon water

1. Write down fortunes or sayings on small strips of paper. Preheat the oven to 350 °F and line a large baking sheet with parchment paper.

2. Mix together all the ingredients in a large bowl. Using a wooden spoon, drop 20 mounds of batter onto the prepared baking sheet, spaced well apart to allow room for the cookies to spread. Bake in the preheated oven for 10–15 minutes.

3. As soon as you remove the cookies from the oven, place a paper strip in the center of each one, then fold the cookie over the handle of a wooden spoon. Place each folded cookie on the rim of a bowl and press the edges together on each side of the bowl to make the traditional fold. Transfer to a wire rack and let cool.

ANOTHER WORLD
of *Baking*

When people think of classic baking, delicacies from France or Italy spring to mind, with Asian baking being less well known. This makes the variety of Asian recipes more surprising, though many of them have been developed in only the last 100 years.

Naan has a plain taste that makes it a great accompaniment to spicy food, yogurt, and tasty dips. It is a surprising fact that this variety of bread was developed in Turkey, where it is consumed in the same way.

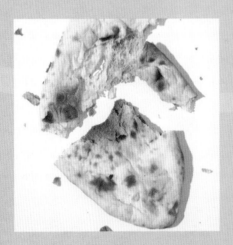

Although moon cakes and fortune cookies appear in Chinese records dating back to the thirteenth and fourteenth centuries, in a food culture dominated by rice dishes, cakes and bread made from grain play a more subordinate role. For this reason, a ceremonial meal without rice cakes in all their various shapes and sizes and in all possible combinations, such as with fruit, cannot be imagined. Their color and exact composition are attuned to the Yin and Yang in order to achieve balance. The composition also depends on the region and the festival. The idea of desserts and cakes in the Western sense evolved much later. Instead, soup was often served as the final course in many southeast Asian countries—the idea being to fill the last remaining space in the stomach. Although bread made with flour does exist from northern China to Beijing, it is also a more expensive food. In Thailand, Laos, and Vietnam, wheat breads are baked in steam ovens. The flatbreads are ready in 20 minutes and are spread with ground meat and baked vegetables. The most popular baked goods in China and Japan are a Western import: French croissants are the epitome of a luxury food.

In other parts of Asia the situation is different. In South Asia (India, Pakistan, Bangladesh) and Central Asia (Afghanistan, Uzbekistan, Tajikistan), as well as in the Near East (Iran, Kurdistan), the baking culture is mainly determined by a naan type of bread. It is usually eaten as an accompaniment to hot food. Naan has a flat, pitalike shape and is elongated prior to baking. The inner part is flat while the outer edge is a little thicker. It resembles a pizza crust. Unlike other Indian breads, naan is made from leavened dough, either by adding yogurt or yeast and also baking powder. The basic ingredients were originally millet and yeast, but nowadays naan is often made with wheat flour. Traditionally, bread is baked over an open fire. This natural baking method, which calls for a great deal of care, is what gives it its characteristic flavor. The word "naan" has both Persian and Afghan roots. In both languages, it simply means "bread."

Ginger Tartlets

MAKES 8

PREP TIME: 25 minutes

COOKING TIME: 15 minutes

INGREDIENTS

28 gingersnaps (about 7 ounces)
⅓ cup blanched almonds
1 stick butter, melted
1¼ cups heavy cream
½ cup cream cheese
¼ cup freshly squeezed orange juice
2 tablespoons confectioners' sugar
1 teaspoon finely grated orange zest
fresh raspberries, to decorate

Ginger is originally from the Asian tropics and is used both as a spice and a medicine. It has a pleasing, aromatic smell and a spicy, pungent flavor. Ginger was often used to replace black pepper, which was scarce in the Middle Ages, but it also lends a special fragrance to sweet treats. Tarts spiced with ginger are widespread in the English-speaking world.

1. Preheat the oven to 325 °F. Put the gingersnap cookies and almonds into a food processor and process until they resemble coarse crumbs.

2. Transfer to a bowl, add the butter, and stir until well combined. Divide the mixture among eight individual 3-inch fluted molds or pans, pressing the crumbs against the bottom and sides. Place the molds on a baking sheet and bake in the preheated oven for 15 minutes. Let cool slightly, then carefully remove the tart shells from the molds and let cool completely.

3. Put the cream, cream cheese, orange juice, confectioners' sugar, and orange zest into a large bowl and mix to combine. Gently beat until smooth. Spoon the filling into the tart shells, decorate with fresh raspberries, and serve.

1.

2.

1.

3.

4.

Chocolate
Samosas

MAKES 16

PREP TIME: 1 hour,
plus 1 hour to chill

COOKING TIME: 10–15 minutes

For centuries, samosas have been a popular filled dough in South Asia, Arabia, and East Africa. The folded triangles can be filled with a variety of ingredients, typically cooked leftovers, and then deep fried. Here, they've been turned into a delightful dessert.

1. To make the filling, put the cream into a small saucepan and bring to a boil over medium heat. Put the chocolate chips into a bowl, pour the boiling cream over them, and stir until melted. Chill in the refrigerator for 1 hour.

2. Sift the flour into a mixing bowl, add the ghee, and rub in. If the dough is too stiff, gradually add a little cold water. Keep covered with a damp cloth.

3. Divide the dough into 16 equal pieces and roll out each piece into a rectangle. Put 1 teaspoon of the filling into each rectangle and fold over the dough to make a triangle shape.

4. Heat enough oil for deep-frying in a large saucepan to 350–375°F, or until a cube of bread browns in 30 seconds. Add the samosas, in batches if necessary, and cook over medium heat until crisp and golden. Do not overcrowd the pan, and be careful that the oil is brought back to the correct temperature between each batch. Drain on paper towels and let cool for 5 minutes. Serve warm.

INGREDIENTS

filling
1 cup heavy cream
1¼ cups semisweet chocolate chips

2 cups all-purpose flour
½ cup ghee (clarified butter)
or vegetable oil

oil, for deep-frying

Gulab Jamun

SYRUP
DUMPLINGS

MAKES 12–14

PREP TIME: 25 minutes,
plus 2 hours to soak

COOKING TIME: 5 minutes

INGREDIENTS

4 cups water
2¼ cups granulated sugar
1 tablespoon ground cardamom
2 tablespoons rose water
4 cups instant dry milk
1½ cups all-purpose flour
1½ teaspoons baking powder
1 cup heavy cream
oil, for oiling and deep-frying

Gulab Jamun is a classic Indian dessert served at large celebrations. Little balls of milk dough are deep fried and then soaked in flavored syrup. The name goes back to the Persian word gulab, for "rose," and it probably refers to the shape of the Jambul berries.

1. Put the water and sugar into a saucepan, bring to a boil, and boil until the sugar is dissolved. Remove from the heat and add the cardamon and rose water. Mix well and set aside.

2. Put the instant milk, flour and baking powder into a bowl and mix together well. Gradually add the cream, a little at a time, kneading the mixture until you have a medium–soft dough that is not sticky. Do not add all the cream unless it is needed to achieve the correct consistency.

3. Divide the dough into walnut-size balls and roll between lightly oiled hands until smooth. Meanwhile, heat enough oil for deep-frying in a large saucepan to 350–375 °F, or until a cube of bread browns in 30 seconds. Add the dumplings, in batches, and fry, stirring frequently to brown all over.

4. Remove the cooked dumplings from the oil, using a slotted spoon, and place in the sugar syrup. Let the dumplings soak in the syrup for at least 2 hours before serving.

1.

2.

3.

1.

2.

3.

Hokkaido Milk Loaf

SERVES 6–8

PREP TIME: 25 minutes, plus about 2 hours to rise

COOKING TIME: 45 minutes

Fresh and instant dry milk from the Japanese island of Hokkaido were originally used for this bread, giving it its name. In Japan, Korea, and other East Asian countries it is a staple food. However, it is more than just a simple soft and sweet white bread—its special texture and fluffiness are legendary.

1. Lightly oil a large bowl. Put all the ingredients into a separate large bowl and mix, using the dough hook of an electric mixer until a walnut-size piece of dough can be rolled out thinly enough for light to pass through it.

2. Place the dough in the prepared bowl, cover with oiled plastic wrap, and let stand for about 1 hour, until doubled in size. Punch down the dough to knock out the air, then divide it into three equal pieces, shape each piece into a ball, and let rise for an additional 20 minutes. Preheat the oven to 350 °F.

3. Flatten the dough and roll up each portion like a jelly roll. Place the rolls side by side in an 8½-inch loaf pan and let rise until the dough fills the pan four-fifths full. Bake in the preheated oven for 45 minutes. Remove from the oven and let cool on a wire rack. Cut into slices and serve.

INGREDIENTS

oil, for oiling
2¼ cups white white flour
3 tablespoons all-purpose flour
1¼ teaspoons active dry yeast
3 tablespoons instant dry milk
¼ cup granulated sugar
1 teaspoon salt
½ egg, beaten
¾ cup milk
⅓ cup heavy cream

Moon Cakes

MAKES 15–20

PREP TIME: 20–30 minutes, plus overnight chilling

COOKING TIME: 30 minutes

INGREDIENTS

5¼ cups all-purpose flour
1 cup instant dry milk
1 tablespoon baking powder
1 teaspoon salt
4 eggs
1¼ cups granulated sugar
1 teaspoon vanilla extract
or 1 vanilla bean, scraped
1 stick butter, melted
2 tablespoons water, for glazing

filling
⅔ cup apricot preserves
⅔ cup chopped dried dates
¾ cup dry unsweetened coconut
½ cup raisins

In ancient times, Chinese emperors used to make offerings to the moon in fall. This tradition evolved into the Mid-Fall Festival, which is still celebrated in China today, and the moon cakes as a delicacy definitely form part of it. Formerly, the pastries were also used to pass on secret information. Like a puzzle, the filling of the cakes would reveal a message when correctly put together.

1. Mix together the flour, instant milk, baking powder, and salt in a bowl. Put three of the eggs, the sugar, vanilla extract, and butter into a separate bowl and beat with an electric mixer for about 5 minutes, until creamy. Stir in the dry ingredients and knead until a smooth dough forms. Wrap in plastic wrap and chill in the refrigerator overnight.

2. To make the filling, mix together the preserves, dates, coconut, and raisins.

3. Preheat the oven to 375 °F. Line two baking sheets with parchment paper.

4. Remove the dough from the refrigerator and divide into 15–20 pieces. Shape each piece into a circle and place 1 tablespoon of the filling in the center of each circle. Fold the edges over the filling and press together.

5. Dust a 2-inch moon cake press or round cutter with flour. Take the filled balls of dough and, one at a time, press them in the moon cake press, then remove. Alternatively, use the cutter to cut out circles.

6. Lightly beat the remaining egg with the water and brush over the moon cakes, then place them on the prepared baking sheets. Bake in the preheated oven for 30 minutes, or until the cakes are golden brown.

4.

5.

MOONLIGHT

Romance

It's not exactly simple, but in China August used to be regarded as the second month of fall, and every year the Moon Festival falls on the 15th day of the eighth month of the lunar calendar.

The production of moon cakes varies much from region to region. However, they are always nicely decorated and sold in beautiful cake boxes that are even more important than the cake itself.

Are you still not sure when it takes place? It doesn't matter! The main thing to note is that in mid to late September, the Moon Festival turns daily life in China upside down. Whoever can't calculate the date just has to wait until the cities are decorated with countless colorful paper lanterns in every conceivable shape and size. They are everywhere—in front of every house, in every street, in every store. Small gifts are bought, especially the 4-inch moon cakes that have all kinds of different decoration and and come in various kinds of packaging. A Moon Festival definitely wouldn't be the same without moon cakes.

There are different theories about how the custom originated. One of them suggests that moon cakes were originally used to convey secret messages from house to house by hiding little notes in the filling. Or the fillings were like a puzzle that, when put together, revealed a secret message. They were, so it would seem, a forerunner of today's fortune cookies. Another theory claims that the people wanted to express their respect for Chang'e, the mystery woman on the moon, by giving away exquisitely prepared desserts. In any case, the Moon Festival can be compared with harvest festivals and is celebrated with sumptuous foods. The status of the cake can be compared with goose or turkey for Christmas or maybe chocolate for Valentine's Day. Its decisive, leading role makes it simply indispensable during the festival. The sheer multitude of flavors and exquisite packaging of the moon cake definitely make it a cultural highlight. Usually they are filled with lotus paste and curdled egg yolks, but there are also many sweet versions based on all kinds of recipes. The surfaces of the cakes are decorated with motifs symbolizing heaven. The moon cake must be round, because this signifies the reunion of lovers for the Chinese. The moon brings people closer together emotionally, because—no matter where they are in the world—they all look up at its silvery light in the same sky.

1.

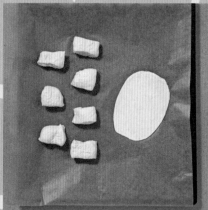

2.

3.

Naan

Naan comes from a Persian word meaning (flat) "bread." For at least two centuries, it has been the typical bread in the western and southern parts of Asia. It is traditionally baked in a stone oven. It is round, soft, and puffs up making light bubbles in the dough. It is always served hot and can be spread with butter or dipped in a sauce.

1. Sift together the flour and salt into a mixing bowl. Gradually add the yogurt and mix with your hands. Gradually add enough water to make a soft, slightly sticky dough. Cover the bowl and let stand at room temperature for 1 hour.

2. Divide the dough into eight equal pieces, shape each piece into a ball, then flatten the balls into 8-inch ovals.

3. Preheat the broiler to high. Put the butter and garlic into a small saucepan and heat over low heat. Stir in the cilantro and keep warm.

4. Place the bread under the preheated broiler and cook for 8–10 minutes, turning halfway through, or until puffed up and there are little brown spots on the surface. Remove from the heat, brush with the butter mixture, and serve immediately.

MAKES 8

PREP TIME: 25 minutes, plus 1 hour to stand

COOKING TIME: 8–10 minutes

INGREDIENTS

2 cups all-purpose flour
2½ teaspoons salt
3 tablespoons plain yogurt
½ cup lukewarm water
3 tablespoons butter
1 garlic clove, peeled and crushed
2 tablespoons chopped fresh cilantro

Baking IN THE Antipodes

The history of the British colonization of Australia began with the founding of New South Wales in 1788. Sheep farming was essentially the main source of nourishment for the settlers, who would often eat lamb for each meal every day of the week. The staple diet of the farm workers consisted of mutton, tea, and damper, a kind of bread made of flour, salt, and water, which was baked directly in the embers of an open fire. The Honorable Robert Dundas Murray made the following remark in his work *A Summer at Port Philip* (published in 1843): "You're eating mutton and damper today—tomorrow they'll be serving mutton and damper as well, and for the rest of the year your meal will consist of good old mutton—be it boiled, grilled, or stewed." The "ritual" of afternoon tea was adopted from England, whereby tea would be served alongside the classic scones. In Australia, scones and tea would typically also include pumpkin puree instead of, or as well as, jam.

In a country once governed by Great Britain, it's no wonder that scones, cookies, cakes, and bread feature highly in Australia's baking repertoire.

Hokey Pokey
COOKIES

MAKES 15–20

PREP TIME: 25 minutes, plus time to cool

COOKING TIME: 20–25 minutes

The cookie dough is incredibly quick and easy to make and it smells delicious as it bakes in the oven. The name "hokey pokey" comes from a vanilla and caramel-flavored ice cream with the same name. It was also used in the nineteenth century by Italian street vendors selling ice cream on the streets of Great Britain and the United States.

1. Preheat the oven to 350°F. Line a large baking sheet with parchment paper. Put the butter, sugar, light corn syrup, and milk into a saucepan and heat, stirring continuously, until the butter is melted and the mixture is just below boiling point. Remove from the heat and let cool to lukewarm.

2. Sift together the flour and baking soda into a bowl, add to the cooled mixture, and stir well.

3. Roll heaping tablespoons of the dough into balls. Place the balls on the prepared sheet, then flatten them with a floured fork to make 3-inch circles.

4. Bake in the preheated oven for 15–20 minutes, or until golden brown. Let cool on the baking sheet for 1–2 minutes, then carefully transfer to a wire rack to cool completely.

5. Dip the cookies halfway vertically into the melted chocolate and sprinkle the chocolate with the chopped nuts. Transfer to wax paper to set.

INGREDIENTS

1 stick butter

½ cup granulated sugar

1 tablespoon light corn syrup

1 tablespoon milk

1⅓ cups all-purpose flour, plus extra for flouring

1 teaspoon baking soda

8 ounces white chocolate, melted

½ cup finely chopped walnuts

1.

2.

3.

Anzac
COOKIES

MAKES 18–20

PREP TIME: 20 minutes

COOKING TIME: 20–25 minutes

INGREDIENTS

1 cup rolled oats
1¼ cups all-purpose flour
¾ cup firmly packed light brown sugar
1¼ cups dry unsweetened coconut
1 stick butter
2 tablespoons light corn syrup
¾ teaspoon baking soda
3 tablespoons water
halved, melted caramels and small chocolate disks, to decorate

This coarse oatmeal cookie is an integral part of the Australian Army tradition, with its name dating back to the Australian and New Zealand Army Corps (ANZAC). During World War I, the wives and mothers of soldiers would send these cookies to their loved ones who were fighting in Europe at the time. These treats from home survived the long journey.

1. Preheat the oven to 300 °F. Line a baking sheet with parchment paper. Mix together the rolled oats, flour, sugar, and coconut in a large bowl.

2. Melt the butter and light corn syrup in a saucepan over low heat. Mix the baking soda with the water and stir into the butter mixture. Remove the pan from the heat, add the contents to the oat mixture, and mix until a moist, firm batter forms.

3. Place tablespoons of the batter onto the prepared sheet, lightly pressing each mound with the back of the spoon until the cookies are about 2 inches in diameter.

4. Bake in the preheated oven for about 12–15 minutes, until golden brown. Let cool on the baking sheet for 1–2 minutes, then carefully transfer to a wire rack to cool completely.

5. To decorate, place half a melted caramel on each cookie and top with a chocolate disk. The cookies can be stored in an airtight container for up to one week.

2.

2.

Lamingtons

MAKES 8–10

PREP TIME: 40 minutes,
plus at least 8 hours to chill

COOKING TIME: 35–45 minutes

INGREDIENTS

2¼ cups all-purpose flour,
plus extra for dusting

3 teaspoon baking powder

¼ teaspoon salt

1¼ sticks butter,
plus extra for greasing

¾ cup granulated sugar

1 vanilla bean, scraped, or 1 teaspoon
vanilla extract

2 eggs

½ cup milk

topping

1⅔ cups confectioners' sugar

⅓ cup unsweetened cocoa powder

½ cup milk

2 tablespoons butter

4 cups dry unsweetened coconut

If you haven't eaten Lamingtons during your childhood, you didn't grow up in Australia. They were first served by the Scottish nobleman Lord Lamington, Governor of Queensland from 1896 to 1901.

1. Preheat the oven to 350 °F. Lightly grease an 8 x 12-inch rectangular cake pan and dust it with flour. Mix together the flour, baking powder, and salt in a large bowl.

2. Put the butter, sugar, and vanilla seeds or vanilla extract into a separate bowl and beat until pale and fluffy. Gradually add the eggs, flour mixture, and milk, making alternate additions and stirring carefully to combine.

3. Spread the batter evenly into the prepared pan and bake in the preheated oven for 30–40 minutes, until a toothpick inserted into the center of the cake comes out clean.

4. Remove from the oven, transfer to a wire rack, and let cool for 5 minutes. Cut the cake into 8–10 rectangles and chill in the refrigerator overnight.

5. To make an icing, mix together the confectioners' sugar and cocoa powder in a bowl. Heat the milk in a saucepan, then add the butter and stir until melted. Pour the warm liquid into the sugar mixture, stirring well until thickened but still runny.

6. Using a fork, dip the cake rectangles in the icing to cover them completely, then place them on a wire rack set over a piece of parchment paper. Put the coconut into a shallow bowl, then add the cakes, one at a time, and turn in the coconut until completely covered. The cakes can be kept in an airtight container for up to one week.

2.

2.

6.

Boston BUN

Traditionally, this recipe makes use of leftover, lightly seasoned mashed potatoes. Raisins and a thick layer of frosting and dry unsweetened coconut are added to this modern version of the cake, which is made in both Australia and New Zealand.

1. Preheat the oven to 350°F. Lightly grease an 8-inch round cake pan. Make sure the potatoes are cold and smooth—push them through a strainer, if necessary. Put the potatoes and sugar into a large bowl and beat together. Add the raisins and beat the mixture until smooth.

2. Sift together the flour, baking powder, and cinnamon into a separate bowl, then add to the potato mixture alternately with the milk.

3. Transfer the batter to the prepared pan, using a spatula to spread it evenly, and bake in the preheated oven for 40–50 minutes. Remove from the oven and transfer to a wire rack to cool in the pan.

4. To make the frosting, mix together the sugar, lemon juice, butter, and coconut. Use a spoon to press the mixture through a strainer, then spread it over the top of the cake in a thick layer. Carefully remove the cake from the pan, cut into slices, and serve.

SERVES 8

PREP TIME: 20 minutes

COOKING TIME: 40–50 minutes

INGREDIENTS

½ cup mashed potatoes
1 cup plus 2 tablespoons granulated sugar
1 cup raisins
2 cups all-purpose flour
1 tablespoon baking powder
1 teaspoon ground cinnamon
1 cup milk

frosting
1⅓ cups confectioners' sugar
2 teaspoons lemon juice
2 tablespoons butter, melted, plus extra for greasing
1 tablespoon dry unsweetened coconut

1.

3.

Coffee
SCROLLS

MAKES 12–15

PREP TIME: 40 minutes,
plus 1 hour to rise

COOKING TIME: 25 minutes

INGREDIENTS

2 cups milk, plus extra for brushing
½ cup vegetable oil
½ cup granulated sugar
2¼ teaspoons active dry yeast
3⅔ cups all-purpose flour,
plus extra for dusting
1 teaspoon baking powder
1 teaspoon baking soda
½ teaspoon salt
6 tablespoons butter
½ cup firmly packed light brown sugar
½ cup golden raisins
ground cinnamon, for sprinkling

icing

¾ cup confectioners' sugar, sifted
1 teaspoon vanilla extract
2–3 tablespoons milk, plus extra if needed
2–3 teaspoons espresso coffee
pinch of salt

These cinnamon rolls are similar to the English Chelsea bun, but with the addition of a coffee-flavored icing, which prevents them from tasting too sweet. They are a popular breakfast food in Australia—especially for late weekend breakfasts when enjoyed with a cup of strong coffee.

1. Put the milk and oil into a large saucepan with the granulated sugar and heat over medium heat until hot but not boiling. Remove from the heat and let cool until lukewarm. Add the yeast and stir to dissolve. Add the flour and mix well. Cover with plastic wrap and let rise for 1 hour at room temperature.

2. Preheat the oven to 350°F and line a baking sheet with some parchment paper. Add the baking powder, baking soda, and salt to the flour mixture and mix to combine.

3. Turn out the dough onto a work surface dusted with flour and roll out to a 28 x 12-inch rectangle. Spread the butter, brown sugar, golden raisins, and cinnamon evenly over the dough. Roll up widthwise and brush the ends with a little milk to seal them.

4. Using a sharp knife, cut the roll into ¾-inch-thick slices and place on the baking sheet, leaving enough space between the slices to allow for spreading. Bake in the middle of the preheated oven for about 20 minutes.

5. Meanwhile, prepare the icing. Mix together all the ingredients in a bowl. The glaze should remain fluid. If it's too thick, add a little milk. Spread the warm rolls with the icing and serve immediately.

1.

3.

4.

Peach Melba Meringue

Auguste Escoffier, the chef at London's Savoy Hotel, created a new dessert to celebrate the 1892 premiere of Lohengrin at Covent Garden. The combination of a peach and two scoops of vanilla ice cream drizzled with raspberry sauce was intended to represent the pose held by the swan at the end of the first act. The Australian opera singer Nellie Melba loved this dessert and it was soon referred to as Peach Melba. Here, it is used as a filling for a meringue roll.

1. Preheat the oven to 300°F. Brush a 14 x 10-inch jelly roll pan with oil and line with wax paper.

2. To make the raspberry coulis, process the raspberries and confectioners' sugar to a puree. Press through a strainer into a bowl and reserve.

3. To make the meringue, sift the cornstarch into a bowl and stir in the sugar. In a separate, grease-free bowl, beat the egg whites until they hold stiff peaks, then beat in the vinegar. Gradually beat in the cornstarch and sugar mixture until stiff and glossy.

4. Spread the mixture evenly in the prepared pan, leaving a ½-inch border. Bake in the center of the preheated oven for 20 minutes, then reduce the heat to 225°F and cook for an additional 25–30 minutes, or until puffed up. Remove from the oven. Let cool for 15 minutes. Turn out onto a sheet of parchment paper and carefully remove the wax paper from the meringue.

5. To make the filling, put the peaches in a bowl with the raspberries. Add 2 tablespoons of the coulis and mix. In a separate bowl, beat together the crème fraîche and cream until thick. Spread over the meringue. Sprinkle the fruit over the cream, leaving a 1¼-inch border at one short edge. Using the parchment paper, lift and roll the meringue, starting at the short edge without the border and finishing with the seam underneath. Transfer to a plate and serve with the coulis.

SERVES 8

PREP TIME: 25 minutes, plus 15 minutes to cool

COOKING TIME: 50 minutes

INGREDIENTS

sunflower oil, for brushing

raspberry coulis
3 cups fresh raspberries
1 cup confectioners' sugar

meringue
2 teaspoon cornstarch
1½ cups superfine sugar
5 extra-large egg whites
1 teaspoon cider vinegar

filling
3 peaches, peeled, pitted, and chopped
2 cups fresh raspberries
1 cup crème fraîche or sour cream
⅔ cup heavy cream

1.

2.

3.

Damper Bread

The damper is a classic bread made by Australian cattlemen, who would bake a few, long-lasting ingredients in the glow of the campfire when they were in the outback alone for weeks on end. As the temperature of the coals tended to vary, the men would knock on the thick bread to check when it was ready. If the bread made a hollow sound, it was ready to eat. Different flavors can be created by adding Parmesan cheese, olives, or dried fruit.

1. Preheat the oven to 400°F. Line a baking sheet with parchment paper. Sift together the flour and salt into a large bowl. Use your fingertips to rub the butter into the flour until the mixture resembles fine bread crumbs.

2. Turn out onto a floured work surface. Add the water, cutting in with a knife until the mixture comes together. Knead gently until smooth.

3. Shape into a 7-inch circle and place on the prepared sheet. Use a sharp knife that has been dipped in flour to mark eight wedges on top. Sprinkle with the poppy seeds and bake in the preheated oven for 30 minutes, or until the damper is cooked through and sounds hollow when tapped on the bottom. Transfer to a wire rack for 5 minutes to cool. Serve warm or at room temperature.

SERVES 8

PREP TIME: 20 minutes

COOKING TIME: 30 minutes

INGREDIENTS

3⅔ cups all-purpose flour, plus extra for dusting

pinch of salt

6 tablespoons butter

¾ cup water, plus extra if needed

1⅓ cups poppy seeds

Louise *Cake*

SERVES 6–8

PREP TIME: 30 minutes

COOKING TIME: 25–30 minutes

INGREDIENTS

1¼ sticks butter, at room temperature, plus extra for greasing

¾ cup superfine sugar

3 egg yolks, at room temperature

2 teaspoons vanilla extract or 2 vanilla beans, scraped

2 cups all-purpose flour

2 teaspoons baking powder

¾ cup raspberry preserves

coconut meringue topping

3 egg whites

pinch of salt

⅓ cup superfine sugar

1 cup dry unsweetened coconut

1 vanilla bean, scraped, or 1 teaspoon vanilla extract

The Louise Cake has been a popular dessert in New Zealand for a long time. A thin layer of sponge cake is topped with raspberry preserves and coconut meringue and then baked. The charming trio goes perfectly with a cup of tea or coffee.

1. Preheat the oven to 350°F. Lightly grease an 8-inch round springform cake pan. Put the butter and sugar into a large bowl and beat until fluffy. Add the egg yolks and beat until incorporated. Add the vanilla extract, then fold in the flour and baking powder. The batter should be crumbly in texture.

2. Spread the batter evenly in the prepared pan and bake in the preheated oven for 10–15 minutes, until golden.

3. Remove from the oven and use a spatula to spread the preserves over the entire surface of the cake.

4. Meanwhile, to make the topping, put the egg whites into a bowl with the salt and beat until they hold soft peaks. Using a wooden spoon, carefully fold in the sugar and coconut. Add the vanilla seeds or vanilla extract and lightly stir to incorporate. Use a spatula to spread the meringue over the preserves.

5. Bake in the oven for an additional 10–15 minutes, until the meringue is light golden brown. Make sure that the meringue doesn't burn. Remove the cake from the oven and let cool in the pan for 10 minutes.

6. Unclip and remove the springform, leaving the cake on the bottom of the pan, then transfer to a wire rack to cool completely. Transfer the cake to a plate, cut into slices, and serve.

2.

3.

4.

INDEX

INDEX

In this beautifully illustrated book, American pastry chef Edward Gee explains the techniques that produce perfect results every time, whether baking small or family cakes, breads, cookies, brownies, macarons, or buns. Since Edward was a small boy of eight, he has loved baking for his family and he has gone on to develop a passion for creating sweet treats for all occasions. Many years later—as an Executive Pastry Chef in big luxury hotels like the Buena Vista Palace, The Swan and Dolphin Hotel, or the Waldorf Astoria—he has now realized his dream to write down his favorite recipes for others to bake and enjoy too. With a baking teacher's precision and a cook's passion, Edward Gee brings the baking world to you — "With easy step-by-step instructions, I can ensure you're always on the right track".

BAKE is the result of an international collaboration between the renowned worldwide publisher Parragon and 99pages, an innovative publishing team based in Europe. Both partners have created a beautiful design with stunning photography, featuring 180 famous baking recipes from all over the world including the USA, Europe, Latin America, Asia, Australasia, and Africa. All of the recipes provide a background into international baking traditions, while also giving practical advice to develop the reader's baking skills. And the cakes, cookies, breads, and buns in this book have two things in common—they look beautiful and taste fantastic.

Books produced by 99pages regularly cause sensations at international cookbook competitions and are enthusiastically received by critics. Edouard Cointreau, President of the Gourmand World Cookbook Awards, says "99pages are one of the greatest surprises on the international cookbook market."

99PAGES

PICTURE ACKNOWLEDGMENTS

The publisher would like to thank the following for permission to reproduce copyright material on the following pages: page 10: Woman grinding corn to make unleavened bread © Richard Hook/Getty Images; page 10: Barley / corn, on white background, cut out © 2010 Creative Crop (Digital Vision)/Getty Images; page 11: Detail of a Harvest Scene. From the tomb of Sennedjem. Mural painting, 19th Dynasty. Necropolis of Deir el-Medina on the West Bank at Luxor, Egypt © Leemage (Universal Images Group)/Getty Images; page 11: Woman with a shovel, 1497 © SSPL/Getty Images; page 13: German chemist Justus Liebig, created Baron von Liebig, (1803 - 1873). Original Artwork: Engraving by J B Hunt after a painting by Trantschold. © Hulton Archive/Getty Images; page 13: Advertisement for Royal Baking Powder by the Royal Baking Powder Company in New York, New York, 1888. © Jay Paull (Archive Photos)/Getty Images; page 14: Political map © Sylvain Sonnet (Photographer's Choice RF)/Getty Images; page 15: American Flag © Jose Luis Pelaez (The Image Bank)/Getty Images; page 15: USA, California, Route 66, Barstow, Route 66 Motel; © Alan Copson (AWL Images)/Getty Images; page 15: Autumn High Resolution Isolated Dry Maple Leaf © Miroslav Boskov (E+)/Getty Images; page 15: The Chrysler Building New York City © 2009 Matthew Mawson (Flickr Select)/Getty Images; page 40: Pink cup cake with cherry on the top on white background, cut out © Creative Crop (Digital Vision)/Getty Images; page 41: Large and small red white and blue cupcakes arranged as an American Flag ©Thatcher Keats (Photonica)/Getty Images; page 41: Hands icing cupcake on table © Line Klein(Cultura)/Getty Images; page 62: Bagel pieces © C Squared Studios (Photodisc)/Getty Images; page 63: Baker taking bagels out of oven in kitchen of bakery, portrait © Mitch Tobias (The Image Bank)/Getty Images; page 63: Neon sign advertising seafood specialties and bagels at delicatessen. © Dennis K. Johnson (Lonely Planet Images)/Getty Images; page 74: Political map © Sylvain Sonnet (Photographer's Choice RF)/Getty Images; page 75: Smashed donkey pinata on floor with candy © Jeffrey Coolidge (Stone)/Getty Images; page 75: Chichen Itza in Mexico. © Xavier Arnau (Vetta)/Getty Images; page 75: Girl wearing a sombrero in Puerto Penasco Mexico during spring. © 2011 Bill Dwyer (Flickr Select)/Getty Images; page 86: Day of the Dead statuettes © Inti St Clair (Blend Images)/Getty Images; page 87: Mexican crafts with skeletons in old town, Albuquerque, New Mexico, USA © Danita Delimont (Gallo Images)/Getty Images; page 87: Mexico, young woman wearing Day of the Dead skull mask © Livia Corona (Stone+)/Getty Images; page 108: Political map © Sylvain Sonnet (Photographer's Choice RF)/Getty Images; page 109: South African giraffes (Giraffa camelopardalis giraffa) running © Art Wolfe (Lifesize)/Getty Images; page 109: Happy maasai with small son outside the village. © Britta Kasholm-Tengve (the Agency Collection)/Getty Images; page 109: Sunrise in savannah, Massai Mara National Park. © 2011 Luis Sánchez Martín (Ismart Photography)/(Flickr)/Getty Images; page 116: Political map © Sylvain Sonnet (Photographer's Choice RF)/Getty Images; page 152: Presentation and tasting of a giant pie, in Denby dale, England. Frontpage of French newspaper Le Petit Journal Illustre, 1928. Private Collection. © Leemage (Universal Images Group)/Getty Images; page 153: Woman holding pie with oven mittens © Angela Wyant (Stone+)/Getty Images; page 166: Political map © Sylvain Sonnet (Photographer's Choice RF)/Getty Images; page 166: Sheep grazing on rural hillside © Henglein and Steets (Cultura)/Getty Images; page 170: Political map © Sylvain Sonnet (Photographer's Choice RF)/Getty Images; page 184: Macaroons © 2012 Neil Langan UK (Photolibrary)/Getty Images; page 185: Colorful French Macarons © Dan Moore (E+)/Getty Images; page 185: France, market, macaroons © Jacques LOIC (Photononstop)/Getty Images; page 212: Political map © Sylvain Sonnet (Photographer's Choice RF)/Getty Images; page 213: Black bull billboard © Shanna Baker (Photographer's Choice RF)/Getty Images; page 213: The view along the Lycian coast trail from Kayakoy to Oludeniz, Turkey © Ron Watts (First Light)/Getty Images; page 213: Didyma, an ancient Ionian sanctuary, in modern Didim, Turkey, containing the Temple of Apollo, the Didymaion. © Chris Cheadle (All Canada Photos)/Getty Images; page 226: Pablo Picasso At Lunch, Vallauris, 1952. © Robert DOISNEAU(2011Gamma-Rapho)/(Masters)/Getty Images; page 227: Salted pretzel stick © Foodcollection/Getty Images; page 250: Political map © Sylvain Sonnet (Photographer's Choice RF)/Getty Images; page 251: Alp digl Plaz, ascent to Alp Flix, Kanton of Grisons, Switzerland © Iris Kuerschner (LOOK)/Getty Images; page 251: Girl with map at Brandenburger Tor © Chris Tobin (Digital Vision)/Getty Images; page 251: German man in lederhosen drinking beer, Hofbrauhaus, Munich, Bavaria, Germany © Laurie Noble (The Image Bank)/Getty Images; page 260: Man breaking bread © Andrew Carmichael (Stone)/Getty Images; page 261: Man kneading bread dough © Howard George (Arthur Woodcroft)/(The Image Bank)/Getty Images; page 261: Bread and pastries in shop window. © Richard I'Anson (Lonely Planet Images)/Getty Images; page 284: Lebkuchenherz, heart-shaped cookies made from Lebkuchen, sold during Oktoberfest. © Dan Herrick (Lonely Planet Images)/Getty Images; page 284: Gingerbread house on white background, close-up © Dag Sundberg (Photographer's Choice)/Getty Images; page 296: Political map © Sylvain Sonnet (Photographer's Choice RF)/Getty Images; page 297: Fishermans Cabin (Rorbuer), Nusfjord, Lofoten Islands, Norway © Banana Pancake (Photolibrary)/Getty Images; page 297: A basket of blueberries, Sweden. © Huerta, Anna/Getty Images; page 297: A moose laying down Sweden. © Plattform/Getty Images; page 304: Storkyrkan (Cathedral) and Stortorget (Parliament). Stockholm. Sweden © Nils-Johan Norenlind (age fotostock)/Getty Images; page 305: Celebration of Fat/Shrove Tuesday with semlor. © 2010 Karin Andersson (Flickr Open)/Getty Images; page 305: Cup of cappuccino with spoon and sugar packet © Inti St. Clair (Inti St.Clair, Inc.)/(Photodisc)/Getty Images; page 324: Political map © Sylvain Sonnet (Photographer's Choice RF)/Getty Images; page 325: Loaf of homemade sourdough bread, small bowl of salt and knife. © 2012 Sarka Babicka (Flickr)/Getty Images; page 325: Wooden nesting dolls © Alan Kearney (Brand X Pictures)/Getty Images; page 325: Saint Basil's Cathedral and The Kremlin in Moscow © Dmitry Mordvintsev (E+)/Getty Images; page 332: Political map © Sylvain Sonnet (Photographer's Choice RF)/Getty Images; page 333: Israel, Judean Mountains, Old Jerusalem, Dome of the Rock © Bertrand Gardel (hemis.fr)/Getty Images; page 333: Jerusalem road sign © Joel Carillet (E+)/Getty Images; page 333: People pray and walk in front of the western wall, wailing wall or kotel. © 2011 Beatriz Pitarch (Flickr)/Getty Images; page 338: Political map © Sylvain Sonnet (Photographer's Choice RF)/Getty Images; page 339: Taj Mahal facade © David Henderson (OJO Images)/Getty Images; page 339: Shanghai Cityscape During the Daytime © 2009 Andrew Rowat (Stone)/Getty Images; page 339: Pagoda and Dragon Snow Mountain © Adam Crowleyd (Digital Vision)/Getty Images; page 344: Naan Bread © Ferran Traite Soler (E+)/Getty Images; page 345: Men making bread at bakery. © Dennis Walton (Lonely Planet Images)/Getty Images; page 345: naan and ginger mango chutney. © Jessica Boone (Photodisc)/Getty Images; page 356: Homemade Mooncake for Chinese mid-autumn festival. © MelindaChan (Flickr)/Getty Images; page 357: mooncake handmade ©Vietnam (Dantoan)/(Flickr Open)/Getty Images; page 357: Early morning in a bakery making moon cakes for the Moon Festival on Hong Kong Island © Oliver Strewe (Lonely Planet Images)/Getty Images; page 360: Political map © Sylvain Sonnet (Photographer's Choice RF)/Getty Images; page 361: sydney opera house at sunrise © David Messent (Photolibrary)/Getty Images; page 361: Rotorua, North Island, New Zealand © LatitudeStock -TTL (Gallo Images)/Getty Images; page 361: ULURU ROCK IN AUSTRALIA © Marc Romanelli (Stone)/Getty Images; page 361: Kangaroo road sign, outback Australia © Josie Elias (Photodisc)/Getty Images; All other incidentals are 99pages and Parragon images.